SESQUICENTENNIAL

1987

D0080764

MICHIGAN

VISIONS OF OUR PAST

MICHIGAN
VISIONS OF OUR PAST

Edited By
Richard J. Hathaway

Michigan State University Press
East Lansing, Michigan
1989

Copyright ©1989 Greater Michigan Foundation
Printed in the United States of America

All Michigan State University Press books are produced on paper
which meets the requirements of American National Standard for
Information Sciences—Permanence of paper for printed materials.
ANSI 239.48-1984

Michigan State University Press
East Lansing, Michigan 48823-5202

Library of Congress Cataloging-in-Publication Data
Michigan: Visions of Our Past / Richard J. Hathaway, editor.
p.   cm.
Includes index.
ISBN 0-87013-265-2 — ISBN 0-87013-267-9 (pbk.)
1. Michigan—History.   I. Hathaway, Richard J.
F566.M689   1989
977.4—dc19

88-43042
CIP

TABLE OF CONTENTS

LIBRARY
ALMA COLLEGE
ALMA, MICHIGAN

ADVISORY BOARD

Dr. James McConnell (chair)
Executive Director
Michigan Commission on the Bicentennial of the United States Constitution

Larry Beckon
Director, Finance and Administration, Michigan Sesquicentennial Office;
and
Special Assistant, Michigan Department of Transportation

Thomas Jones
Executive Director
Historical Society of Michigan

Dr. William Mulligan
Director, Clarke Historical Library
Central Michigan University

Sharon Peters
Assistant Secretary of State

Jerry Roe
Member, Michigan Historical Commission, and Michigan Sesquicentennial
Commission

Gene Walter
Historical Observances Coordinator
Michigan Sesquicentennial Office

PREFACE

Michigan's Sesquicentennial celebration offered the state's citizens a chance to reflect on their past and plan for the future. All of what we are and much of what we will become is contained in the struggles, tragedies, and triumphs of our past.

Throughout Michigan's varied and fascinating history, its people have been leaders. They have led the nation in the production of automobiles, iron and copper, lumber, and many agricultural products. Of even greater importance, Michigan citizens have been leaders in the movements for equitable working conditions, civil rights, and a clean environment.

Michigan: Visions of Our Past presents our state's heritage in an exciting and compelling manner. The authors have brought their individual research, analysis, and interpretive skills to themes from Michigan's past. Each chapter provides new information and insights. The illustrations serve as graphic time capsules, providing glimpses of bygone eras.

As you read this book you will experience the Michigan of yesterday. Most importantly, you will gain ideas and understandings to help our state deal with the challenges of the future.

Michigan: Visions of Our Past is a gift to the people of Michigan; a gift of knowledge, pride and hope.

William G. Milliken   James J. Blanchard

George Romney   John Swainson

THE GREAT SEAL OF THE STATE OF MICHIGAN

E PLURIBUS UNUM

TUEBOR

SI QUÆRIS PENINSULAM AMŒNAM
CIRCUMSPICE

A.D. MDCCCXXXV.

Michigan's Great Seal was designed by Lewis Cass from the pattern of the Seal of the Hudson Bay Fur Company. It was presented to the Constitutional Convention of 1835 and adopted June 2, 1835, as the Great Seal of Michigan.

At the top of the Seal are the words, "E Pluribus Unum." These words come from our national motto meaning, "From many, one," formation of one nation from many states.

Below is the American Eagle, our national bird. This symbolizes the superior authority and jurisdiction of the United States. In his talons he holds three arrows and an olive branch with 13 olives. The arrows emphasize that our nation is ready to defend its principles. The olive branch signifies our desire for peace. The olives represent the first 13 states.

"Tuebor," meaning, "I will defend," refers to Michigan's frontier position.

The shield is supported by two animals representing Michigan . . . the elk on the left and the moose on the right.

Michigan is on an international boundary, and the figure of the man shows his right hand upraised symbolizing peace. The left hand holds a gunstock to indicate that although we love peace we are ready to defend our State and nation.

"Si Quaeris Peninsulam Amoenam Circumspice" means, "If you seek a pleasant peninsula, look about you." Evidently this refers to the Lower Peninsula. The Upper Peninsula was added in 1837, in compensation for the loss of a strip of land on our southern border obtained by Ohio when Congress recognized Michigan as a state.

The words, "The Great Seal of the State of Michigan, A.D. MDCCCXXXV," complete the State Seal. Omitting this legend, it was adopted as the Coat of Arms of the State of Michigan.

Changes in the Seal have been made from time to time. However, in 1911, the Legislature adopted the present Seal in the original design. It has remained unchanged since that year.

The law forbids its use in commercial advertising.

By Authority of

Secretary of State

Richard H. Austin

INTRODUCTION

RICHARD J. HATHAWAY

Michigan's sesquicentennial celebration was highlighted in Lansing, Marquette, and Detroit on 26 January 1987 with glittering balls recognizing 150 years of statehood. For nearly two years, parades, festivals, school programs, historical markers, magazine and newspaper articles, local histories, and conferences explored the state's past and probed into its future. No single work, however, attempted to summarize Michigan's heritage.

Initiated by its Historical Observances Committee, the Michigan Sesquicentennial Commission recognized this need. Through the Statehood 150 Fund, support was provided to produce this book. The result was to be a lasting memorial of the sesquicentennial, a gift to the people of Michigan.

An advisory board was appointed and an editor selected. The book would consist of a number of chapters on particular themes and time periods to be written by various authors. The authors were selected after extensive contact with historians throughout Michigan and evaluation by the editor and advisory board.

The authors were directed to bring the best of current scholarship to their research, to be true to their own writing style, and to include interpretation and opinion. The result which follows in these pages is a completely new, generously illustrated history of Michigan. Many well-known events are recounted, but with different interpretations. Other lesser-known but significant occurrences and trends are examined and analyzed. Together, the authors have provided a thought-provoking picture of Michigan which extends from before the retreat of the glaciers to yesterday's headlines.

The book would not have been possible without the dedication and enthusiasm of Jerry Roe, member of the Michigan Historical Commission and former chair of the Sesquicentennial Commission's Historical Observances Committee. Each member of the book's advisory board also spent hours reviewing manuscripts and providing direction for the project. The work of Larry Beckon has been especially significant in unraveling the strands of financial and administrative procedures.

The staff of the Michigan State University Press, including Richard Chapin and Julie Loehr, has provided great skill and commitment. The assistance of the Greater Michigan Foundation has also been crucial to the project's success.

Richard J. Hathaway

The result of all these efforts awaits the reader in the following pages. Continuing themes, such as social justice and discontent, population growth and environmental protection, economic growth and recession, and sectional and political rivalry, thread their way through nearly every essay. One chapter, dealing with Michigan's unique entry into the Union, is particularly reflective of the book's sesquicentennial origin. Each author has also provided a list of suggested readings to aid those readers who wish to further pursue a particular topic.

The authors have provided a tool for the teacher, a source for the scholar, and a pleasurable trip through Michigan history. *Michigan: Visions of Our Past* also provides a challenge: a challenge to the citizens of Michigan to understand their past, and apply its lessons to their future.

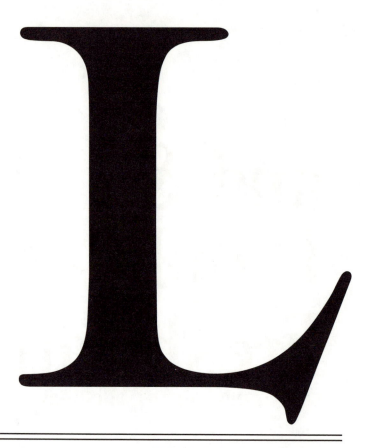

RICHARD A. SANTER

Professor Santer received his elementary and secondary education in Detroit and graduated from Redford High School in 1965. He earned bachelor's and master's degrees from Eastern Michigan University. His doctorate in geography was awarded at Michigan State University in 1970. He has contributed to and has authored numerous Michigan-related publications, notably *Michigan: Heart of the Great Lakes*.

and &
People of
Freshwater:
The Geography of Michigan

In 1917 with the few words, ". . . history furnishes a foundation for enduring patriotism and better government,"[1] former governor Woodbridge Ferris put into perspective the important work of the Michigan Historical Commission which was organized during his first year in office. Today the understanding and appreciation of the *what* and *when* perspectives of history remain essential for progress in a democratic society faced with global competition and interdependence. Yet, without a sense of *where*—geography—one is easily disoriented and history loses some of its relevance. George Fuller, the early twentieth-century Michigan historian, advanced this point in his insightful quote of Ellen Churchill Semple:

> . . . all historical problems ought to be studied geographically and all geographic problems must be studied historically.[2]

Having noted the inseparable tie between history and geography, this chapter is devoted to a summary of the location and the physiographic and demographic relationships of Michigan.

MICHIGAN: HEART OF THE GREAT LAKES

Michigan is a prominent place partly because it is a big state—in area and number of people. Its 96,791 square miles include 58,216 of land and 38,575 of non-inland water which makes it larger than many notable nations, i.e., the United Kingdom, Greece, and Switzerland. Michigan's population of 9.2 million is larger than two-thirds of the nations of the world.

A FITTING NAME

Where is Michigan? How did it get its identity? The answers are revealed in the translation of its name from two native Algonquian words: *michi* 'great, big or large' and *gama* 'lake'. The first use of the name on a map by the French occurred in 1681 as *Lac de Michigami du Lac Illinois* (Lake Michigan).[3] In the post-American Revolution years, *Michigania* came into use in reference to a land area, specifically as a proposed state name for the area of present-day northern Wisconsin and the southwest Upper Peninsula.[4] Michigan, as a land and water area, came into common usage associated with the Lower Peninsula when the Territory of Michigan was set apart from Indiana Territory in 1805. The territorial boundary ran due east from the "... southern bend or extreme of Lake Michigan."[5] Today when an astronaut sees from outer space the distinctive Upper and Lower peninsulas of the North American continent shaped from the heart of four of the great freshwater lakes of the world, the idealness of the name 'Michigan' is reaffirmed.

CONTEMPORARY GEOMETRIC LOCATIONS

During the diffusion of rail transportation and the Industrial Revolution, the world longitude/latitude and time systems became focused on Greenwich, England. As a result, Michigan became located in the center of both the Western and Northern hemispheres. The state's Mid-Polar/Equator Recreation Trail follows the 45th parallel (45°N) between lakes Michigan and Huron. Communities near 45°N include Menominee, Leland, Gaylord, Atlanta, and Alpena.

TIME ZONES

Ironwood (46°28′N – 90°10′W) and Little Girl's Point near the western end of the Upper Peninsula are situated west of St. Louis, Missouri. The eastern extremity of the state, Port Huron (43°N – 82°30′W) is located east of St. Petersburg, Florida. Given the state's relative geometric location and the pressure from railroad interests, the Michigan legislature in the 1880s placed it in the central (Chicago) time zone. Energy-saving needs, brought on by World War I and Michigan's increasing economic ties to the East, promoted a move to place Michigan on daylight saving time. After decades of disputes, farm interest opposition, and votes with varying results, a consensus emerged to shift the state, except for four western Upper Peninsula counties, into the eastern standard time zone (year round daylight time). Eastern daylight time (double daylight saving time to some) was accepted reluctantly by many. Presently, Michigan banks are striving for Midwest financial leadership by moving into the Chicago market area. Such economic relocations and the apparent advantages of reducing to three continental time zones, as in Australia, could foster additional time zone changes.[6]

CHANGING SECTIONAL PERCEPTION

As the nation has become more evenly settled, a confusion of sectional terms is still associated with the state, prompting, "In what section of the country is Michigan?" Pioneers commonly referred to their peninsula destination as a *western* or *northwestern* place. Now such terms as *Old Northwest, North, Eastern, Central, North-Central,* and *Midwest* are often used. Some universities affiliate themselves with the *Mid-American* or *Great Lakes* conferences while the Detroit baseball club competes in the *East Division*. In contrast, that city's basketball and football teams compete in *Central Divisions*. The United States Department of Commerce categorizes and maps Michigan as an *East-North Central* state. To contemporary international business people who have connections with both coasts plus Michigan and Colorado, 'Midwest' is old-fashioned. Recently, the National Collegiate Athletic Association (NCAA) has placed Michigan teams in the *Mideast* Regionals for tournament competition.[7] This geographic grouping recognizes a maturing national view. It also serves to highlight the importance of the state's north-south interactions via Interstate 75, whose number denotes a route located three-fourths of the way across the country from the Pacific coast. Given Michigan's responsibility, along with Ontario and seven other states, for the wise use of over 20 percent of the earth's fresh water, perhaps the best sectional term is the *Great Lakes Region*.

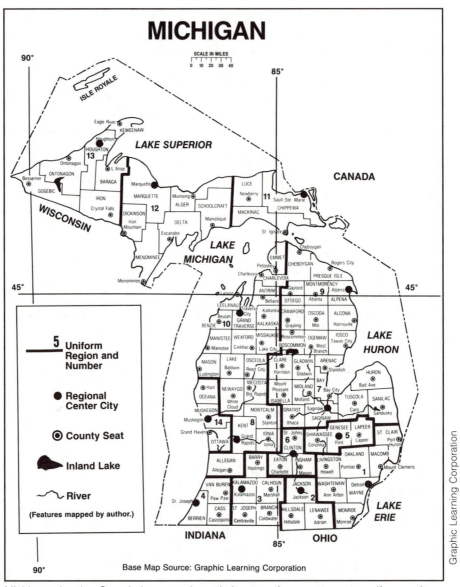

Michigan, showing Great Lakes water boundaries, counties, county seats, uniform regions, central cities, largest inland lakes, and longest rivers.

SHAPE, AREA AND DISTANCES — MORE THAN A MITTEN

Typically, Michigan is described as 'mitten' shaped. Even though the mitten—or *mittens*, to include both peninsulas—is useful to suggest Michigan's *land shape*, it is a misleading example. A more precise perception of the state includes its peninsulas, islands, and Great Lakes water boundaries.

Perhaps with more people acquiring a holistic perception of the shape of the state, Isle Royale National Park will not be so frequently left off or mislocated on maps. Similarly, 300 square miles of Lake Erie may not have been awarded to Ohio as recently as 1972, nor would Upper Peninsula residents be so inclined to form a separate state if people had a more inclusive perception of the state.[8]

AREA

Most government publications rank Michigan twenty-third in size based on its land area, including 1,573 square miles of water held in over ten thousand inland lakes.[9] In reality, the land area constantly changes due to shoreline erosion, soil deposition, and lake level fluctuations. Michigan ranks eleventh, the largest state east of the Mississippi River, when the land boundaries are recognized in conjunction with the water borders.[10] In 1915, when the North Cape of Maumee Bay had eroded somewhat north and the city of Toledo was experiencing growth which encroached on Michigan, governors Frank Willis of Ohio and Woodbridge Ferris of Michigan brought the 1835 Toledo boundary war to a modern-day peaceful settlement. To determine and mark the contemporary boundary, they organized a joint survey with teams from both states and the federal government. The survey group's results, after consulting local landowners, was a modestly zigzagging line with seventy 5-foot granite markers placed at one-mile intervals between Indiana and Lake Erie at the Lost Peninsula.[11]

DISTANCES AND CENTERS

The 315-mile-long Upper Peninsula is about twenty-five miles longer than the Lower Peninsula's distance between Morenci (41°50′N – 84°50′W) on the Ohio line and Mackinac City (45°45′N – 84°45′W). The air distance between Monroe and Ironwood is greater than that from Detroit to St. Louis or New York City. As a consequence of its bulky extent, Michigan's east to west, north to south geographic center is near Traverse City. However, its population center lies in the area

Richard A. Santer

Michigan Department of Natural Resources

Govs. Woodbridge Ferris of Michigan and Frank Willis of Ohio at a November 1915 ceremony concluding a peaceful end to the 1835 Toledo War after completion of a joint survey of the Michigan-Ohio border. Printed in *Biennial Report of the Director and Report on Retracement and Permanent Monumenting of the Michigan-Ohio Boundary*, Publication 22, series 18 (Lansing: Michigan Geological and Biological Survey, 1916), facing page 48.

between Flint, Lansing, and Jackson, west of metropolitan Detroit, where one-half of the state's citizens reside.

POLITICAL GEOGRAPHIC DIVISION

Since 1897, the shape and number of counties have remained unchanged at eighty-three. Between 1818, when the state's first land office opened, and 1897, frequent adjustments in county organization were made as settlement patterns changed.[12] Contrary to widespread belief, most of the state's county seats are nongeographically centered. The majority have been located in shoreline communities, places with relatively easy access, or at locations with the greatest population.

Michigan is served by two distinct types of townships. *Survey Townships*, also known as Jefferson, Congressional, and Federal townships, are used for legal land description. They resulted from the Land Ordinance of 1785. The intent of the ordinance was to establish a fair system to raise funds from land sales for the depleted national treasury and to create an orderly system to spread pioneers into the interior as a defense against reencroachment by the British and Spanish. Today when one observes a county map or air photo of the state, the most prominent cultural landscape feature is the grid Town Range/Section Line square-mile-road pattern. The Survey Townships of 36 square miles were formed, starting in 1815, from Town and Range lines placed at six-mile intervals north and south from the Baseline (Eight Mile Road, Detroit) and east and west from the Michigan Meridian, which was run due north and south from the flagpole base at Fort Defiance, Ohio, near the confluence of the Maumee and Auglaze rivers. Because of cumbersome equipment, tortuous conditions and trying to fit a square system to a round earth, the Baseline and Meridian intersect each other with a 937.4-foot mismatch in Jackson County at Baseline-Meridian State Park.

Each Survey Township is identified and divided with its individualized Town and Range coordinate and Section Number 1–36. T4S R12W Section 2, for example, identifies a specific township, range, and 640 acre section. Usually, pioneer village developers or farmers could not afford to purchase an entire section. Thus, half- (320 acres), quarter- (160 acres), and quarter-quarter (40 acres) sections were most commonly bought. For example, Horace Blackman of Tioga County, New York, the founder of Jackson, began that city on the Grand River by purchasing at the Monroe Land Office on 10 July 1829: T2S R1W Section 34 SE 1/4 160 acres.

Civil Townships were established beginning in 1827 and are identified by name, i.e., Prairie Ronde. They are organized for rural government general services. Civil Townships are served by an elected board consisting of a supervisor, clerk, treasurer, and trustees. In area they may be the same size, larger, or smaller than a Survey Township. Charter Townships have been created in some metropolitan areas to provide more administrative flexibility in order to cope with urbanization pressures. Charter Townships differ from Civil Townships in that they have additional taxing authority and the same ordinance-making power as cities.

Unlike the counties and only three of the state's approximately 1,375 communities, 349 of the state's 1,245 Civil Townships have duplicate names. Most duplicate names occur in the northern Lower Peninsula, which was settled after 1851, the year the legislature shifted place naming from state to county control. Most Michigan places have names related to Indians, natural features, pioneer home towns, and local individuals.

School districts are another form of local government which influence the state's political geography. Since 1912 consolidation has reduced the number of public school districts from 7,362 to 566.

Because school borders are based in part on local concerns and family preference (not arbitrary geometric areas), their irregular patterns most nearly bound economic and social/sports communities of interest.

In 1945 regional units of government became legal entities to help cope with migrations, population growth, fragmented communities, and the flow of state and federal money into local areas. To overcome the random proliferation of service regions, fourteen Uniform Planning and Development Regions were created in 1973. They focused on major urban centers, with boundary considerations given to modern-day shopping patterns, newspaper circulation, intercounty commuting, agricultural patterns and driving time.[13]

TWENTY-FIRST CENTURY POLITICAL GEOGRAPHIC ORGANIZATION

Given the precedents of nineteenth century county and twentieth century school boundary changes, plus the emergence of interdependent global competition, should the fourteen Uniform Planning and Development Regions be designated counties and the school districts become the basis for contemporary civil townships or incorporated cities? Such a political/geographic evolution would allow local communities, with their greater area and human resources, to become less dependent on Lansing and Washington to solve local problems. The new counties would also reduce fragmentation by fitting boundaries to contemporary settlement patterns, free duplicated local service resources for international competition, and eliminate the current layer of appointed and indirectly funded regional governments.

DEMOGRAPHY AND FOOD

Respected authorities generally fix the number of prehistoric and early tribal inhabitants in Michigan at less than fifteen thousand.[14] Table 1 summarizes the daily and decade population increases of the territory and state since 1810. Further, the table indicates that the "Baby Boom" of the 1950s and 1960s was six to eight times greater than the "Pioneer Boom" of the 1830s and 1840s, thus illustrating the remarkable population increase in Michigan during the mid-twentieth century (Table 1).

More important than population numbers alone is the relationship of people to food resources and environmental qualities necessary to sustain life. As a comparison, Michigan's current population density is similar to that of China when it came into the twentieth century. Seventy-one percent of the state's residents, however, live in urban communities.

TABLE 1

**Michigan Population by Decade and
Average Daily Increase, 1810–1987**

Year	Population	Average Daily Increase*	Year	Population	Average Daily Increase*
1810	4,762	—	1910	2,810,173	106
1820	8,896	1	1920	3,668,412	235
1830	31,639	6	1930	4,842,325	321
1840	212,267	49	1940	5,256,106	113
1850	397,654	50	1950	6,371,766	305
1860	749,113	96	1960	7,823,194	397
1870	1,184,059	119	1970	8,881,826	288
1880	1,636,937	124	1980	9,262,078	103
1890	2,093,890	125	1985	9,088,326	–
1900	2,420,982	89	1987	9,200,000 + –

Sources: *Michigan Statistical Abstract: 1986–87*, 20th ed., 13; *Population Today* 16 (2) (February 1988) citing United States Census Bureau News Release CB87-295, 30 December 1987.

*For preceding decade.

The state's growth, coupled with strip development, freeway expansion, decentralization of shopping and industry along highway corridors, and population movement to suburbs have combined into costly urban sprawl and led to enormous losses of foodland, as well as wetlands so critical to maintaining the earth's genetic pool.

As recently as 1927, Clyde Newnom estimated that Michigan was self-sufficient in basic food products. Less than fifty years later in 1972, Donald Isleib was warning that continued farmland losses would lead to a human/land ratio in A.D. 2000 similar to over-populated Taiwan. Even during the out-migration to the Sun/Drought Belt in the early 1980s, it was estimated that an economy-sapping $7.5 billion of the state's total $16 billion spent annually for food went for transportation and purchase of food grown outside the state.[15] The release of industrial toxins into the food chain, such as PBB (polybrominated biphenyl) in 1973, demonstrates that such contaminations can also undo progress in balancing population with resources and foodland preservation.

SEX, RACE, AND ETHNIC COMPOSITION

Since 1920, the sex ratio peak has dropped from 110 to 95 males per 100 females. Black citizens now comprise nearly 13 percent of the state total. Over 755,000 blacks live in the six-county Detroit standardized Metropolitan Statistical Area. Today American Indians comprise .5 percent of state residents with most living in urban areas rather than on the reservations at Mt. Pleasant, Bay Mills, L'Anse, and Hannahville. The state's Hispanic and Asian people comprise 1.7 and .7 percent of the population, respectively. Nearly half of the Mexican residents are found in the vicinity of south Detroit's Holy Trinity Church. The Arab-Muslim population has created a notable cultural landscape in the south end of Dearborn. Increasing numbers of Amish are locating in rural areas of the central Lower Peninsula.[16] All of these groups also have a significant impact on the education system. The state's birthrate of 15 to 16 per 1,000 far exceeds the death rate of about 8 per 1,000, which provides a yearly natural increase of about 65,000—far exceeding a natural zero population growth rate.[17] Even though fewer people lived in Michigan in 1988 than in 1980, from 1986 to 1987 the state's population increased 61,000, with a net in-migration of 13,226 residents.[18] However recent offsetting trends of in-out migration are interpreted, relocation of talented Michiganians to other more prosperous areas of the country remains a crucial problem.

ICONOGRAPHY — SYMBOLS OF STATEHOOD

Since Michigan's days as a territory, a variety of symbols, or icons, have been identified to indicate legal authority and to build citizen cohesiveness. The Territorial Seal had a shield held by two eagles with a lone deciduous tree and a motto proclaiming: *Tamdem fit surculus arbor* (from the sapling comes the tree). Today Michigan's iconography includes a flag (blue background with the seal in the center), a bird (robin), a flower (apple blossom), a stone (Petoskey stone, a fossilized coral), a gem (greenstone), a fish (the brook trout), and the Great Seal with two unofficial animals (the moose and elk), plus the motto. In analyzing these symbols, mixed emotions can be experienced from unbounded pride and joy to disquieting pangs of conscience. For instance, the white pine—the state tree—has been timbered and burned relentlessly. Now it remains in its original grandeur at only a few sites, such as the forty acres at the Hartwick Pines State Park near Grayling. Even when a few remnant giants are found in the Upper Peninsula, most are quickly harvested.[19] Nevertheless, the state's motto in Latin endures as a beacon of truth: *Si quaeris peninsulam amoenan circumspice* (if you seek a pleasant peninsula, look about you). Further, *Tuebor* (I defend), given the central spot in the Great Seal, identifies a basic responsibility and challenges all citizens to protect the state.

PHYSICAL AND GEOLOGICAL RESOURCES

The beauty and opportunities for wealth and pleasant living that are available in Michigan have attracted people for twelve millennia and are directly traceable to the region's basic physical assets. The array of renewable and nonrenewable resources includes metallic and non-metallic bedrock minerals; an ever-changing four-season climate; intriguing flora and fauna from delicate wildflowers and insects to beefy bulls; tranquilizing inland lakes, scores of waterfalls, and 36,140 miles of flowing rivers; awe-inspiring post-glacial morrain hilltop and sand dune vistas; plus the Great Lakes in all their breathtaking moods. Perhaps the contemporary puffy advertising slogan does sum up the state's assets best—Yes Michigan!

GEOLOGIC RESOURCES

The Michigan Basin bedrock foundation of the region dates from the Precambrian and Paleozoic eras, scientifically dating between 3.5 billion to 220 million years ago. The western Upper Peninsula Precambrian igneous rock resources include major deposits of iron and copper, plus small reserves of gold, silver, lead, zinc, nickel, cobalt, uranium, and platinum ores. The sedimentary deposits of the six Paleozoic seas era, beginning about 600 million years ago, include: sandstones, limestones, salts, brines, corals, shale, gypsum, alabaster, and coal. Most waterfalls are associated with the resistant Cambrian sandstone, while most of the bays are formed in the easily erodable Ordivician rock. The state's chemical industry is based on the Silurian deposits, while the cement, oil, and natural gas producers tap the Devonian formation.

Between sixteen and ten thousand years ago, the Wisconsin stage of the Pliestocene era's mile-thick ice lobes retreated to the north. At the same time, warming temperatures produced changing climate-vegetation belts. Left behind, in addition to the skeletal remains of ice age mammals (mammoths, mastodons, musk ox), were huge deposits of sand and gravel held in hilly end morrains, kames, eskers, and drumlins. These upland features, if not mined, are used for woodlots, pastures, and scenic home sites, but seldom held or identified as unique park landforms. The muck land and peat bogs of naturally eutrophicated former inland lakes are important for soil conditioners and sod farming. Sand dunes have been extensively mined for casting molds. Former

17

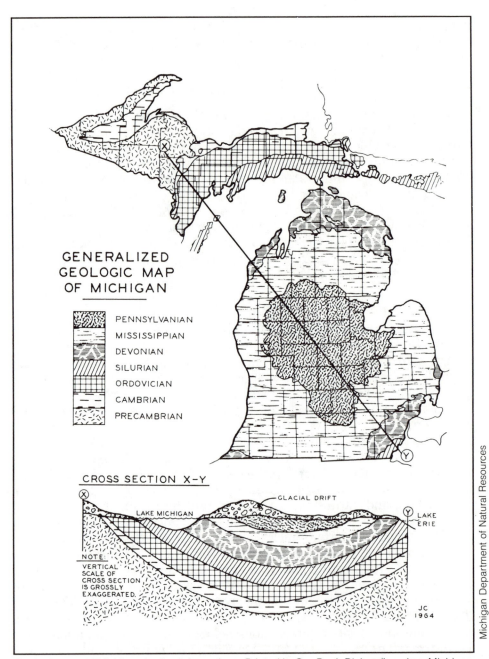

GENERALIZED
GEOLOGIC MAP
OF MICHIGAN

PENNSYLVANIAN
MISSISSIPPIAN
DEVONIAN
SILURIAN
ORDOVICIAN
CAMBRIAN
PRECAMBRIAN

CROSS SECTION X-Y

GLACIAL DRIFT

LAKE MICHIGAN

LAKE
ERIE

NOTE:
VERTICAL
SCALE OF
CROSS SECTION
IS GROSSLY
EXAGGERATED.

JC
1964

Michigan Department of Natural Resources

Geologic map of Michigan bedrock formations. Printed in *Our Rock Riches* (Lansing: Michigan Geological Survey, 1946), 84.

glacial lake bottom lacustrine plains, ice-recession till plains and melt-water outwash plains provide important airport and industrial sites. However, their primary value, after painstaking drainage, is for agriculture—the state's second-ranking economic activity.

RIVERS

Most Michigan rivers are relatively short; however, they are useful for hydroelectric power generation, transportation, water supplies, and recreation. The Grand River is the longest and flows 260 miles from Jackson County to Grand Haven. The innovative fish ladder at Grand Rapids allows planted salmon to reach Lansing, the state capital. The Saginaw watershed drains an area of nearly 6,000 square miles. Because of the dynamics of new pollution identification, recent clean-up efforts, and very limited total watershed ecosystem research, the exact miles of river segments, number of lakes, and watershed sites contaminated to the point of unsafe swimming or fish consumption is not known. Evidence of contamination has been found in several hundred miles of river and at well over one hundred sites.[20]

TABLE 2

Michigan's Largest Lakes

Lakes	Area m² Total	/	In State	Detention Years†	Depth in feet	Elevation above sea level
Great:						
Superior	31,699	/	16,231	191	1335	600
Huron	22,973	/	8,975	22	748	581
Michigan	22,278	/	13,037	99	925	581
Erie	9,906	/	216	2.6	210	571
Connecting:						
St. Clair	460	/	116	—	40	575
Inland:						
Houghton	31	/	31	—	—	1220
Gogebic*	20	/	20	—	—	1289

Sources: Michigan Sea Grant Program, Michigan State University, East Lansing; *Statistical Abstract of the United States: 1985*, 197; Hudgins, *Michigan Geographic Backgrounds*, 29.

*Largest in the Upper Peninsula, sixth largest in the state.

†The time needed to drain or flush and refill, or recharge a lake.

Richard A. Santer

ISLANDS

Islands with interesting historic roles include: Isle Royale, the state's largest (45 miles long, 539,280 acres), situated about forty-eight miles from the Keweenaw Peninsula but much closer to Minnesota; Mackinac, Drummond, Bois Blanc at the head of Lake Huron; North and South Fox, North and South Manitou, High, Beaver, Hog, and Garden off the northwest shore of the Lower Peninsula; the Green Bay group south of the Garden Peninsula; and Harsens, Belle, and Grosse Isle in the Lower Straits area of the St. Clair and Detroit rivers. These islands, plus hundreds of smaller ones, some of which have been recently transferred to the state from federal jurisdiction, play important roles in recreational use and wetlands ecology.

CLIMATE, VEGETATION AND SOIL RELATIONSHIPS

The state is situated in the Humid Continental Long and Short Climate regions. The two regions are divided by a shifting climate zone, and the tension line is observable in changing soil, vegetation, economic activity, and population patterns north and south of the area between Bay and Muskegon counties. Temperature averages vary between 50°F in the south to 40°F on the Keweenaw Peninsula to the far north. Record highs and lows are 112°F at Mio and -51°F at Vanderbilt. The frost-free or growing season length varies between 180 days in the south to about 65 days in interior parts of the northern Upper and Lower peninsulas. Average snowfall accumulations vary between Detroit's 30 and the Keweenaw's 180 inches. Great Lakes levels fluctuate yearly and somewhat cyclically in response to variations from average precipitation and temperature. Lake Michigan significantly influences fall and winter cloudiness, lake effect snow, and the narrow shoreline pattern of the bountiful western "Fruit Belt." In response to climate, trees generally vary from southern broadleaf deciduous to northern mixed deciduous and needleleaf coniferous species. Soil patterns closely follow those of climate and vegetation with highly productive loamy gray-brown podzolic (udalfs) in the south to acidic sandy podzols (spodosols) in the north. Small prairie grasslands and open areas dotted with oak trees were found by pioneers in the southern counties.

OBSERVATIONS AND CONCLUSIONS

Continued urban sprawl threatens food production on the state's most fertile southern lands. In an attempt to relieve such destructive sprawl, one can look to Canada. While most Ontarioans live south of

Ludington, Michigan (44°N), four of their attractive metropolitan cities are located further north but within the range of Michigan's latitudes and climate regions. Perhaps, then, metropolitan centers in this electronic age can also be developed in northern Michigan.

Whether driving through a city or in the country, a reassuring variety of domesticated, native, introduced and reintroduced birds and mammals can be seen and heard. What is often overlooked is the unnatural pattern of their distribution, which provides warning that the food chain and habitats, especially wetlands, continue to be negatively altered.[21]

In the quest for a healthful environment, perhaps the current generation of Michiganians can assume educational leadership and bring into successful operation an innovative, international, interstate water-grant college system similar to the land-grant system of colleges pioneered at what is now Michigan State University. Then, in the near future, well-schooled, talented and knowledgeable extension agents could be assigned to each major creek and river watershed. Given authority, they could help assure healthy water quality standards and guide the resolution of conflicts relating to economic development and settlement activities between competing units of government.

From a geographic point of view, Michigan is a wealthy, attractive, pleasant place with a robust history and dynamic opportunities exceeding many other less well-endowed areas of the world. If we significantly overcome our current self-defeating ways relating to environmental health, our great-great-great grandchildren will be able to again write a laudable history for the tricentennial in 2137.

◆

NOTES

1. Roy Newton, ed. "Life and Works of W. N. Ferris," (unpublished manuscript, Ferris State University, 1960), 329.

2. George N. Fuller, *Economic and Social Beginnings of Michigan* (Lansing: Wynkoop Hallenbeck Crawford Co., 1916), 11.

3. Louis C. Karpinski, *Bibliography of Maps of Michigan 1804–1880* (Lansing: Michigan Historical Commission, 1931), 105.

4. Ibid., 176; *Thomas Jefferson 1743–1943: A Guide to the Rare Books, Maps and Manuscripts exhibited at the University of Michigan* (Ann Arbor: The William L. Clements Library, 1943), 13–14.

5. Karpinski, 203; Fuller, lxviii–lxix.; Earl J. Senninger, Jr., *Atlas of Michigan*, 3d ed. (Flint: Flint Geographical Press, 1970), 84; United States in Congress Assembled, *An Ordinance for the Government of the Territory of the United States, Northwest of the River Ohio* (13 July 1787) Article 5 lines 10–12.

6. Eric Starkman, "State Banks Build Second Home in Chicago," *The Detroit News*, 31 January 1988, F1; Edward B. Espenshade, Jr., ed., *Goode's World Atlas*, 17th ed. (Chicago: Rand McNally and Company, 1986), xvi.

7. "Mideast Region Names Miller Coach of Year," *The Pioneer*, Big Rapids, 26 February 1988, 6A. See also *National Collegiate Championship Handbooks* (National Collegiate Athletic Association, 1987 or 1988 maps).

8. Richard A. Santer, *Michigan: Heart of the Great Lakes* (Dubuque, Iowa: Kendall/Hunt Publishing Co., 1977) 8–10, 50–53; Richard A. Santer, "Where is Isle Royale," *Michigan History* 69, no. 3 (May-June 1985), 2–3.

9. United States Department of Commerce, Bureau of the Census, *Statistical Abstract of the United States: 1985*, 105th ed. (Washington, D.C.: 1984), 191; Bert Hudgins, *Michigan: Geographic Backgrounds in the Development of the Commonwealth*, 4th ed. (Detroit: Edwards Brothers of Ann Arbor, 1961), 2–4.

10. Espenshade, *Goode's World Atlas*, 14th ed. (1974), 229; and 17th ed. (1986), 243.

11. Michigan Geological and Biological Survey, *Biennial Report of the Director and Report on Retracement and Permanent Monumenting of the Michigan-Ohio Boundary*, Pub. 22, Geol. Sur. 18 (Lansing: State Printers, 1916); United States Department of Interior, Geological Survey, *Oregon Quadrangle Ohio-Michigan*, a map.

12. Richard W. Welch, *County Evolution in Michigan 1790–1897*, Occasional Paper 2 (Lansing: Michigan Department of Education, 1972).

13. Executive Office of the Governor, State Planning Division, "Guidelines for Recognition of Regional Planning and Development Organizations" (Lansing: Mimeographed, n.d.); Bureau of Planning and Program Development, Office of Planning Coordination, *Planning and Development Regions for Michigan*, Technical Report No. 14 (February 1968); Bureau of Programs and Budget, Office of Planning Coordination, "An Investigation of Locally Established Regional Bodies in Michigan" (Lansing: Work Item A.I.A., December 1970, mimeographed with maps).

14. Helen H. Tanner, ed., *Atlas of Great Lakes Indian History* (Norman: University of Oklahoma Press for Newberry Library, 1987), 65–66.

15. Clyde L. Newnom, *Michigan's Thirty-Seven Million Acres of Diamonds* (Detroit: The Book of Michigan Company, 1927), 25; Michigan Department of Agriculture, *Michigan Agricultural Land Requirements: A Projection to 2000 A.D.* (Lansing, February 1973, mimeographed); Richard Struthers and Rosemary Lewando, *The Michigan Food System: Increasing Dependence or Self-Reliance?* (Emmaus, Penn.: The Cornucopia Project of Rodale Press, 1982), 2.

16. L. M. Sommers, J. T. Darden, J. R. Harmon, and L. K. Sommers, *Michigan: A Geography* (Boulder, Colo.: Westview Press, 1984), 184–202.

17. United States Department of Commerce, Bureau of the Census, *City and County Data Book: 1983* 10th ed. (Washington, D.C.: 1983), 256–58.

18. *Detroit Free Press,* 11 September 1988, 2B.

19. Russell McKee, "Tombstones of a Lost Forest," *Audubon*, March 1988, 72.

20. Wayne A. Schmidt, "700 Miles of Streams Fouled: DNR," *The Grand Rapids Press*, 15 March 1988, A1; Mark Best, "DNR Study Surprises Local Officials," *The Pioneer*, Big Rapids, 17 March 1988, 1.

21. Wayne A. Schmidt, "Other Wild Creatures Suffer Ill Effects of Lake Pollution," *The Grand Rapids Press*, 28 February 1988, A16; Environment Canada, United States Environmental Protection Agency, Brock University, and Northwestern University, *The Great Lakes: An Environmental Atlas and Resource Book*, a joint publication (Toronto, Chicago, St. Catherines, Ont., Evanston, Ill.: 1987), 29–35.

---- ◆ ----

SUGGESTED READINGS

Dorr, John, Jr. and Donald F. Eschman. *Geology of Michigan*. Ann Arbor: The University of Michigan Press, 1970.

Egginton, Joyce. *The Poisoning of Michigan*. New York: W. W. Norton and Company, 1980.

Environment Canada and United States Environmental Protection Agency. *The Great Lakes: An Environmental Atlas and Resource Book*. A Joint Publication. Toronto, Chicago, St. Catherines, Ont., Evanston, Ill., 1987.

Fitting, James E. *The Archaeology of Michigan*. Bloomfield Hills: Cranbrook Institute of Science, 1975.

Michigan Department of Agriculture, Michigan Weather Service. *Climate of Michigan by Stations*. 2nd rev. ed. East Lansing, 1971.

Michigan Natural Resources Magazine. *Mapbook of Michigan Counties*. Lansing: Two Peninsula Press, 1984.

Press, Charles, et al. *Michigan Political Atlas*. East Lansing: Michigan State University Center for Cartographic Research and Spatial Analysis, 1984.

Santer, Richard A. *Michigan: Heart of the Great Lakes*. Dubuque, Iowa: Kendall/Hunt Publishing Company, 1977.

Sommers, Lawrence M., ed. *Atlas of Michigan*. Grand Rapids: Michigan State University Press, 1977.

Sommers, Lawrence M., et al. *Michigan: A Geography*. Boulder: Westview Press, 1984.

Tanner, Helen H., ed. *Atlas of Great Lakes Indian History*. Norman: University of Oklahoma Press, 1987.

Verway, David I., ed. *Michigan Statistical Abstract*. Detroit: Wayne State University Bureau of Business Research, Annual.

Welch, Richard W. *County Evolution in Michigan 1790–1897*. Occasional Paper 2. Lansing: Michigan Department of Education, 1972.

GEORGE L. CORNELL

Born in Highland Park, Michigan, Dr. Cornell received his bachelor's, master's and doctorate degrees from Michigan State University. Presently he is director of the Native American Institute, Center for Urban Affairs, and Assistant Professor of English and American Studies at Michigan State University. Dr. Cornell has published widely in the field of native American affairs and studies, and has served on the Michigan Commission on Indian Affairs. He is a co-author of *People of the Three Fires: The Ottawa, Potawatomi and Ojibway of Michigan.*

nconquered Nations:
The Native Peoples of Michigan

Long before Étienne Brulé became the first white man to come in contact with the natives of the upper Great Lakes, diverse groups of peoples lived in the region. The earliest known inhabitants of the area are called Paleo-Indians. Their appearance in the upper Great Lakes is dated from 12,000 B.C.; and, most likely, they migrated into the region from the south as the glaciers receded. The Paleo-Indians hunted large mammals and gathered natural foods from the land. Over time, though, the climate in the Great Lakes began to change as the glaciers continued to recede to the north.

The mean temperature of the region increased, and new plants and animals began to populate the land. These changes, which occurred over thousands of years, marked the end of the Paleo-Indian period and gave rise to the Archaic period. The Archaic period is divided into three classifications: The Early Archaic, from 8000 B.C. to 6000 B.C.; the Middle Archaic, from 6000 B.C. to 3000 B.C.; and the Late Archaic, from 3000 B.C. to 1000 B.C.

During the entire Archaic period, major changes occurred that would shape native lifestyle. The conifer (pine) forests were gradually replaced by hardwoods in much of southern Michigan and mammals such as the moose, deer, caribou, and bear became staples in the local diet. These, and other mammals, had become much more abundant as the glaciers moved further north. Technological changes also made life easier. Pestles for grinding foods came into use sometime during the Middle Archaic period. Hunting weapons also became more sophisticated as smaller projectile points were manufactured. These smaller points allowed native peoples to hunt faster and more agile animals. These innovations, in concert with the increased availability of plant foods, insured the survival of native peoples.

The Archaic period gave rise to what is now called the Woodland period. This period is dated from 1000 B.C. to A.D. 1650. During this period agriculture began to flourish in the Great Lakes. Native peoples grew squash and sunflowers and approximately 300 B.C. acquired corn. These crops, as well as beans and nuts, supplemented a diet of meat and fish. The environment that was created after the recession of the glaciers provided the environmental basis to support larger populations.

Like the Archaic period, the Woodland period is divided into three phases. It was during the Middle Woodland period, from 300 B.C. to A.D. 500, that the mound builders moved into the region. These cultures, referred to as the Hopewell, built large conical mounds, many of which are still visible in southern Michigan. The influence of the Hopewell cultures began to diminish after A.D. 1000. The demise of the mound builders gave rise to the cultural patterns of the primary groups of native peoples who inhabited the upper Great Lakes region when Europeans came into contact with them. These groups are the Ojibway (Chippewa), Ottawa, and Potawatomi. Collectively, they referred to themselves as the Anishnabeg—the 'original' or 'first' people.

The Anishnabeg were not, however, original inhabitants of the upper Great Lakes. They migrated into the region from the "Great Salt Sea" to the east. The oral traditions of the Anishnabeg clearly state that they moved into the region from the east, and the people were sick and suffering much hardship. The migration of the Anishnabeg most likely began on the Atlantic seaboard and, over a period of many years, they came to settle in Michigan and the surrounding area.

They moved from one aquatic environment to another and were well prepared to utilize the abundant resources of the upper Great Lakes. Many scholars have pondered the question of what triggered the migration of the Anishnabeg from their homelands in the east. It may have been that the Viking colonies that were established in North America shortly after 1000 B.C. introduced new diseases to the continent. These diseases, as witnessed during the later colonial period, had devastating consequences for American Indian populations.

Native peoples of the Americas had no resistance to the major diseases of Europe. Even common diseases such as chicken pox and measles often proved fatal to American Indians. The Viking settlements probably introduced new diseases which killed large numbers of indigenous peoples and forced severe disruptions of native culture, including major relocations. By 1500 the Anishnabeg were firmly established in the upper Great Lakes and had made successful transitions to the local environment.

The vast resources of the Great Lakes provided subsistence for the Anishnabeg. Fish and mammals were available in large numbers and were the primary proteins in the diet. In addition, the Anishnabeg cultivated large gardens which provided corn, beans, squash, sunflower seeds, potatoes, and pumpkins. They gathered wild rice, which is really a grain, from lakes and rivers and also made large quantities of maple sugar during the spring. These food sources, in combination with nuts, fruits and other naturally occurring plants, insured the nutritional needs of the Anishnabeg. Foods were also stored for use in winter and provided a degree of safety from the harsh climate.

The life of the Anishnabeg was predicated on the availability of foodstuffs and suitable village sites. They used the rivers and lakes as travel routes, and villages were always located near water. Birchbark canoes, as well as dugout canoes, were the primary transportation. These vessels were perfectly suited for use on Michigan's waterways and allowed people the mobility to visit and socialize with their relatives at distant villages.

Anishnabeg society was then, as it is today, organized along family lines. The lineages of the Anishnabeg are commonly referred to as clans. Originally, there were five great clans of the Anishnabeg: the Great Fish Clan, the Loon Clan, the Marten Clan, the Crane Clan, and the Bear Clan. These clans provided the identity of children born into them, and clan affiliation was determined via the father's lineage. Thus, if the father was a Crane Clan member, all children born to him and his wife would be members of that clan. Clans played a very important role in Anishnabeg life. All members of the same clan, whether they were related by blood or not, were considered to be brothers and sisters. Marriage rules among the Anishnabeg only allowed unions between members of different clans. These marriages extended the kin of families. This was important since clan members were formally obligated to assist other members of the same clan. This social system provided a degree of security for Anishnabeg families because they could depend

George L. Cornell

and rely on their clan/relatives should they encounter hard times or suffer personal misfortune.

Clans have been referred to as the "super families" of the Anishnabeg. In reality, clans formed the social fabric of society and tied people

Wissegong, Michigan Chippewa (Ojibway) woman about 1842. Printed in François Comte de Castelnau, *Vues et Souvenirs de'l Amerique du Nord* (Paris: A. Bertrand, 1842), plate 15.

Library of Congress; Michigan State Archives

together in an intricate, formal system that provided support and nurturance. Of course, leadership in the clans was also important to village life. Political leadership was provided by older, respected members of the community. Elders provided wise counsel based on years of experience. There was political specialization among the Anishnabeg, as well as in other areas. Like all groups of people, Anishnabeg society had individuals who were better able to perform certain tasks than others. Usually, the most skilled people in a specific area would provide leadership when it was necessary.

Anishnabeg life was directed by spiritual perceptions of the land, and their existence was attributed to divine action. The Anishnabeg were very religious and the earth, plants, and animals had spiritual connotations. All things were a part of the Creation and were to be carefully used and treated with respect. These beliefs regarding the environment were the basis for Anishnabeg lifeways and dictated the hunting practices and agricultural patterns of the people.

Prior to contact with Europeans, the Anishnabeg enjoyed a lifestyle that provided for their wants and needs. Without question, their lifeways required a great deal of work, yet they possessed the requisite knowledge and skills to provide a good quality of life. The land provided their building materials and their food. Over the centuries, they had perfected their environmental knowledge and were familiar with medicinal plants and the regional flora and fauna. Their life was based on an intimate understanding of the land and the habits of animals. The Anishnabeg, for the most part, lived in peace with themselves and others. The people had a spiritual philosophy which directed their lives and they were generally content. Crimes were infrequent and children were well fed. Laughter and good will were ever-present. All of this would change as the Anishnabeg came into contact with Europeans who settled the North American continent.

In the early 1600s, the French began to exert an influence in the upper Great Lakes. In 1622, Brulé traveled to the present site of Sault Ste. Marie and became the first recorded white man to meet with the Ojibway. He was employed by Samuel de Champlain, who founded Quebec and was the governor of New France. Contact with the French ushered in a new period of Anishnabeg life.

The French were actively seeking a water passage to China and the Orient. They were also very interested in obtaining native furs, which could be shipped back to Europe for a handsome profit. The fur trade between the French and representatives of the Anishnabeg caused many changes in native communities. The French introduced a market economy which was based on the accumulation of raw materials for profit. In return for furs, they offered technological goods which made life easier for the Anishnabeg. Initially, furs were traded for textiles, metal implements, glass beads and other curios. The trade was conducted in such a fashion, though, that native peoples were grossly underpaid for their furs. The fur trade provided profits of 600 percent to 700 percent on initial investments for the French. The trade also had the effect of binding the Anishnabeg to trade items, and eventually they became dependent on manufactured goods. The Anishnabeg also became political allies of the French as a result of diplomacy and the missionary efforts of French priests. This alliance between the French and the Anishnabeg would eventually entangle them in wars of international scope.

The French also introduced disease into the region and alcohol was frequently used to induce the Anishnabeg to trade. This situation was compounded when the French began to extend credit to Anishnabeg trappers, thereby binding them to select trading houses and forcing them to step up efforts in obtaining furs. The Anishnabeg began to spend much more time trapping fur-bearing mammals than they had previously. This disrupted their seasonal hunting/agricultural patterns and made them more dependent on items of foreign manufacture. By 1670, hundreds of fur-laden canoes were leaving the Great Lakes for Montreal and Quebec. The French were prospering, while the Anishnabeg were depleting valuable fur resources for a pittance of their true worth in the international market. This system was carefully orchestrated for French benefit; eventually, the Anishnabeg would be left to their own devices.

By the mid-1700s, tensions between the French and the English in the New World were ready to explode. The English, with their strong influence on the eastern seaboard, were intent on political and economic control of North America. The tensions erupted in 1754 in the French and Indian War. This war, fought between the French and British, along with their respective Indian allies, resulted in France losing political control on the continent. The surrender of Fort Ponchartrain at Detroit in the fall of 1760 marked the transition from French to British rule in the Great Lakes. During the conflict, the Anishnabeg were allied with the French. With the demise of French influence, the Anishnabeg bore the brunt of punitive policies levied on them by the British. The British governor-general of North America, Jeffrey Amherst, ordered his troops and garrisons to withhold supplies and gifts from the former French allies, the Anishnabeg.

Interestingly, the Anishnabeg did not consider themselves to be defeated nations at the conclusion of the French and Indian War.

Rather, they considered themselves political successors in the region. Anishnabeg leadership resented the high-handed policies of the British, and relations between the Ojibway, Ottawa, and Potawatomi and the British newcomers were strained.

The harsh trade policies of the British infuriated the Anishnabeg. Mistrust and discontent increased between the rival groups, while French nationals still residing in the Great Lakes spread rumors of British plans to war against the Anishnabeg. By 1763, elements of the Anishnabeg were staunchly antagonistic to the British. This situation was exacerbated by the presence of the Ottawa leader Pontiac, who actively incited his relatives to war on the British. Hostilities between the Anishnabeg and the British began in May 1763. The conflict has been referred to as Pontiac's 'Revolt' or 'Uprising.' The war was more of a general response to the unacceptable trade policies of the British than a result of Pontiac's leadership and oratorical abilities. The Anishnabeg and their Indian allies, the Huron and Delaware, seriously disrupted British military actions in the Great Lakes. The failure of Pontiac and his followers to seize the fort at Detroit proved to be a disappointment to his Indian allies, and by early fall the revolt was losing support.

The insurrection was short-lived, and by the fall of 1763 most of the Anishnabeg who participated in the struggle had returned to their villages to prepare for winter. In October 1764, peace between the Anishnabeg and the British was formally concluded and relations were stabilized. The Anishnabeg recognized British influence in the Great Lakes, and life returned to normal patterns. Resources were still abundant in the Great Lakes, although fur-bearing mammals were declining. The Anishnabeg still had access to important resources to insure the well-being of villages. All of this was to change in the very near future.

The beginning of the American Revolution in 1775 signaled major changes in Anishnabeg life. The conflict between emerging American interests and British political control marked yet another upheaval for the Anishnabeg. The defeat of the British in the revolution and the subsequent changes in policies caused uncertainty and consternation. The Anishnabeg continued to recognize their former alliance with the British, even after the revolution, and resisted American encroachment into the Great Lakes. Elements of the Anishnabeg, fueled by British Loyalists who remained in the region, participated in the defeat of Gen. Josiah Harmar's army in 1790. The Anishnabeg were also a major factor in the route of Gen. Arthur St. Clair's forces in 1791.

The turning point came in 1794, when Anishnabeg allies were soundly defeated by the army of Gen. Anthony Wayne at the Battle of Fallen Timbers in Ohio. This defeat led to the Treaty of Greenville in

1795, whereby large tracts of Indian land were ceded to the United States. These land cessions opened the door to settlement in the southern Great Lakes region, and settlers began to move into the area in large numbers. The Treaty of Greenville also ushered in the treaty period for the Anishnabeg, and their land holdings would continue to shrink during the nineteenth century.

As an example, the Treaty at Detroit in 1807 between the Anishnabeg and the United States resulted in one-fourth of Michigan's Lower Peninsula being transferred from Indian possession to the United States government. The creation of the Territory of Michigan by Congress in 1805 proved to be an important motivation in acquiring Anishnabeg lands. Without the transfer of lands from Indians to the United States, statehood for Michigan would have been difficult to obtain. Interestingly, the newly created territory was formally referred to as Michigan, which is a corruption of the Anishnabeg word *kitchigami*, meaning 'great water' or 'lake.'

The War of 1812 between Great Britain and the United States interfered with Indian relations in the Great Lakes for a brief period. Many Anishnabeg villages supported the Shawnee leader Tecumseh in his effort to dislodge American interests in the Great Lakes and along the frontier. The Anishnabeg, allied with the British, supported the Indian confederation which Tecumseh promoted. The idea of unified Indian resistance to American expansion died along with Tecumseh at the Battle of Thames in 1813. With the defeat of the British and their Anishnabeg allies, efforts were renewed by the United States to obtain Indian lands in the Territory.

With new vigor, the United States sent representatives to the Anishnabeg to treat for their lands. Treaties were negotiated in quick succession: the Foot of the Rapids Treaty in 1817, the Treaty of Saginaw in 1819, the Treaty at Sault Ste. Marie in 1820, the L'Arbe Croche Treaty of 1820, and the Treaty of Chicago in 1821. These treaties had one thing in common: they transferred Anishnabeg lands to the United States and increased the political control of the United States in the Territory of Michigan.

These treaties had the effect of reducing the resource base which the Anishnabeg could use to support their villages. By this period, the fur trade was no longer a lucrative source of economic support, and increasing settlement further heightened competition for resources. Without access to previously abundant resources, Anishnabeg life became much more difficult. Disease epidemics also compounded an already precarious situation. The cholera outbreak of 1832 killed many Anishnabeg in the Territory of Michigan and undermined the quality of life in native villages.

An already bad situation would get worse, as the Territory of Michigan began efforts to achieve statehood. The Treaty of Washington in 1836 was concluded, allowing Michigan to become a state in 1837. This treaty, which conveyed almost one-third of the Lower Peninsula and the eastern half of the Upper Peninsula to the federal government, was crucial to Michigan being admitted to the union. The Treaty of Washington, without question, provided the resource base for Michigan's developing economy. Vast resources, such as minerals, timber, and the freshwater fishery, were transferred from Anishnabeg communities to the United States. These same lands and resources would later be sold to citizens of Michigan, allowing them economic opportunity.

The threat of removal west to Indian Territory, as proposed by the federal Removal Act of 1830 and reiterated by Article Eight of the Treaty of Washington, induced many Anishnabeg leaders to cede lands via this treaty. Anishnabeg communities were under tremendous pressure during this period and had little choice but to accommodate the federal government. Attempts were made to remove Indians from Michigan west to Kansas and other territories. Despite intense resistance, a number of Ottawa and Potawatomi were relocated to the west where their descendants still live today. Meanwhile, the United States was embarking on a policy of assimilating the Anishnabeg and other Indian groups into the mainstream of American life. In other words, the federal government wanted Indians to "walk the white man's road."

It was to this end that the Treaty of Detroit was signed in 1855 between the Anishnabeg and the United States. Under the provisions of the treaty, individual Anishnabeg families made selections of property, which would be held in fee simple as private property. This process of allotment undermined the communal nature of Anishnabeg village life and forced Indians to recognize property as a private commodity which could be used for subsistence or investment purposes. Unfortunately, most Anishnabeg families were unaware of the taxing authority of the state or simply did not have the money to pay taxes on their selected land holdings. Many of the land selections made under the 1855 treaty were quickly transferred to the non-Indian sector of the economy. Unscrupulous land speculators took advantage of the situation and profiteered at the expense of landless, impoverished Anishnabeg families.

The 1855 Treaty of Detroit marked the conclusion of the treaty period for Michigan Indians. In the aftermath of this treaty, most Anishnabeg communities found themselves in dire circumstances. They no longer had access to vast resources and land holdings, and communities were weakened by disease and federal neglect. The Anishnabeg made transitions to the situation and found work in the emerging industries in Michigan. They worked in the lumber camps and factories when possible and plied their traditional skills, such as basket making, to provide income for their families. It was an extremely difficult period of time, yet they adapted and made important transitions into the twentieth century.

Throughout the nineteenth century the Anishnabeg had witnessed enormous changes. Their land base had been reduced to almost nothing, and the natural resources on which they depended had come under severe pressure from the increasing population in Michigan. In less than one hundred years, the Anishnabeg had gone from being the possessors and stewards of the land to paupers in a society that sought to ignore their existence. Opportunity was limited and conditions in communities deteriorated, but they did survive.

The early decades of the twentieth century were also very difficult years for the Anishnabeg. The depression years after the economic crash of 1929 were particularly hard. Even though times were bad, Anishnabeg communities, with their strong sense of family, made the

Indian family at Sault Ste. Marie selling baskets during the 1890s.

Clarke Historical Library, Central Michigan University

34

necessary transitions to maintain and continue their heritage and culture. Many groups of Ojibway, Ottawa, and Potawatomi resided on lands near reservations that were created by treaty or allotments selected under the provisions of the 1855 treaty. These settlements were the centers of Indian activity in Michigan, along with urban areas which were becoming home to large numbers of the Anishnabeg.

World War II was a critical event for Anishnabeg families in Michigan. Many members of the Ojibway, Ottawa, and Potawatomi served in the armed forces during the conflict while others found employment in the war industries. The economic activity associated with the war also induced many Anishnabeg to relocate to urban areas in southern Michigan. It was in the postwar years, though, that many members of Anishnabeg communities began to reexamine their past relationship with the federal government and initiate efforts to seek redress for illegal activities which had resulted in the loss of their lands.

Many Michigan Indians filed claims against the federal government under the provisions of the Indian Claims Commission Act of 1946. These cases, which focused on land issues, provided an opportunity for Michigan Indian communities that were not federally recognized as Indian tribes to reorganize and to collectively work to create a better future. The postwar years witnessed increased Indian activity, yet socioeconomic conditions on Indian reservations in Michigan were poor. Housing and sanitation were substandard, and employment opportunities on reservations were scarce. Educational levels were also low in comparison to levels of achievement for other Americans.

During this same time period, Michigan Indians began to assert the treaty rights they had reserved during the treaty process. What Indians had not ceded in a treaty, they retained. One issue that came to national prominence was the fishing rights controversy. Michigan Indians had fished the Great Lakes for centuries to provide food for families and surplus to trade for other commodities. Over the years, the Ottawa and Ojibway of northern Michigan had continued to fish in Michigan waters without regulation by the state. The tribes were empowered to fish in such a manner by provisions contained in the 1836 Treaty of Washington. They had not ceded the specific right to fish in "their usual and accustomed manner" and, thus, were able to continue their age-old right.

Unfortunately, the state of Michigan decided to challenge the tribes' right to commercially fish Michigan waters. This decision led to years of litigation, and in every case, Michigan Indian tribes and their rights were upheld. The fishing case was finally settled in late 1981 when the United States Supreme Court declined to review the lower court's decision.

Numerous allegations were leveled against the Indian fishery during this period of time. The vast majority of these charges were never substantiated. In hindsight, the issue seems to have centered on the economic uses of the Great Lakes. The state of Michigan determined that more revenue could be produced from the Great Lakes fishery if it was primarily utilized as a sport fishery, and so moved to reduce the influence of commercial fishing on the lakes, including the Indian fishery.

The Indian commercial fishery played a valuable role in the economies of northern tribes. In essence, the state of Michigan was attempting to undermine one of the major economic activities on reservations in northern Michigan. It is no wonder that Michigan Indians resisted the state and eventually had their day in court. Today, the tribal fishery is managed by tribal conservation departments, in cooperation with the state of Michigan and the United States Department of Interior. The fishery is closely monitored and regulated so as to insure future resources.

The fishing rights issue focused attention on Indian resource use patterns while ignoring the environmental history of Michigan and the use of resources by non-Indians. Interestingly, the Great Lakes fishery was initially overfished by non-Indians. The white pine forests were cut by non-Indians who sought to maximize profits while destroying trout streams and causing serious erosion problems. Market hunters killed large numbers of mammals for sale in commercial outlets and were instrumental in the extermination of the grayling and passenger pigeon. All of these activities were forgotten during the fishing rights issue while Indians were being singled out as environmental culprits. In reality, nothing could be further from the truth.

Michigan Indians are interested in preserving the Great Lakes fishery and other resources of the state. It must be clearly remembered that the resources of the region were abundant when treaties transferred lands from Indians to non-Indians. The Anishnabeg, like other indigenous peoples, have always advocated the intelligent use of the land. The earth is the mother of native peoples, and the integrity of the land must be preserved for future generations.

Anishnabeg communities in Michigan are currently faring much better than they have in the past. Michigan is the home of six federally recognized tribes: the Sault Ste. Marie Tribe of Chippewa, the Bay Mills Indian Community (Chippewa), the Grand Traverse Ottawa, the Saginaw-Isabella Chippewa, the Hannahville Potawatomi, and the Keweenaw Bay Community (Chippewa). In addition, there are four historic tribes resident in the state that are not yet federally recognized: the Pokagon Potawatomi, the Huron Potawatomi, the Burt Lake Band

David Kenyon, Michigan Department of Natural Resources

Don and Ray Massey, Indian commercial fishermen, near Ste. Ignace, 1980s.

of Ottawa and Chippewa, and the Lac Vieux Desert Band of Chippewa. There are also Indian centers in Michigan cities which provide valuable services to Anishnabeg who reside in those areas.

All of the six federally recognized tribes have reservations and govern community activities. The tribes run preschool and other educational programs for Indian children and adults. Tribal governments are recognized by the federal government and function much like cities in Michigan. The one major exception is that state government cannot regulate the affairs of Indian tribes. That power is reserved by the Congress of the United States.

It was the inability of the state to regulate tribal affairs that allowed the tribes to create gaming establishments. Initially, the tribes operated bingo games which offered larger prizes than other charitable games that were licensed by the state. The tribal bingo games, with larger prizes, appealed to a broad segment of the Michigan population, and the games proved to be profitable for tribal governments. The bingo games gave rise to casinos on the reservations, and currently, every tribal government in Michigan operates Las Vegas-style gambling entertainment.

The casinos are prohibited from using mechanical devices such as slot machines, but they do offer card and dice games. The United States Supreme Court issued a decision in 1987 that reaffirmed the right of the tribe to operate gaming facilities. Federal legislation to regulate the casinos is pending. The casinos and bingo games have proven to be valuable economic assets for tribal governments in Michigan. Large numbers of tribal members have been employed in these establishments, and the tribes are generating revenues from the businesses to fund other governmental services. Much like the state of Michigan and lottery proceeds, the tribes are using their new-found income to provide services to tribal membership. The tribes are using revenues to diversify tribal economies, and business development is coming of age on Michigan Indian reservations. This is a far cry from the situation that existed only twenty years ago.

The history of the Anishnabeg and other Indians who reside in Michigan has been difficult. It has been a strenuous task to maintain tribal sovereignty and rights in the face of federal and state opposition. Michigan Indians, like native peoples across the United States, have had to assert their strength and courage as peoples to retain their heritage and culture. In the recent past, relations between the state of Michigan and Indian communities have improved. There are good reasons for this progress. Indian tribes have become important economic factors in the regional economies of Michigan. The Sault Ste. Marie Tribe is the largest employer in the eastern end of the Upper Peninsula, and other tribes in the state exert an influence in local regions. These positive contributions to the well-being of Michigan are finally being acknowledged and applauded. When one considers the land and resource contributions of the Anishnabeg to the making of Michigan, it seems long overdue.

The Anishnabeg have existed in the Great Lakes region for hundreds of years. Over time, they have adapted and changed. They are partners with other citizens of the state in our collective future. As a part of that future, they advocate the integrity of the earth and opportunity for all people. They are concerned about the world of tomorrow and the well-being of their children. In the future, though, they will have a larger voice in the course we steer. They cannot be ignored, as in past generations, for their cooperation and guidance will prove to be wise counsel as we face new and unprecedented challenges.

———————————◆———————————

SUGGESTED READINGS

Catton, Bruce. *Michigan: A Bicentennial History*. New York: W. W. Norton and Company, Inc., 1976.

Cleland, Charles E. *A Brief History of Michigan Indians*. Lansing: Michigan History Division, Michigan Department of State, 1975.

Clifton, James A. *The Pokagons, 1683–1983: Catholic Potawatomi Indians of the St. Joseph River Valley*. Washington, D.C.: University Press of America, 1984.

Clifton, James A., George L. Cornell, and James M. McClurken. *People of the Three Fires*. Grand Rapids: Grand Rapids Inter-Tribal Council, 1986.

Danzinger, Edmund Jefferson, Jr. *The Chippewas of Lake Superior*. Norman: University of Oklahoma Press, 1978.

Edmunds, R. David. *The Potawatomis: Keepers of the Fire*. Norman: University of Oklahoma Press, 1978.

Feest, Johanna E., and Christian F. Feest. "Ottawa," in *Handbook of North American Indians*, vol. 15, edited by Bruce G. Trigger. Washington, D.C.: Smithsonian Institution, 1978.

Fitting, James E. *The Archaeology of Michigan*. Bloomfield Hills: Cranbrook Institute of Science, 1975.

Kinietz, W. Vernon. *Indians of the Western Great Lakes, 1615–1760*. Ann Arbor: The University of Michigan Press, 1972.

George L. Cornell

Peckham, Howard H. *Pontiac and the Indian Uprising.* New York: Russell and Russell, 1947.

Rubenstein, Bruce A., and Lawrence E. Ziewacz. *Michigan: A History of the Great Lakes State.* St. Louis: Forum Press, 1981.

Tanner, Helen Hornbrock, ed. *Atlas of Great Lakes Indian History.* Norman: University of Oklahoma Press, 1987.

DAVID A. ARMOUR

David Armour was born in Grove City, Pennsylvania. He received a bachelor's degree from Calvin College in Grand Rapids, and a master's and doctorate degree in Colonial American History from Northwestern University. Presently David Armour is deputy director of the Mackinac Island State Park Commission. He is the author of numerous articles and books including (with Keith R. Widder) *At the Crossroads: Michilimackinac During the American Revolution,* and entries in the *Dictionary of Canadian Biography.* Dr. Armour has also served as editor of *Historical Archaeology,* and as a trustee of the Historical Society of Michigan.

urs,
Faith &
Fleur-de-lys:
The French Experience in Michigan

A HERITAGE THAT SURVIVES

From the early seventeenth century until 1760, the land we now call Michigan was within the sphere of influence of France. Though Michigan was not a defined area, the upper Great Lakes, which surround Michigan, was a significant part of the expanding territory of New France. French politicians, geographers, and religious leaders were concerned about events taking place in North America as the nation of France and the Catholic Counter Reformation expanded. The average French peasant had no desire to emigrate to the far and formidable land, and few French emigrants ever went to New France. Only ten thousand or so crossed the Atlantic to become colonists.[1] A few of these hardy people or their descendants took up residence in Michigan. At no time during the French era did as many as fifteen hundred permanent French residents live within the modern boundaries of the state.

Yet, the French left a major imprint on the state of Michigan. A glance at a present map reflects many French names for towns, rivers, waterways, and geographical features. Detroit, Grosse Isle, Rouge

River, Raisin River, Bois Blanc Island, Grand Traverse Bay, Grand River, AuSable River, Presque Isle, L'Anse, and Lake Superior are only a few French-named places. The French Catholic heritage is reflected in places named for saints, such as Sault Ste. Marie, St. Joseph, Lake St. Clair, St. Helene Island, St. Martin Island, and St. Ignace. At both Detroit and Mackinac Island the name Ste. Anne (patron saint of the voyageurs) still adorns churches whose parish registers date back to the eighteenth century. The names of prominent French explorers and missionaries are found in Marquette County and the town of Charlevoix. The map reveals French names clustering where the French presence was most pronounced. During the seventeenth and eighteenth centuries Michigan was a forest-covered wilderness, and nearly all travel was by water. The French, using Indian-designed birchbark canoes, followed the interconnected lakes and streams into the interior of North America. Thus, French names predominate along the shores of the Great Lakes and their interconnecting rivers.

At places where waterways met, the French established small settlements such as Sault Ste. Marie on the St. Mary's River connecting Lakes Superior and Huron, Michilimackinac at the Straits of Mackinac linking Lakes Huron and Michigan, Detroit on the Straits between Lakes Huron and Erie, and St. Joseph on the river connecting southward into the rivers of the Illinois country. At Detroit, the largest French settlement in the Great Lakes, street names such as Cadieux, Cadillac, Moross, Livernois, Dequindre, and Vernier still bear testimony to the city's French beginnings.

The French brought their land settlement patterns with them. Farms, with narrow fronts on the waterways, stretched inland in long narrow ribbons. These ribbon farms are still very evident from an airplane as one crosses the Detroit River. The French land patterns have left a permanent mark on the landscape in the Detroit, Monroe, and St. Ignace areas and are even more pronounced on the less-developed Canadian side.

Descendants of the colonial French still live in Michigan. Genealogists of the French-Canadian Heritage Society actively trace their roots. While many have dispersed to other areas, clusters of French descendants live at the Straits of Mackinac and in the Monroe County area. Only in the Monroe area, however, are a few remnants of the colonial French language and cultural patterns maintained. Muskrat, a French-Canadian delicacy, is still revered there. At the Straits of Mackinac, many of the French share an Indian heritage reflecting the blending of the French and the native American population. These *metis*, who combine both French and Indian blood and lifestyles, have developed their own distinctive heritage.

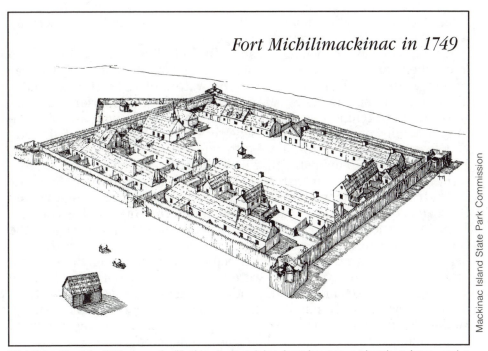

Fort Michilimackinac in 1749

Mackinac Island State Park Commission

Michilimackinac in 1749 was a fortified town containing forty houses, a church, a forge, and a powder magazine. Bake ovens, barns, and an icehouse were located outside the twelve-foot high palisaded walls. This artist's reconstruction is based on a detailed map drawn by a French engineer.

FURS AND FORTUNE

The French came to Michigan in search of riches, unsaved souls, geographical knowledge, imperial control, and adventure. Where they went was determined by geography and frequently by wars and conflicts with other peoples.

French fishermen along the Canadian coast and St. Lawrence River valley discovered, in the furs that the natives brought to trade, the prime economic base of New France. Light, storable, and of tremendous value in Europe, the glistening pelts of North American animals found ready buyers in the markets of Europe.[2] By the time Samuel de Champlain settled at Quebec on the banks of the St. Lawrence in 1608, fur was the most valuable export commodity. The cold climate of the Great Lakes area was ideal for a thick growth of fur and native American hunters were already skilled in trapping the animals. Trade with the

David A. Armour

Great Lakes tribes began almost immediately with the Ottawa serving as middlemen to the more western nations.

Champlain sent the young Étienne Brûlé to live with the Indians to learn their language, their customs, and the lay of their land. He was probably the first European to see the waters of Lake Huron, and in about 1622 ascended the St. Mary's River to Lake Superior. The vast waterways stretching westward intrigued the French, who were searching for an all-water route to the riches of China. During the 1630s Jean Nicolet was dispatched to the west to explore for a route to the Orient. Recent scholarship indicates that he made the trip in 1638 and that he went into Lake Superior instead of Green Bay as was earlier thought.[3]

The time-consuming job of hunting and trapping was done by the thousands of native Americans who inhabited the Great Lakes country. Very few Frenchmen were necessary to trade with them and to pack the furs aboard ships. Even after the 1650s, when hardy French traders began to penetrate the Great Lakes region themselves, only a few hundred canoe-paddling voyageurs were needed to transport merchandise and furs. A couple hundred independent traders, who eventually settled in the interior, easily handled all the furs that the Indians secured. While the fur trade made a few people wealthy, it never provided employment for more than a thousand Frenchmen.[4]

There was always the hope that gold or other precious metals might be found in the region, but except for copper, no minerals of value were discovered. The copper deposits on the southern shore of Lake Superior were too distant and their value not sufficient to make their exploitation worthwhile for the French.

Farming could and did provide a livelihood for a few French families. Except for the food they ate themselves, the only market for the farmers at Detroit, Michilimackinac, St. Joseph, and Sault Ste. Marie was the voyageurs and soldiers who purchased their corn and peas. The local Ottawa, Potawatomi, and Huron were agricultural peoples who raised most of the food that supported the fur trade. With no export market for crops raised in the Michigan area, farmers had no reason, except for a desire to be independent, to move to the region.

Efforts to entice farmers to the Detroit area in 1701 and 1749 added only a few families to the small settlement. By 1750 about five hundred people, including thirty-three Indian slaves, lived in the approximately seventy-five farms along both sides of the Detroit River. Their log houses with high-pitched roofs faced the river, and their fields stretched back in long strips. Less than two square miles of land had been cleared for farming and 1,070 acres were planted with wheat, oats, and corn. The farmers owned 160 horses, 211 oxen, 471 cows, 251 hogs, and 2,187 chickens and other fowl. Two mills had been constructed to grind grain.[5] Not until the nineteenth century, when the Erie Canal opened Michigan to eastern agricultural markets, was there a demand for Michigan-grown farm products.

The geographical location of Michigan in a northern climate brought isolation when the ice of winter solidified the waterways. From April to November, however, the lakes and rivers were open. Summer brought a rush of voyageurs who came and went. But the remainder of the year the residents were cut off from each other, the rest of New France, and the world. Some who remained during the winter scattered to live in the Indian winter hunting camps in order to purchase prime furs as soon as they were caught.

The close contact with the native peoples, so vital to a successful trade, was frequently strengthened by marriages between French traders and Indian women. Sometimes these alliances were temporary, "after the fashion of the country," but frequently they were lifelong commitments. Marriage opened up an invaluable network of suppliers and customers to the trader, because trade was a very personal relationship between people who knew and trusted each other. Also, an Indian wife brought the added advantage of knowing how to survive in the wilderness by making clothes, preparing food, and even repairing canoes.

From these marriages developed a growing population of *metis*, people who combined the cultural heritage of their French and Indian parents. While the girls retained a stronger affinity to the Indian culture of their mothers, the boys tended to identify with their French fathers and occasionally were sent east to Montreal for their education. As the eighteenth century progresssed, some *metis*, such as Charles de Langlade, became part of the French military and played a prominent role in events in Michigan.[6]

Not all Frenchmen had Indian or *metis* wives. Lamothe Cadillac and Alphonse de Tonty brought their wives to Detroit in 1701, and by 1716 there were a number of French women at Michilimackinac. These women, frequently the wives of the more well-to-do traders or soldiers, did much to maintain French cultural tradition in the wilderness.

The fur trade was dependent on moving furs and merchandise vast distances in the short summer season. Following the watercourses, lugging ninety-pound bales over innumerable portages, hugging the Great Lakes shoreline, and paddling an average of fifty miles a day, some Frenchmen spent months in a canoe. Incredibly mobile and few in number, they were well-acquainted and frequently related. Like inhabitants of small towns today, everyone knew each other. The difference was that their community extended over an area of several hundred miles. Undeterred by vast distances, people embarked on trips that would take weeks, months, or even a year or more, with much greater frequency than do people today.

New France was headed by a governor who supervised the military and Indian affairs, and an intendant who administered justice, finance, and civil affairs. They tried to control the fur trade to the government's advantage. The official policy varied from time to time. Usually, the government in Quebec tried to limit trade to a few locations, such as Detroit and Michilimackinac, and to restrict the number of traders who were licensed to carry merchandise into the interior. Sometimes they granted monopolies to the commandants of the interior forts in an effort to reward favorites or generate sufficient funds to pay for the operation of the posts.[7] Occasionally, such as in 1696 when there were too many beaver furs flowing out of the upper lakes, the government attempted to stop the trade until markets improved.

Despite the efforts of the government, about two hundred free-spirited, unlicensed traders called *coureurs de bois* roamed the Great Lakes trading with the Indians for furs. They surreptitiously took their packs either to Montreal or to the English at Albany, New York, or, after the 1720s, to Oswego on Lake Ontario.[8] When a large profit is at stake, people find ways to make it. Perhaps the greatest negative result from the government's restrictive policy came about when Pierre-Espirit Radisson and Médard Chouart des Groseilliers had their furs confiscated in 1660 for trading in the upper Great Lakes without a license. Intrigued with the rich fur trade possibilities of the territory north of Lake Superior, they took their knowledge and enthusiasm to the English. Eventually, they persuaded some English merchants and politicians to tap that area from the north by way of Hudson Bay. In 1670 their dreams were rewarded by the founding of the Hudson Bay Company which sent traders to the region. From that time on, French traders had to compete with aggressive English merchants whose skill was such that their company survives to this day.[9]

Throughout the colonial period, the native American peoples of Michigan vastly outnumbered the French, whom they permitted in their midst. Chippewa, Ottawa, Potawatomi, Huron, Miami, Fox and others numbered in the thousands. Trade with the French had a tremendous impact on the Indians. Initially the guns, knives, kettles, and cloth raised their standard of living. Hunting was made easier and cooking more efficient. Woolen cloth was much more comfortable than cold clammy deerskin. However, with the acceptance of European goods came a dependency upon the traders.

To obtain coveted items, the Indians increased their hunting and trapping. No longer hunting only for food, their goal became fur. They soon eliminated the valuable beaver from nearby areas and had to move their hunting grounds. Frequently, this led to clashes over hunting grounds with other tribes.

A most detrimental aspect of the trade was the introduction of alcohol into Indian society. French brandy or "milk," as it was called, had no counterpart in Indian culture. Thus, they were not equipped to handle it in moderation. Traders considered alcohol to be an ideal commodity; it was easily transportable, could be extended by adding water, befuddled the senses of the customers making them easier to exploit, and was rapidly consumed, leaving a continuing demand. Throughout the French era, the clergy, seeing the destruction of Indian society, wanted to ban the brandy trade while the traders, realizing its profitability, sought to continue the sale of alcohol. Indian leaders could not decide whether to permit or exclude it from their villages, but those who counseled prohibition usually lost.

Along with European goods came European diseases. Frequently, epidemics raged well in advance of the actual traders as infected Indians spread smallpox and measles. How many Indians died of these plagues, to which the natives had little or no resistance, is a question which historians are debating; but there is no question that at various times the Huron, Ottawa, and other tribes were decimated.[10]

FAITH

Some Frenchmen came to Michigan in search of souls. During the seventeenth century, the Catholic Counter Reformation aggressively sought to convert people to the "true faith." The Jesuits, founded by St. Ignatius Loyola and composed of highly educated and dedicated men, were among the leaders of the missionary effort. Supporting the order were a host of pious lay people who contributed funds and followed with great interest the success of the mission activity. To keep their supporters informed, the Jesuits annually published a volume of the *Jesuit Relations*, recounting their activities in the past year. Thanks to these reports, historians have a considerable amount of information about these early missionaries. When the *Jesuit Relations* ceased publication in 1673, the quantity of available data decreased, and consequently the missionaries of the eighteenth century are not as well known as their earlier forebears.

The initial Jesuit efforts were with the Huron and Ottawa tribes. In 1641 Fathers Charles Raymbaut and Isaac Jogues accompanied an Ottawa band to Sault Ste. Marie. There they found two thousand Indians and held a mass, the first in what is now Michigan. When the Hurons in present-day Ontario were overrun by the Iroquois during the 1640s and 1650s, a number of refugees fled to the southern shore of Lake Superior. Jesuit missionaries followed them. Fathers Claude Dablon and Claude Allouez explored the shores of Lake Superior. Their geographical observations resulted in a superb map of Lake Superior published in 1670. Some of the refugees migrated to Sault Ste. Marie where Father Jacques Marquette ministered to them and the neighboring Chippewa. When the Huron moved again to the Straits of Mackinac in 1670 the mission followed.

From this location, Father Marquette left in May 1673 with Louis Joliet to search for the reported Mississippi River and to make contact with the tribes of Illinois. During the next few years, missions were established in Wisconsin and the Illinois country and at the mouth of the St. Joseph River. The missionaries were frequently appalled by the irreligious activities of the "Christian" traders, whose alcohol caused such misery. Tension between the clergy and the traders persisted throughout the French era.

Occasionally, Jesuit fathers accompanied Indians to their winter hunting camps, but missions were usually located close to Indian villages. These villages frequently moved after the Indians exhausted the fertility of their corn fields. To stay close to his people, the priest moved the mission to the new village. In the Straits of Mackinac, the mission, first established on Mackinac Island in 1670, was moved to the mainland on the north side of the Straits in 1671. About 1715, the mission of St. Ignace followed the Ottawa village to the south side; and in 1741 it was moved again to L'Arbre Croche (Cross Village) on the northeast shore of Lake Michigan when the Ottawa migrated in search of new farmland. By this time, the Jesuits had established at Michilimackinac the church of Ste. Anne for the French families, and operated the mission of St. Ignace for the Indians.[11]

The mission at St. Joseph followed a similar pattern. First established at the mouth of the St. Joseph River in the late 1680s, the mission was moved twenty-five miles upriver, near present-day Niles, sometime between 1718 and 1720. There it was visited in 1721 by Father Pierre de Charlevoix who described the mission in his book *Histoire et Description Générale de la Nouvelle France* (Paris: 1744). Because missions usually kept the same name, it is difficult to know exactly where some missions were located.[12]

As missionary zeal in Europe cooled during the eighteenth century, the number of missionaries sent to Michigan declined. In 1761 only two priests at Detroit and Michilimackinac remained within the area of present-day Michigan, and the one at Michilimackinac left in 1765. Consequently, priests had to travel to the various posts to say Mass, marry couples, and baptize their children, who were often several years old. Despite years of effort by this hardy band of dedicated Jesuits, most native peoples preferred their old ways rather than the foreign ideas of the Jesuit "black robes." It was even remarked by some that Frenchmen tended to become Indian easier than the Indians became Frenchmen.[13]

The most active church endeavors were at Detroit, where there was a major concentration of both French and Indians after 1701. Founded by Cadillac in that year as an effort to consolidate the Indian population and trade in the face of an English threat, Detroit became the largest population center of French and Indians in the Great Lakes country. By 1750 the fortified town located on the west bank of the river had a winter population of about two hundred that swelled to four hundred in the summer. Local farmers numbered about five hundred. Sizable villages of Huron, Ottawa, and Potawatomi numbering twenty-six hundred, provided ample missionary opportunity, though work among the Huron met with the most success.

FLEUR-DE-LYS

The Jesuit missions were supported by the French government, which perceived them to be a part of the expansion of French authority. By the 1660s, France, under Louis XIV, was in an expansionist mood. Thus, in 1671 the intendant of New France, Jean Talon, sent Daumont de Saint-Lusson with a group of traders and missionaries to Sault Ste. Marie to conduct a formal ceremony establishing French hegemony. While the Indians from fourteen tribes watched with awe, the French laid claim to their lands. The ceremony, however, was really directed at the English who had recently established posts on Hudson Bay.[14]

In order to establish an imperial presence in the Great Lakes country, Cavelier de LaSalle received permission from Governor Louis de Buade de Frontenac to establish posts on the Great Lakes. The effort was to be financed by profits of the fur trade. To more effectively conduct the trade, in 1679 LaSalle constructed, near the eastern end of Lake Erie, a small ship, *Le Griffon*. Its shallow draft passed the bars in the St. Clair River, sailed to Mackinac, and then on to Green Bay. Heavily loaded with furs, it bent its sails back toward Mackinac while LaSalle continued his journey. Never seen again, *Le Griffon*'s fate remains one of Michigan's intriguing mysteries. It was months before LaSalle knew the vessel was missing. He had pressed on and established a post at Fort Miami at the mouth of the St. Joseph River.[15]

David A. Armour

Cavelier de La Salle's ship *Le Griffon* disappeared during its maiden voyage on the Great Lakes in 1679. (Painting by Robert Thom)

Michigan State Archives

During the 1680s, French control of the Great Lakes was severely threatened by two English trading expeditions from Albany, New York to the Straits of Mackinac. The first venture was enormously successful. The second group, however, was captured by the French under Oliver de La Durantaye and taken prisoner to Montreal. This English penetration frightened French officials, who decided to fortify the Straits of Mackinac by erecting Fort DeBaude on the north shore in 1689. Daniel Duluth also erected, at present-day Port Huron, a small post, Fort St. Joseph, in 1686. Initially garissoned by fifty men, it was maintained for only two years.[16]

The English threat was the major rationale behind Cadillac's plan to establish a fort at Detroit. In 1701 he succeeded in bringing one hundred soldiers and settlers to Detroit and also attracting a sizable number of Huron, Ottawa, and Potawatomi to settle nearby. However, despite his aim of keeping the Indians from contact with the English by bringing them further south, he only brought them closer together.

To show French authority and to police the fur trade, a small contingent of soldiers of the Campagnies Franches de la Marine was stationed

52

at each post. Beginning in 1683 with La Durantaye's appointment at Michilimackinac, officers were sent to command at the western posts. Commandants usually stayed for three years, during which time they hoped to make their fortune in the fur trade.[17]

Not all was trade and profits for the commandants because the Great Lakes region was wracked by war. Many tribes harbored long-standing animosities against other groups. War parties frequently took the forest trail to avenge some long-remembered outrage. But war blocked trade, and the goal of the French was profits. Thus, the commandants spent much of their energy diplomatically trying to maintain peace.

During the seventeenth century, the expansive Iroquois sent raiding parties from their homeland in New York to attack Sault Ste. Marie and St. Joseph. Their fierce warriors also attacked tribes in the Illinois country. Due to the Iroquois threat, southeast Michigan was virtually depopulated during the seventeenth century, and the French used the Ottawa River/Lake Nipissing route to the west rather than the Lake Erie/St. Clair River route. During the late seventeenth century, when France and England were torn by King William's War, 1689–1697, the Iroquois took the brunt of the fighting. They lost so many warriors that in 1701 they signed a treaty of neutrality with the French and agreed to stay out of future conflicts. As a result, it was possible for the first time to settle Detroit and surround it with friendly tribes. The Lake Erie shipping route was now open, though cautious Cadillac brought his men to Detroit by the traditional Ottawa River route.

The Iroquois was not the only troublesome tribe. At Cadillac's invitation, a thousand Fox Indians moved from Wisconsin to the Detroit area, but within a short time they were in armed conflict with the Ottawa, Potawatomi, and French. In 1712 a nineteen-day siege of the Fox camp by Jacques Dubuisson resulted in a severe defeat for the Fox in the bloodiest battle ever fought on Michigan soil.[18] The survivors retreated to Wisconsin where they sought to block French expansion to the west. A series of devastating wars against the Fox raged from 1711 to 1740, resulting in their near extinction. The defeat of the Fox was only accomplished when the French sent a sizable force of heavily armed troops to the west to lay siege to the fortified Fox villages. As a result of the war, in 1715 it was decided to regarrison Michilimackinac, which had been abandoned in 1698. The fort was relocated to the south shore of the Straits.

Another tribe at some distance created a threat. The Chickasaw, along the Mississippi River, harassed French trade. Two expeditions were mounted from Michilimackinac in 1736 and 1739 to eliminate this threat. Local French militia and Indians accompanied these expeditions.

David A. Armour

One of the roles of the post commandant was to keep the local tribes friendly and to recruit them in time of war. The eighteenth century was disturbed by a series of wars between the French and English: Queen Anne's War, 1702–1714; King George's War, 1739–1745; and the French and Indian War, 1754–1760. During wartime, the superior English fleet frequently blocked the mouth of the St. Lawrence River, cutting off or curtailing imports.

Much of the fighting took place along the New York frontier, but the French, who were heavily outnumbered by the English, recruited

The Great Lakes area during the mid- to late-eighteenth century. Printed in Paul Christer Phillips, *The Fur Trade*, 1 (Norman: University of Oklahoma Press, 1961), 557.

western tribes from the Michigan area to assist them. Raiding parties of Great Lakes Indians ravaged the New York frontier during King George's War.

During the 1740s, English traders were moving into the Ohio country. Despite a futile effort by Céloron de Blainville in 1749 to persuade the British to leave, they strengthened their position and recruited Indian allies. The threat of an Indian uprising against the French frightened both Mackinac and Detroit. Finally, in 1752, Charles de Langlade led a force of Michilimackinac Indians to Ohio where they destroyed the English post at Pickawillany.[19] Full-scale warfare broke out in western Pennsylvania in 1754, and Michigan tribes went to defeat Gen. Edward Braddock near present-day Pittsburgh.

Soon, French and English were locked in a titanic struggle for control of North America. The English colonies had been growing rapidly in population and now numbered more than a million. Canada's growth was slow, and in all of New France there were only seventy thousand people. Both France and England committed increasing numbers of professional troops to the fray. When British Gen. James Wolfe captured Quebec in 1759 and Montreal fell in 1760, France's rule in New France came to an abrupt end.

Robert Rogers and a force of rangers quickly paddled to Detroit to raise the British Union Jack on 29 November 1760, while Beaujeau de Villemomble led the French troops down the Mississippi to Louisiana, which had not capitulated.

French political control of Michigan had come to an end. Most of the French people remained, however, and the remnants of their culture continue to be an important part of the mosaic that is Michigan.

NOTES

1. Marcel Trudel, "New France, 1524–1713," in *Dictionary of Canadian Biography*, 4 vols. (Toronto, 1966–1979), 1:35.

2. W. J. Eccles, *The Canadian Frontier: 1534–1760*, rev. ed. (Albuquerque, 1983), 19–20.

3. Ibid., xi, 37.

4. Ibid., 8, 82; Trudel, 1:35.

5. George Paré, *The Catholic Church in Detroit* (Detroit, 1951), 178–180; R. Cole Harris, ed., *Historical Atlas of Canada*, vol. 1 (Toronto, 1987), plate 41.

6. Jacqueline Peterson, "Many Roads to Red River: Metis Genesis in the Great Lakes Region, 1680–1815," in *The New Peoples; Being and Becoming Metis in North America*, ed. Jacqueline Peterson and Jennifer S. H. Brown (Lincoln, 1986), 37–71.

7. J. F. Bosher, *The Canada Merchants, 1713–1763* (Oxford, 1987), 79–84; Eccles, 146–47.

8. Eccles, 128.

9. *Dictionary of Canadian Biography*, 1:223–28, 2:535–40.

10. Paré, 113; Eccles, 52–53.

11. See Eugene T. Petersen, *France at Mackinac 1715–1750* (Mackinac Island, 1968).

12. See Dunning Idle, "The Post of the St. Joseph River During the French Regime: 1679–1761" (Ph.D. diss., University of Illinois-Urbana, 1946).

13. *Dictionary of Canadian Biography*, 1:618.

14. Ibid., 1:248–50.

15. Ibid., 1:172–84.

16. Ibid., 2:261–64.

17. Eccles, 116, 146–48.

18. Paré, 166.

19. *Dictionary of Canadian Biography*, 4:563–64.

———————◆———————

SUGGESTED READINGS

Brown, George W., Frances G. Halpenny, and David M. Haynes, eds. *Dictionary of Canadian Biography, 1000–1800.* 4 vols. Toronto, 1966–1979. These volumes contain scholarly and well-written biographies of the prominent people in Canada and Michigan during the French regime.

Eccles, W. J. *The Canadian Frontier: 1534–1760.* Rev. ed. Albuquerque, 1983. A perceptive, interpretive analysis of the Canadian frontier which included Michigan.

Harris, R. Cole, ed. *Historical Atlas of Canada.* Vol. 1, *From the Beginning to 1800.* Toronto, 1987. This volume contains numerous detailed maps and descriptive text about the Great Lakes area during the French period.

Paré, George. *The Catholic Church in Detroit 1701–1888.* Detroit, 1951. Despite its title, the book is not limited to Detroit but presents the religious history of Michigan during the French era.

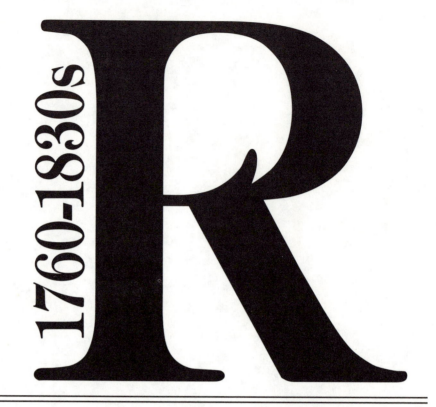

1760-1830s

JOHN CUMMING

A graduate of Eastern Michigan University and the University of Michigan, John Cumming served as director of the Clarke Historical Library at Central Michigan University for twenty-two years before retiring in 1983. He has been a frequent contributor of articles to Michigan historical magazines and is the author of several books such as *Runners and Walkers: A Nineteenth Century Sports Chronicle*. John Cumming is also a printer who has produced more than twenty-seven titles on his own private press, most notably a series of narratives of Michiganians who left the state for the California Gold Rush.

evolution in the Wilderness:
Michigan as Colony and Territory

The defeat of the French troops at Montreal, and the subsequent capitulation by the governor of Canada, yielded to the British all claims to that province which included the western Great Lakes and the Ohio Valley. The long struggle between these two nations came to an end on 8 September 1760. A few days later, Maj. Robert Rogers, under orders from Sir Jeffrey Amherst, commander in chief of the British forces, started for Detroit and Michilimackinac with two hundred men in fifteen whale boats.

Major Rogers stopped en route at Presqu'Isle to take on additional supplies and to report to Brig. Gen. Robert Monckton at Fort Pitt. Here the general ordered Capt. Donald Campbell to join the expedition with a company of soldiers and to remain in Detroit. George Croghan, an Irish trader who had experience in dealing with the Indians, was also added to the company to aid in conferences with the Indians. They stopped at several points in an effort to win their friendship.

Indian messengers had been sent on ahead to announce their approach to Detroit, which was reached on 29 November 1760. Upon presenting a copy of the capitulation to the French commandant, Capt. Francois de Bellestre, the British assumed possession of Detroit. A few days later the French commandant and his troops were sent under guard as prisoners of war to Fort Pitt.[1] Accompanying them were fifteen former English captives found among the Indians at Detroit.

The presence of English captives at Detroit was an indication of the active involvement of the Indians on behalf of the French in the recent war. Some of the prisoners were English traders who had been captured in the Ohio Valley, years before the outbreak of war. The French had laid claim to the lands from present-day Erie, Pennsylvania to Pittsburgh, and north of the Ohio River. Finding that English traders were operating in what they considered their territory, the French, with the aid of the Indians, took steps to prevent these incursions by English traders.

The occupation of Detroit marked the end of this war. Major Rogers had planned to proceed on to Michilimackinac to occupy the fort there, but the onset of winter weather prevented that endeavor. He left Detroit on 23 December and marched overland to Fort Pitt, leaving Captain Campbell in command.

Captain Campbell was an intelligent and observant officer. He spoke French and soon made friends of the French settlers in the area. Although he maintained friendly relationships with the Indians, he was not equipped to distribute gifts and ammunition among them as the French had done. This caused some stress. In the spring of 1761, the arrival of English traders promised to alleviate this situation. However, differences in the manners and practices of the English traders from their French predecessors gave rise to complaints from the Indians. Indeed, a general unrest existed among most of the Indian tribes, including those that had been allied with the British during the late war.

Under the French, the Indians had become accustomed to receiving gifts and provisions when needed, as well as the services of a gunsmith. To General Amherst, a stern and unyielding leader, this practice of purchasing good behavior from the Indians with gifts was reprehensible. He ordered it discontinued and established a new set of rules governing exchanges between the traders and Indians.

General Amherst failed to recognize a basic difference between Indians and whites. The Indians had no concept of private property, they believed in sharing their goods and wealth freely with friends and allies. Tension between the Indians and the British grew. In September 1762, an Indian from Detroit informed George Croghan at his home near Pittsburgh that the Indians were plotting against the British. Thomas

Hutchings, a surveyor who had been assigned the task of mapping the Great Lakes region, returned with a similar report, which expressed the Indians' disappointment in not receiving gifts and an adequate supply of ammunition. Croghan's reports to General Amherst of imminent trouble were ignored. In the meantime, Maj. Henry Gladwin had been elevated to the command at Detroit by Amherst.[2]

In the Ohio Valley among the Delawares, an Indian, called the Prophet, had begun to exhort the Indians to rise against all whites and to drive them from their lands. With evangelical fervor, he urged the Indians to return to their old ways before the coming of the Europeans. The Prophet was heard by the Indians. Their beliefs in the validity of the Prophet's warnings were reinforced by the large number of white settlers who were beginning to cross the mountains into western Pennsylvania and Kentucky. A climate for war existed.

In the Detroit area an Ottawa leader, Pontiac, had risen to a position of influence. Early in 1763, he summoned Indian tribes who were allied with his group to a meeting. At a later meeting, he outlined a plot for a surprise attack upon Detroit. With sixty carefully chosen warriors, he would enter the fort for a council with Major Gladwin. Under their blankets, Indian warriors would carry weapons concealed from the English. The rest of the Ottawa were to follow the warriors into the fort with weapons concealed in a like manner. At a given signal, the Indians were to attack.

Pontiac's secret was not well kept. Major Gladwin had been informed of the plot in advance and had his troops fully armed and ready when the visitors arrived. Recognizing that his plans had been disclosed, Pontiac did not give the signal for attack. He and his followers departed. When other ruses failed, Pontiac gave the war cry and began the attack on the English who resided outside the fort. At the end of the first week of hostilities, the Indians had killed fifteen men and women, wounded five, and captured fifteen. With but one hundred soldiers and about twenty merchants to defend the fort against Pontiac's eight hundred warriors, Major Gladwin saw that the fort was in peril unless relief could be obtained.

The Indian uprising spread throughout the area west of the Alleghenies. Pontiac's command, however, did not extend beyond the Detroit area. In short order Fort Sandusky in Ohio, Fort St. Joseph in southwestern Michigan, and the fort at Michilimackinac fell.

Fort Michilimackinac was surprised by a group of Chippewa and Sauk Indians who were engaged in a game of lacrosse outside the fort. While the braves were engaged in their game, women moved toward the gate and into the enclosure with knives and tomahawks concealed under their blankets. The ball was thrown in the direction of the gate, and the Indians followed it. Grasping their weapons from the women, the warriors attacked the soldiers, killing most of them.

The first effort to aid the besieged fort at Detroit ended in defeat when a force of one hundred men was attacked by Pontiac's forces while encamped at Point Pelee on Lake Erie. Unaware that the Indians were already at war against Detroit, Lieut. Abraham Cuyler and his men fell easy victims to the Indians, with more than half of the company being killed or captured.

The next relief expedition, consisting of 260 men in twenty-two batteaux under the command of Capt. James Dalyell and accompanied by Maj. Robert Rogers, arrived at Detroit from Fort Niagara on 29 July. Almost immediately, Captain Dalyell persuaded Major Gladwin to permit him to lead an attack upon the Ottawa village. Forewarned by cooperating Frenchmen in the fort, Pontiac lay in wait for Captain Dalyell's troops, ambushing them at Parent's Creek. The British troops were forced to retreat, suffering the loss of fifty-eight officers and men either killed or wounded. Since that day, the creek has been known as Bloody Run.

As the war wore on, a number of Indians began to lose interest and made moves toward peace with Major Gladwin. Although hostilities continued, the British won minor skirmishes, helping to discourage the Indians further. As signs of winter approached, more Indians deserted the cause. Throughout the war, Pontiac had hoped to receive word of support from the French commandant at Fort Chartes in Illinois. When word was finally received on 29 October, it was not a promise of aid but a notice that the war in Europe between the British and the French had ended and that there would be no further French presence in the Great Lakes area or the Ohio Valley. Pontiac dispatched a note, translated into French, to Major Gladwin offering to make peace. Major Gladwin responded that the note would be forwarded to General Amherst for his decision. Without waiting for a reply, Pontiac, and a few followers, departed for the Maumee. The Indian uprising was at an end.[3]

One of the major complaints of the Indians was the encroachment of settlers upon what they considered to be their territory. Siding with the Indians on this issue were the traders, who wished to maintain the *status quo* for their own profit. In 1763 the British government issued a proclamation that, among other points, ruled that a line be drawn along the crest of the Alleghenies. Settlers could not go beyond this line. In addition, the Crown ruled that trade with the Indians and other matters concerning them should be governed henceforth by the Crown rather than by the colonies.

For the colonists, these rules were a great disappointment. Many a resident of the colonies harbored a dream of moving into the wilderness to establish a home and clear a farm. Indeed, some had already done so. Others in more prosperous circumstances entertained prospects of winning further wealth by acquiring huge tracts of land for development. Thus, in attempting to solve one problem with the Indians, the Crown replaced it with one that soon would be a contributing factor in the outbreak of a rebellion against the mother country by the colonists.

With the end of Indian hostilities in the Ohio Valley and the Great Lakes, a new set of traders moved into the area. Many of them were Scots, Irish, and Dutch from Albany, while some were New Englanders and entrepreneurs from other colonies. These traders soon learned to deal with the Indians as effectively as the French had. Many of them became permanent settlers at Detroit and allied themselves to the French through marriage.

When the Revolutionary War began in 1775, Lieut. Gov. Henry Hamilton was in charge at Detroit and had jurisdiction over other posts in the area. Although Michigan was not the scene of any battles in this conflict, Detroit became a center for mustering Indian bands for attacks upon the settlements in Kentucky.

The major Revolutionary War conflict west of the Alleghenies took place when Col. George Rogers Clark led a small detachment of soldiers into the Illinois country to capture British posts there in order to reduce the number of attacks upon the Kentucky settlements. Upon learning of Colonel Clark's conquests, Lieutenant Governor Hamilton left Detroit with a small army of soldiers, volunteers, and Indians to recapture Fort Sackville at Vincennes, which was defended by a small garrison left there by Colonel Clark. Informed of the recapture, Colonel Clark promptly turned about and returned to surprise the British and to force them to surrender on 25 February 1779. Hamilton and his aides were taken prisoner and sent to Virginia for the duration of the war.

The British feared that Colonel Clark would mount an attack upon Detroit and Michilimackinac. As a precaution, Maj. Patrick Sinclair moved his troops from the south side of the Straits to Mackinac Island, where during 1779–1781 he erected a new fort.

The raids against the Kentucky settlements did not cease with the capture of Hamilton. Col. Arent Schuyler, the commandant at Michilimackinac, took over the command at Detroit and continued to send raiding parties to Kentucky.

Fort St. Joseph, at the site of present-day Niles, had no military garrison but was occupied by British traders. In December 1780, a party of French *habitants* from the Illinois country occupied the old fort, but upon learning that a party of British traders was approaching, they quickly left. Many of them were slain by the British as they retreated. In February 1781, a company of Spaniards, French, and Indians returned to capture the fort. This time they raised the Spanish flag. Although Spain was not allied with the colonists, it was at war with England. This incident permits Niles today to call itself the "Land of Four Flags," since it has been under the flags of France, Great Britain, Spain, and the United States.

When the Revolution was over and the treaty of peace signed in 1783, England ceded all of Michigan to the new nation. However, Britain held on to Detroit and Michigan in spite of the treaty and continued to incite the Indians against the settlers, who were now moving into western Pennsylvania and the Ohio Valley in large numbers.

In an effort to end the Indian raids, Pres. George Washington in 1790 appointed Gen. Josiah Harmar to lead a force of fifteen hundred men in a punitive expedition against the Indians. Harmar's troops, however, were not well trained, and the army was defeated by the Indians. A year later, a larger force, under Gov. Arthur St. Clair, met the same fate. President Washington then named Gen. Anthony Wayne to lead still another army. Aware that lack of training was the cause of the defeats, General Wayne spent more than a year whipping his troops into fighting form. In August 1794, General Wayne and his troops met the Indians and British volunteers in an engagement near present-day Maumee, Ohio. The well-drilled American forces soundly defeated the Indians and British in what has become known as the Battle of Fallen Timbers. To secure the area, General Wayne built a fort at what is now Fort Wayne, Indiana, and left a detachment of soldiers there. The next summer, the Indian tribes met at Fort Greenville to make peace with the Americans.

The success of General Wayne's troops was sufficient to convince the British they should finally surrender the western posts. At war again with the French, Britain was reluctant to become engaged in another conflict with the Americans. On 11 July 1796, the British flag was lowered at Detroit, and Capt. Moses Porter and his American soldiers marched into Fort Lernoult (Detroit) to raise the stars and stripes. Two months later, the American flag was also flying over Fort Mackinac.

Following the Revolution, the question of how to deal with the vast tract of land acquired west of the Alleghenies was one of the major problems facing the new nation. States along the Atlantic coast maintained claims to the territory based on their original charters from the British Crown. These claims were often overlapping and conflicting because when the charters were granted the Crown had no real concept of what lands existed beyond the mountains. The settlement finally reached resulted in the states ceding to the federal government all claims to the territory, reserving only a few tracts of land to be sold to settle war debts and to reward those who served in the Revolutionary War.

The flood gates for western settlement and land speculation were opened. Huge tracts of land measured in millions of acres were sold or acquired by hastily organized companies, some fraudulently. One group even attempted to bribe congressmen in an effort to acquire title to all the Lower Peninsula of Michigan. Each Congress for more than half a century would face the task of devising a solution for an equitable system of land sales and distribution.[4]

As a means of providing an orderly administration of the territory, the government passed a series of ordinances—in 1784, 1785, and 1787. The last, known as the Northwest Ordinance, provided a plan of government or constitution for the Northwest Territory. It guaranteed the inhabitants freedom of religion, the right of *habeas corpus*, trial by jury, free passage on all navigable waters, and a number of other basic rights. It also stated that ". . . schools and the means of education shall forever be encouraged."

Slavery was also banned under the Northwest Ordinance. However, British subjects who possessed slaves before 11 July 1796 were allowed to keep them under the terms of the Jay Treaty (1795), which declared that British subjects would not be deprived of their property. Some of the slaves had been captured by the Indians in their raids on Kentucky. As late as 1830, the census showed that there were still thirty-two slaves in Michigan. Six years later, they had all been freed or had died.

With the raising of the American flag over Detroit, Lieut. Col. John Francis Hamtramck was placed in charge of the military and civilians. Unlike Ohio, Michigan was not immediately inundated with settlers and speculators. A few merchants came from the eastern states to start businesses, and there were a few notable attorneys among the newcomers. In 1798, Father Gabriel Richard, a Catholic priest, arrived to serve as assistant to Father Michel Levadoux. A refugee from France, Father Richard became a major contributor to the early development of Detroit and Michigan.

Until 1803 when it was attached to the Indiana Territory, Michigan remained a part of the Northwest Territory. During this period, most of what is today Michigan was simply an immense county within the territories; a county named in honor of Gen. Anthony Wayne. In January 1805, Pres. Thomas Jefferson approved an act establishing the Territory of Michigan, which included those lands within a line running east from the lower end of Lake Michigan and a line running north through the middle of that lake. This excluded much of the Upper Peninsula.

Appointed by President Jefferson to administer the territory were William Hull of Massachusetts, governor; Stanley Griswold of New Hampshire, secretary; Samuel Huntington of Ohio, Augustus Brevoort Woodward of Washington, D.C., and Frederick Bates of Detroit and, formerly, Virginia, judges. Huntington declined the appointment. Under the act of Congress, these officials were to assume office on 1 July 1805, the date on which Michigan was to become a territory.

Governor Hull, his family, and Stanley Griswold arrived in Detroit on 1 July to find an unexpected reception. Detroit was in ashes. A disastrous fire on 11 June had destroyed the town, leaving only a blockhouse and the fort standing.

The governor's first task was to rebuild Detroit. Judge Woodward prepared a plan modeled upon that of the nation's new capital at Washington, providing for wide streets and avenues radiating from hubs. A plan for distributing lots in the new town was also adopted. Congress approved the plans. However, Governor Hull faced a difficult task in carrying out the plans, encountering bitter complaints over lot assignments and opposition to Judge Woodward's progressive plan.

Added to the problem was the status of land titles. Under the French and British, little attention had been given to providing proper titles to land. Unraveling this entanglement required the action of Congress. Gradually, the claims of those who could prove possession before 1 July 1796 were approved.

From the American legal viewpoint, the Indians still held title to most of the lands in the Territory of Michigan. Surveys and settlement could not begin until title to the land had been acquired by the United States. Governor Hull was commissioned and ordered to negotiate a treaty with the Indians to acquire title to lands. The result was the Treaty of Brownstown (1807), which ceded to the United States an area of land in the southeastern part of the territory.

One of the losses in the fire of 1805 was the school for boys, which had been established in 1804 by Father Gabriel Richard and his assistant Father John Dilhet. Father Richard also started a training school for Indian and white boys and succeeded in obtaining some federal assistance for the program. From the East, he brought equipment for the school. At the same time, he also brought a printing press to Michigan.

As early as 1796, there had been a printing press in Detroit that produced some legal forms and an act of Congress in pamphlet form. By 1800, the press had been moved from Detroit. Father Richard's press printed the first book in Michigan, and, in 1809, Michigan's first newspaper was issued. Entitled *The Michigan Essay; or The Impartial Observer,* the newspaper seems to have been limited to one issue.

Rumors of unrest among the Indians were often heard during these early years of the Territory of Michigan. Tecumseh, a Shawnee leader, and his brother Elsquataw, known as the Prophet, were making hostile threats as they attempted to organize the tribes of Ohio, Indiana, and Michigan into a unified group to stem the tide of white settlement. Fears of Indian attacks on such a remote outpost as Detroit discouraged settlers from moving to the area.

As hostilities between Indians and whites increased, the settlers appealed to Pres. James Madison for help. A detachment of soldiers was sent to Vincennes. Gov. William Henry Harrison of Indiana assembled these soldiers and a number of militia and volunteers from Indiana and Kentucky. They marched to the Prophet's town on the Tippecanoe, a branch of the Wabash River, where they engaged the Indians in battle on 6 November 1811. Both sides suffered heavy casualties in the fight but the Indians were routed and fled. Governor Harrison burned the village and retired with his troops.

At the same time, relations between Britain and the United States were rapidly deteriorating, resulting in a declaration of war by Congress on 18 June 1812. In March 1812, Governor Hull had warned the secretary of war that in the event of war with Britain, a large military force at Detroit would be required to defend the post from attack. He also pointed out that these troops would be handicapped because the British controlled the lakes. All United States troops and supplies would have to pass through the wilderness to reach Detroit. On 8 April 1812, Governor Hull was named brigadier general and assigned the command of the Northwestern Army.

General Hull traveled to Dayton, Ohio, to take command of three regiments of Ohio militia. Marching northward toward Detroit, they picked up the United States troops who had fought earlier in the Battle of Tippecanoe. The road ahead was difficult. Soldiers had to be detailed for clearing the road, and the heavy rains and flooding further impeded their progress. At Maumee, General Hull chartered two small schooners. The boats were sent on to Detroit on 1 July. The next day General Hull received a notice by messenger from the War Department that war had been declared. Four days earlier, the British commander at Fort Malden, across the river from Detroit, had received a similar notice. The British were ready and waiting when General Hull's schooners appeared. They captured one carrying equipment and General Hull's records.

General Hull had received instructions to proceed to Detroit and to await further orders. Being an experienced army officer, General Hull obeyed, in spite of urging from his young officers—one of whom was Lewis Cass—to attack Malden at once. When General Hull did receive instructions from the secretary of war to take Fort Malden if he could without endangering Detroit, he crossed the river with his forces. After a few skirmishes, General Hull, to the disappointment of his officers, decided not to attack Fort Malden and ordered his troops to return to Detroit.

Capt. Henry Brush had arrived at the River Raisin south of Detroit with supplies, but could not go on to Detroit without the protection of an escort of troops. Three efforts to send troops to escort Captain Brush to Detroit failed. In the meantime, Fort Malden had been reinforced with troops and Indian allies. The heavy artillery of Fort Malden and Detroit exchanged salvos. Gen. Sir Isaac Brock, the new commandant at Fort Malden, crossed the river with his troops, reinforced by Tecumseh with a large body of Indians. They advanced on Detroit. General Hull, recognizing that his position was untenable and not willing to expose the inhabitants of Detroit to the perils of war, surrendered to the British. Once again, Michigan was under British rule.[5]

At Mackinac Island, Lieut. Porter Hanks was unaware that war had begun when, on the morning of 17 July 1812, a large force under British Capt. Charles Roberts appeared on the island and demanded that the Americans surrender. Hopelessly outnumbered, Lieutenant Hanks had no option but to surrender. Fort Mackinac fell without a shot being fired.

Gen. William Henry Harrison was appointed commander of the Northwestern Army with orders to defend the frontier, recapture Detroit, and conquer Canada. One of the first suggestions that General Harrison made to the secretary of war was that a fleet of naval vessels be built on Lake Erie, a recommendation that General Hull had made a year before.

At the River Raisin, residents of Frenchtown (now Monroe) complained that a force of British soldiers and Indians garrisoned near that town were harassing them. A detachment of men under Capt. William Lewis was dispatched on 17 January 1813 to aid the settlers. In the initial encounter, Captain Lewis and his men routed the enemy. Fearing that the enemy would regroup with reinforcements, Captain Lewis called for aid from Gen. James Winchester, who moved up from Maumee with three hundred men. On the morning of 22 January, the British and Indians attacked, catching General Winchester and his Kentuckians by surprise, and driving them across the river. In the battle,

General Winchester was taken prisoner. The British commander, Colonel Proctor, persuaded General Winchester that nothing could be done to protect them from the Indians unless he surrendered his force. General Winchester and the men who could walk were taken to Fort Malden as prisoners. The wounded were left at Frenchtown to be cared for by the settlers. Next morning, the Indians swept down upon the village, killing the wounded soldiers.

The government, finally recognizing that control of the lakes would be necessary to defeat the British, sent a young naval lieutenant, Oliver Hazzard Perry, to Erie, Pennsylvania, to build ships. By mid-summer Lieutenant Perry's fleet was ready for combat. In the first week of August, he sailed out into Lake Erie.

In the meantime, General Harrison had built Fort Meigs on the Maumee and had repulsed an attack by Colonel Proctor and the British, although one unit of General Harrison's troops suffered heavy casualties in the battle. By September, however, Harrison had eleven thousand men in his command, including three thousand mounted soldiers.

On 10 September, while Perry and his fleet were at Put-in-Bay, the enemy was sighted; Lieutenant Perry sailed forth to battle. After a bitter contest, the British commander was compelled to strike his colors. Lieutenant Perry sent General Harrison his famous message: "We have met the enemy and they are ours."

Ten days later, General Harrison started to move his large force toward Detroit and Fort Malden. Learning of General Harrison's advance, Colonel Proctor made haste to abandon Detroit and head east for Toronto. Now aided by a fleet of ships for transporting supplies and equipment and a large mounted force, General Harrison was able to make rapid pursuit. He overtook the enemy at the river Thames. After a brief attack by General Harrison's troops, the enemy broke ranks and surrendered. The Indians held on for a while longer before fleeing into the woods. Their leader, Tecumseh, died in the battle.

A month earlier, an attack upon Mackinac by the Americans had failed. The return of that post had to await the signing of the Treaty of Ghent in December 1814, which affirmed the prewar boundary between the United States and Canada along the Great Lakes.[6]

Gen. Lewis Cass was placed in command of Detroit and on 29 October 1813 he was named governor of the Territory of Michigan by Pres. James Madison. Little was known about Michigan when Lewis Cass assumed the duties of territorial governor. When the newly-appointed territorial secretary, William Woodbridge, wrote to Gen. Duncan McArthur at Detroit to request information about the Territory of Michigan, he was told that Michigan was not worth defending. "The

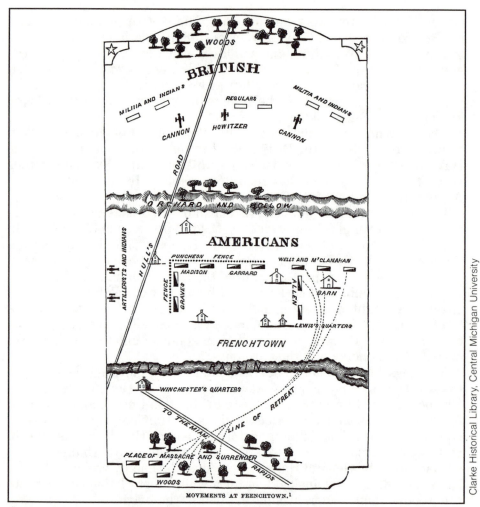

BRITISH

WOODS

MILITIA AND INDIANS

REGULARS

MILITIA AND INDIANS

CANNON

HOWITZER

CANNON

ROAD

ORCHARD AND HOLLOW

AMERICANS

HULL'S

PUNCHEON FENCE

WELLS AND M'CLANAHAN

FENCE

MADISON

GARRARD

ARTILLERISTS AND INDIANS

ALLEN

BARN

GRAVES

LEWIS'S QUARTERS

FRENCHTOWN

RIVER RAISIN

WINCHESTER'S QUARTERS

LINE OF RETREAT

TO THE MIAMI

PLACE OF MASSACRE AND SURRENDER

RAPIDS

WOODS

MOVEMENTS AT FRENCHTOWN.[1]

Plan of the Battle of Frenchtown (22 Jan. 1813). Printed in Benson J. Lossing, *Pictorial Field Book of the War of 1812* (New York: Harper and Brothers, 1896), 358. The Clarke Historical Library, Central Michigan University owns an original manuscript of this map.

Clarke Historical Library, Central Michigan University

banks of the Detroit River are handsome, but nine-tenths of the land in the Territory is unfit for cultivation," he wrote. Edward Tiffin, the surveyor general of Ohio, on 30 November 1815, agreed:

> Taking the country altogether so far as it has been explored, and to all appearances, together with the information received in regard to the balance, it is so bad there would not be one acre out of one hundred, if there would be more than one out of a thousand, that would in any case admit of cultivation.

The government at this time was planning to grant bounty lands in Michigan to veterans of the War of 1812. On the basis of these reports, it changed its mind and instead made grants in Illinois and Missouri.

The cause of much of the slow development of Michigan during this period has been attributed to Tiffin's unfavorable report. There were other reasons, however. Ohio had been settled rapidly because it was more easily accessible and had been well explored. Settlers floated down the Ohio River to claim lands in that area; others found easy access to the lands along Lake Erie. In addition, large tracts of land in Ohio were in possession of companies of speculators who energetically promoted settlement. Then, too, Michigan was not ready for settlement. With the exception of the one road from the Maumee Rapids to Detroit, there were no roads in Michigan.

Since the only land acquired from the Indians was that obtained by Governor Hull in 1807, Governor Cass faced the task of making further treaties to acquire additional lands. In 1817 he obtained a small tract along the southern boundary of the territory; in 1819, by the Treaty of Saginaw, he acquired a large tract north and west of the 1807 acquisition; and in 1821, at Chicago, he acquired an area in the southwestern part of the territory south of the Grand River, except a small corner in the extreme southwest that was obtained later. The Treaty of Washington in 1836 ceded the balance of the Lower Peninsula and a portion of the Upper Peninsula.

In 1810 the population of the Territory of Michigan was 4,762. By 1820 it had increased to only 8,765. There were, however, some signs of progress. In 1817 the *Detroit Gazette* was printed and continued publication until 1830. The *Walk-in-the-Water*, the first steamboat on the western lakes, arrived in Detroit 27 August 1818. In 1817 Judge Augustus B. Woodward presented a plan for the *Catholepistemiad* or "University of Michigania," which would have provided a school system for the primary level through the university. Reverend John Montieth, a Presbyterian minister, and Father Gabriel Richard were appointed president and vice president, respectively. Although the plan never really materialized, it did signal an interest in education that would eventually develop and flourish.

Despite the slow growth of population in the territory, a few counties were established. Monroe County was organized in 1817. In 1818

John Cumming

Macomb and Mackinac counties were established, followed by Oakland County in 1819 and St. Clair County in 1820.

In 1820 Governor Cass led an expedition to the Lake Superior country both for exploration and for becoming acquainted with the Indians of the area. With him was Henry Rowe Schoolcraft, who served as geologist to study mineral formations. Traveling in three large canoes, the expedition first visited Mackinac, followed by Sault Ste. Marie, where the reception by the Indians fell short of friendliness. Bold action on the part of Governor Cass impressed the Indians and convinced them that they must acknowledge the sovereignty of the United States. The expedition continued along the southern shore of Lake Superior and visited parts of Wisconsin and Minnesota.[7]

The lack of roads in Michigan still remained a barrier to settlement of the interior. During the decade of the 1820s, appropriations from Congress made possible the construction of roads, the first of which was from Perrysburgh, Ohio, to Detroit. Other roads planned and started were from Detroit to Chicago, Detroit to Fort Gratiot, Detroit to Saginaw Bay, and Detroit to Grand Rapids. Each session of Congress provided funds for

Detroit in 1820 from the Canadian shore with the *Walk-in-the-Water*, the first steamboat on the upper Great Lakes, in the center. This engraving was taken from an original painting by George W. Whistler, owned by the Dossin Great Lakes Museum in Detroit.

Clarke Historical Library, Central Michigan University

extending these roads. The road to Chicago, for example, was surveyed and started in 1825 but was not completed until 1835.

Settlement during the first half of the decade of the 1820s moved at a slow pace but accelerated considerably with the opening of the Erie Canal in 1825. The canal provided easy access to Lake Erie from New York and New England. By 1830 the population of Michigan had grown to 31,640. A decade later it would be 212,267.

By 1830 Michigan was accessible to immigrants from the East. Roads were extended into the interior. Most of the lands in Ohio, Indiana, and Illinois were occupied or were in the hands of land companies and speculators and were no longer bargains. Michigan's day had come.[8]

The fact that Michigan was slow in winning the attention of settlers and speculators finally worked to its advantage. The land acts had been reformed in each session of Congress so that now lots were available at prices that many more settlers could afford to pay. Because the experience with speculators in Ohio had ended in such a debacle, there were no million-acre grants to speculators in Michigan, thus freeing the land for individual purchase. In addition, the government was now in a position to extend help to the territory by providing funds for roads.

Towns and cities were being promoted across the whole southern portion of the Territory of Michigan. A site was selected, preferably near water power or along one of the main roads, and a village was platted. They did not even wait for the road. As soon as surveys were completed, developers platted the towns and villages and waited for the road to arrive, in the meantime selling lots for the metropolis-to-be.

With the towns came schools, newspapers, churches, stores, mills, factories, and all the appurtenances for civilization. In 1827 the Territorial Council enacted a law that required every township with a population of fifty or more to engage a schoolteacher. Although these were not free schools, reading instruction was offered by many churches in free Sunday schools. By the time Michigan was ready for statehood, there were newspapers in Detroit, Monroe, Ann Arbor, Pontiac, White Pigeon, Adrian, Kalamazoo, Marshall, Constantine, and Niles.

The growth in population brought a demand from the territory's citizens for more representative government. As early as 1818, the United States Congress passed an act authorizing a delegate to Congress from the Territory of Michigan. In 1823, another congressional act raised Michigan to the second degree of territorial government. The voters were empowered to choose eighteen men from which the President would choose nine to serve as a Legislative Council. Four years later, the council was made completely elective and superceded the governor and judges as the lawmaking body of the territory.

Gov. Lewis Cass ended his tenure as governor of the Territory of Michigan in 1831, when Pres. Andrew Jackson named Cass to his cabinet as secretary of war. The citizens of the territory held a banquet in Detroit in Governor Cass's honor on 24 July 1831, before his departure for Washington. On the same day, Governor Cass swore into duty as secretary of the Territory of Michigan Stevens T. Mason, a nineteen-year-old youth whom President Jackson had appointed to that office. George B. Porter was appointed governor by President Jackson.

Governor Porter did not spend a great deal of time in Michigan and died of cholera three years after being appointed. During his absences and after his death, Secretary Mason served as acting governor. Although many had initially opposed Secretary Mason's appointment, they soon became impressed with his energy and leadership.

Clarke Historical Library, Central Michigan University

Lewis Cass, soldier, diplomat, and politician, was a dynamic force for development during Michigan's territorial and early statehood period.

With dynamic leadership, the Territory of Michigan looked forward to rapid growth and statehood in the near future. Towns were springing up in every direction. Investors, tradesmen, artisans, and professionals were swarming to Michigan. By 1832, Michigan had grown sufficiently in population to qualify for statehood. The transition from territory to state, however, would not be easy.

NOTES

1. Maj. Robert Rogers kept a journal of this expedition to Detroit, which was published first in London in 1765 and later in *Bulletin of the New York Public Library* (1933): 265–76. George Croghan's journal covering the same trip was published in the *Massachusetts Historical Society Collections,* 4th series (1871): 362–79.

2. Nicholas B. Wainwright, ed., "George Croghan's Journal, 1759–1763," *Pennsylvania Magazine of History and Biography* (1947): 303–444.

3. There are a number of eyewitness accounts of the Pontiac War. Most of these were used in Francis Parkman's *Conspiracy of Pontiac* (Boston, 1892); and in Howard Peckham's *Pontiac and the Indian Uprising* (Princeton, 1947).

4. A comprehensive review of the land policies and acts of Congress is Roy M. Robbins, *Our Landed Heritage, The Public Domain, 1776–1936* (Lincoln, Neb., 1942).

5. General Hull was tried in a court-martial in January 1814 and found guilty of cowardice and neglect of duty. Sentenced to be shot, General Hull's execution was remitted by Pres. James Madison. He retired to his home in Massachusetts, where he wrote *Memoirs of the Campaign of the Northwestern Army* in an effort to exonerate himself.

6. A number of excellent eyewitness accounts of the War of 1812 in Michigan have been written. Notable are *War on Detroit, the Chronicles of Thomas Vercheres de Boucherville and the Capitulation by an Ohio Volunteer,* ed. Milo Quaife (Chicago, 1940); *A Narrative of the Battle of Brownstown During the Campaign under General Hull* (New York, 1816); Adam Walker, *A Journal of Two Campaigns of the Fourth Regiment of the United States Infantry, in the Michigan and Indiana Territories, 1811–1813* (Keene, N.H., 1816); and John Richardson, *War of 1812* (Toronto, 1902).

7. Several members of Governor Cass's expedition kept journals that have been published. Best known is Henry Schoolcraft, *Narrative Journal of Travels through the Northwestern Regions of the United States, Extending from Detroit through the Great Chain of American Lakes to the Sources of the Mississippi River. Performed as a Member of the Expedition under Governor Cass. In the Year 1820* (Albany, N.Y., 1821).

8. Early travelers to Michigan published their impressions of the territory in books which were eagerly read by easterners who were contemplating emigration. William Darby's *A Tour from the City of New York to Detroit, in the Michigan Territory, Made between the 2nd of May and the 22nd of September, 1818* (New York, 1818), and Estwick Evans's *A Pedestrious Tour, of Four Thousand Miles Through the Western States and Territories, during the Winter and Spring of 1818* (Concord, N.H., 1819) are good pictures of the early period. For a picture of Michigan during the later territorial period, one of the best accounts is Charles Fenno Hoffman's *A Winter in the West*. He traveled through Michigan in 1833, writing accounts of the land for eastern newspapers, which were subsequently published in book form.

◆

SUGGESTED READINGS

THE BRITISH TAKE POSSESSION OF MICHIGAN

Croghan, George. "George Croghan's Journal 1759–1763." *Pennsylvania Magazine of History and Biography.* Edited by Nicholas B. Wainwright. *Pennsylvania Magazine of History and Biography* 71 (1947): 303–444.

————. "Journal of George Croghan, 1760–61." *Massachusetts Historical Society Collections*, 4th series, 9 (1871): 362–79.

Rogers, Robert. "Journal of Robert Rogers on his Expedition for Receiving the Capitulation of Western French Forts." *Bulletin of the New York Public Library*, 37 (1933): 265–76.

THE PONTIAC WAR

Morris, Thomas. *Miscellanies in Prose and Verse.* London, 1791. Reprinted in Reuben G. Thwaites. *Early Western Travels, 1748–1846.* Cleveland, 1904–1907.

Navarre, Robert. *Journal of the Conspiracy of Pontiac.* Translated by R. Clyde Ford. Detroit, 1910.

Parkman, Francis. *History of the Conspiracy of Pontiac, and the Indian Wars after the Conquest of Canada.* Boston, 1913.

Peckham, Howard H. *Pontiac and the Indian Uprising.* Princeton, 1947.

INDIAN CAPTIVES—
UNWILLING VISITORS TO MICHIGAN

Henry, Alexander. *Alexander Henry's Travels and Adventures in Canada and the Indian Territories between 1760 and 1776.* Edited by Milo Quaife. Chicago, 1921.

Jefferies, Ewell. *A Short Biography of John Leeth.* Reprinted in Reuben G. Thwaites. *Early Western Travels, 1748–1846.* Cleveland, 1904–1907.

Peckham, Howard H. *Captured by Indians.* New Brunswick, N.J., 1954.

————. "Thomas Gist's Indian Captivity." *Pennsylvania Magazine of History and Biography* 80 (1956): 287–311.

Tanner, John. *A Narrative of the Captivity of John Tanner, During Thirty Years in Residence among the Indians in the Interior of North America.* Recorded by Edwin James. New York, 1830.

THE WAR OF 1812

Clift, G. Glenn. *Remember the Raisin! Kentucky and Kentuckians in the Battles and Massacre at Frenchtown, Michigan Territory, in the War of 1812.* Frankfort, Ky., 1961.

Darnell, Elias. *A Journal Containing an Accurate and Interesting Account of the Hardships, Sufferings, Battles, Defeats, and Captivity of Those Heroic Volunteers Commanded by General Winchester in the Years 1812–1813.* Paris, Ky., 1813.

Foster, James. *The Capitulation, or a History of the Expedition Conducted by William Hull, Brigadier General of the Northwestern Army.* Chillicothe, Ohio, 1812. Reprinted in *War on the Detroit.* Edited by Milo Quaife. Chicago, 1940.

THE TERRITORIAL PERIOD

Darby, William. *A Tour from the City of New York to Detroit in the Michigan Territory, Made between the 2nd of May and the 22nd of September, 1818.* New York, 1818.

Evans, Estwick. *A Pedestrious Tour, of Four Thousand Miles Through the Western States and Territories, during the Winter and Spring of 1818.* Concord, N.H., 1819.

Hoffman, Charles Fenno. *A Winter in the West; by a New Yorker.* 2 vols. Albany, N.Y., 1835.

Michigan Pioneer and Historical Collections. 40 vols. Lansing, 1877–1913. In anticipation of the Centennial of the United States, in the 1870s pioneer societies were organized throughout Michigan. At the meetings of these societies, members presented papers containing their recollections of pioneer life in Michigan. The best of these were collected and published by the state in this series. In addition to the reminiscences, documents, and diaries, letters of historical importance were also published in these volumes.

Nowlin, William. *The Bark Covered House.* Detroit, 1876.

Schoolcraft, Henry R. *A Narrative Journal of Travels through the Northwestern Regions of the United States, Extending from Detroit through the Great Chain of American Lakes to the Sources of the Mississippi River. Performed as a Member of the Expedition under Governor Cass. In the Year 1820.* Albany, N.Y., 1821.

1832-1837

ROGER L. ROSENTRETER

Roger Rosentreter, acting editor of *Michigan History* magazine, has been with the Bureau of History, Michigan Department of State since 1979. A native Michiganian, he received a bachelor's degree from Western Michigan University and master's and doctorate degrees from Michigan State University. He has written numerous articles on Michigan history, and is the author of the "Michigan's 83 Counties" series which appears regularly in *Michigan History* magazine.

ichigan's Quest for Statehood

On 12 January 1835, acting Michigan Territorial Governor Stevens T. Mason announced to the legislative council that Michigan faced a crisis. Michigan's effort to join the Union as a state had failed. Its request to Congress for an enabling act—congressional permission to call a constitutional convention—had been rejected. The twenty-three-year-old governor declared that Michigan had a "right" to be admitted to the Union, and he asked the legislative council to call a constitutional convention. Twelve days later the council concurred; delegates would be elected in April and gather in Detroit in early May.[1]

Born in Virginia and raised in Kentucky, Stevens T. Mason came to the Territory of Michigan when his father, John Mason, was appointed territorial secretary in 1830. In 1831, following his father's resignation, the nineteen-year-old Mason was appointed secretary by Pres. Andrew Jackson. During the frequent absences of Michigan Territorial Governor George Porter, Mason acted as the ex officio executive. Following Porter's death in July 1834, Mason, known as the "Boy Governor," aggressively campaigned to make Michigan a state.

The January 1835 decision to call a constitutional convention without congressional approval followed several years of frustration. In October 1832 Michigan voters had agreed to initiate the statehood process. In December 1833 Congress received the first formal petition requesting Michigan's admission to the Union. The following year, Congress rejected the request to call a convention, despite a census that showed the Territory of Michigan had twenty-five thousand more persons than the sixty thousand necessary to admit a territory into the Union under the provisions of the Northwest Ordinance of 1787.

The call for a constitutional convention, an act of defiance to federal authority, also precipitated the Toledo War, a conflict between the Territory of Michigan and the state of Ohio over less than five hundred square miles of land dominated by the community of Toledo (originally named Port Lawrence). That conflict was to delay Michigan's admission to the Union for two more years.

Disagreement over who owned the Toledo Strip, especially the mouth of the Maumee River which empties into Lake Erie, began in the early nineteenth century. According to the Northwest Ordinance, the boundary between the northern and southern states in the Northwest Territory would be an east-west line that intersected the southern tip of Lake Michigan. Because of the uncertainty of the exact location of the lake's southernmost point, as well as the absence of a good survey marking the east-west line, Ohio included a provision in its 1803 state constitution that gave the mouth of the Maumee River to Ohio, regardless of where the Northwest Ordinance placed the line. For the next thirty years, both Michigan and Ohio claimed the Toledo Strip. One survey, conducted by William Harris and known as the Harris Line, placed the strip in Ohio. Harris had been ordered to make the survey in accordance with Ohio's constitutional proviso. Two later surveys, including one in 1834 by United States Army engineers, put the disputed land in Michigan.[2] The mouth of the Maumee River was important because it was the terminus of a proposed canal that would connect the Great Lakes with the Ohio River via the Maumee and Wabash rivers. Congress's refusal to grant Michigan an enabling act was directly tied to this border dispute. With twenty-one congressmen, Ohio was the strongest state in the West. The Territory of Michigan had but one non-voting congressional delegate.

Michigan's decision to call a constitutional convention left Ohioans, especially Gov. Robert Lucas, uneasy. Lucas realized that if the boundary issue were not resolved before Michigan joined the Union, Ohio would lose its advantage in Congress. More importantly, once Michigan was a state, it could submit the border dispute to the United States Supreme Court—something it could not do as a territory.

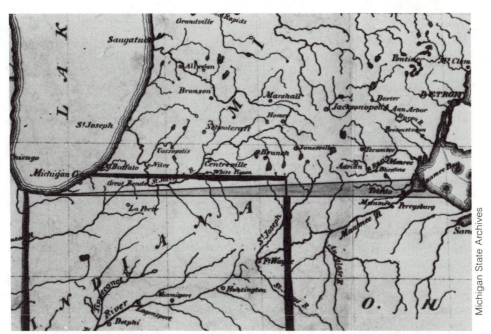

Map (ca. 1835) showing the disputed Toledo Strip, cause of the Michigan and Ohio conflict.

Ohio responded to Michigan's call for a constitutional convention by annexing the disputed territory. Michigan retaliated in February 1835 with the Pains and Penalties Act, which made illegal any attempt by non-Michigan residents (except federal officials) to exercise official jurisdiction in the Toledo Strip upon "pain" of a thousand-dollar fine and five years imprisonment. Describing Ohio's annexation of the disputed territory as "unjustifiable" and "high-handed," a confident Governor Mason declared,

> We are the weaker party, it is true, but we are on the side of justice; and, with the guidance of Him who never forsakes the weak, or hesitates to pursue with punishment the unjust, we cannot fail to maintain our rights against the encroachments of a powerful neighboring State.[3]

The situation along the border intensified as Ohio and Michigan prepared to defend their rights. In early March, Detroiters petitioned Pres. Andrew Jackson to keep Ohio from annexing territory that operated under the jurisdiction of the federal government. At about the same time, the Michigan legislative council declared that Michigan would resist "by all the measures in our power" any Ohio effort to establish jurisdiction over the Toledo Strip.[4]

United States secretary of state John Forsyth heightened tensions when he informed Mason that if the Pains and Penalties Act remained in effect, Congress might use federal prerogatives over a territory to force a compromise with Ohio. A dismayed Mason offered to resign if the president would not support him. Jackson did not ask for Mason's resignation; instead, he sought to resolve the issue by seeking an opinion on the border dispute from his attorney general. Though neutral on the merits of the conflicting claims, Jackson was anxious to maintain the support of Ohio's congressional delegation.

To Jackson's consternation, United States attorney general Benjamin Butler sustained Michigan's position and concluded that Ohio had no right to assume jurisdiction in the Toledo Strip without Congress's approval. Butler also argued that the Pains and Penalties Act was a legitimate measure for Michigan to use to resist incursions into its territory. The attorney general noted that since the president had jurisdiction over territorial officials, he could remove them; however, the same was not true of state officials. Jackson responded to Butler's opinion by appointing two commissioners to negotiate a resolution of the dispute: Benjamin C. Howard of Baltimore and Richard Rush of Philadelphia.[5]

The presidential commissioners arrived at Toledo in time to witness the first hostilities of the Toledo War. On 1 April 1835, Michigan partisans held elections in the disputed area; five days later, Ohio partisans, who represented a majority of Toledo's citizenry, went to the polls. On 8 April, Monroe County sheriff Nathan Hubble and a small posse arrived in Toledo to arrest George McKay and Naaman Goodsell for aiding another Toledoan in resisting Michigan authorities. Hubble found Goodsell at the home of Major Benjamin Stickney, an outspoken Ohio partisan. Goodsell threatened Hubble with bodily harm, and, only after breaking down a door, was the Monroe sheriff able to make his arrest. Hubble arrested McKay after wrestling a gun from him. During this altercation, Goodsell's wife and one of Stickney's daughters escaped from the house and ran toward town screaming for help. According to Hubble, Toledo came alive with gunfire and blowing horns, and the Monroe posse was chased by fifty to sixty armed Ohioans. Nevertheless, the Michiganians escaped with their prisoners.[6]

As Michigan continued to enforce the Pains and Penalties Act, President Jackson's commissioners conferred with Mason and Lucas in hopes of resolving the worsening border dispute. After meeting with Lucas, Commissioner Howard observed that he was "very firm in his character and though doing what nine-tenths of the nation will hereafter pronounce wrong . . . will listen to no argument upon the point." The commissioners found Mason equally determined. According to Howard, Mason agreed not to take "any step that will lead to a broil," as long as Ohio did not attempt to establish its jurisdiction over the territory.[7]

The commissioners then proposed a compromise: Michigan would suspend the Pains and Penalties Act and stop prosecuting those who had violated it; Ohio would re-run the Harris Line, and Ohio and Michigan would establish joint jurisdiction in the disputed territory until the matter was resolved by Congress. Because the proposal recognized Ohio's claim, Mason labeled it "dishonorable and disruptable"; Lucas responded favorably to it.[8]

In early April, Governor Lucas ordered the re-marking of the Harris Line, but the arrests of Toledoans by the Monroe County sheriff left the Ohioans chosen to conduct the survey apprehensive. Lucas urged the surveying crew to move as rapidly as possible; and if confronted by a "superior force," to "immediately" retreat until forces "sufficient to protect them" could be collected. As a word of encouragement, the governor concluded, "Be cautious,—keep a sharp look out,—do not suffer yourselves to be surprised."[9]

The surveyors apparently failed to heed this advice. At noon on 26 April, fourteen miles south of Adrian, Michigan, a posse of approximately thirty Michiganians, commanded by Lenawee County under-sheriff William McNair, surprised the Ohio surveyors, who were camped in a field owned by "Mr. Phillips." Nine Ohioans were taken into custody and imprisoned at Tecumseh; several others escaped. Two of the prisoners were released for lack of evidence, and six others posted bail ranging from four hundred dollars to eight hundred dollars. One Ohioan, Col. J. E. Fletcher, refused bail and remained a prisoner, under orders, he claimed, from Governor Lucas. No one was injured in the "Battle of Phillips Corners," despite an Ohio claim that a Michigan musketball "passed through the clothing" of a member of their party.[10] Professing that "an armed force of several hundred men" stretched across the Michigan/Ohio border, the three Ohio survey commissioners who successfully eluded McNair's men reported to Governor Lucas that they deemed it "prudent" to halt their work until "some efficient preparatory measures" could be taken.[11]

In the meantime, Michiganians gathered in Detroit to write a constitution. After meeting for forty-five days, the delegates completed their work in mid-June. The constitution was similar to existing state constitutions: it included a bill of rights, established a bicameral state legislature, and enfranchised all twenty-one-year-old white males. The document's most farsighted provision concerned education. A state superintendent of public instruction was created, making Michigan the first state to constitutionally establish this position. The constitution also placed the proceeds from the sale of the public lands set aside in each township for education (Section 16) in a central school fund. Since the value of these lands differed, this unique proviso allowed for a more equitable distribution of state funds for education and was Michigan's first step toward the equalization of educational opportunity.[12]

While Michigan finished its constitution, the Ohio State Legislature met in a special session to "adopt prompt measures" to sustain Ohio's rights in the Toledo Strip. Inflamed by Governor Lucas, who characterized Michigan's actions as "reckless vengeance, scarcely paralleled in the history of the civilized nations," the lawmakers adopted legislation enforcing Ohio's claim to the Toledo Strip. The laws made the forcible abduction of an Ohio citizen a crime punishable by three to seven years at hard labor; formed the disputed territory into Lucas County with Toledo as its county seat; appropriated $300,000 to implement these measures; gave the governor the authority to borrow another $300,000; and, to symbolically establish jurisdiction over the strip, ordered the Court of Common Pleas to hold session at Toledo on the first Monday in September.[13]

In midsummer, tensions along the border worsened. On 15 July, Monroe County deputy sheriff Joseph Wood arrived in Toledo to arrest Two Stickney, one of Benjamin's sons, for helping another Toledoan resist arrest. (Major Stickney named his sons after numbers and his daughters after states.) Wood confronted Two Stickney at the Davis Inn, a hotbed of Ohio partisans. Stickney resisted arrest and stabbed the deputy with a small penknife. Wood was taken to a nearby inn where a local physician pronounced him mortally wounded. After the attack, the Ohioans at the Davis Inn warned Michigan officials to "keep away" for they had "their knives sharpened and rifles loaded." On the day after Wood was wounded, Monroe County district attorney J. Q. Adams observed that "all law and authority emanating from Michigan is openly trampled upon and set at defiance by a large portion of the citizens of Toledo." It was also reported that fifty to seventy-five of Toledo's leading citizens pledged to resist further Michigan arrests as long as they had "a drop of blood left."[14]

The Ohioans soon had their chance. In retaliation for wounding Wood, who recovered and was the only human casualty of the Toledo War, Mason ordered the Monroe County sheriff and an armed posse of over two hundred men to arrest Stickney. When the Michiganians reached Toledo, they discovered that Stickney and the other Ohio

Michigan's first Constitution, 1835.

stalwarts had fled. Mason requested that Lucas extradite Stickney, but the Ohio governor refused.[15]

On 17 August, at the urging of President Jackson, Governor Mason convened the legislative council to consider the compromise measures proposed by the presidential commissioners. Arguing that Michigan had taken "no improper step" in resisting Ohio efforts "to extend her

85

boundaries," the Council rejected the compromise. Mason sent their report to Jackson with a note that concluded, "The General Government may expect a serious collision. . . . The consequences attending such a state of things are deeply to be regretted, but they must rest with those who might prevent their occurrence."[16]

On 29 August, citing Mason's overzealous defense of Michigan's rights, Jackson fired the young acting governor. Political expediency demanded that the Toledo Strip controversy be resolved by Congress; until then Michigan would have to yield. In the meantime, Mason ordered that two hundred mounted men be raised to help the Monroe County sheriff prevent Toledo's early-September court session. Unaware that he had been fired, Mason joined the men as they marched toward Toledo.[17]

The Michigan militiamen enjoyed themselves on their march to Toledo. J. Wilkie Moore, a twenty-one-year-old who had come to Michigan from New York in 1833, later recalled that between Detroit and Toledo, the Michigan militia "had a vast amount of fun . . . [as] the farming people en route generally welcomed us enthusiastically because we were 'fighting for Michigan.'" Despite their gaiety, Moore and the other Michiganians "were all very much in earnest" in their efforts to stop the Ohioans. On the evening of 6 September, the Michigan militiamen (some estimates placed the number at over one thousand men) camped eight miles from Toledo; they expected "bloodshed" the next day.[18]

Late on the morning of 7 September, the Michiganians entered Toledo. No Ohio soldiers nor governmental officials met them. The Michiganians remained in Toledo for several days and entertained themselves by tearing up Major Stickney's gardens and stripping his orchards. Following a public review of the troops, Mason and his men returned home, confident that they had thwarted Governor Lucas's plans.[19]

Their confidence was unwarranted. At 3:00 A.M., while the Michigan militia slept, a party of Ohio judges, court officials, and twenty armed men had stealthily crept to an old schoolhouse in Toledo. There, they declared court in session. The proceedings were hastily recorded on bits of paper and deposited in the clerk's bell-crowned hat. The court then adjourned to a nearby tavern to celebrate. The festivities were rudely disrupted when word arrived that the Michiganians were nearby. The alarm proved false, but in their haste to escape, the Ohioans lost the clerk's hat. It was retrieved, and by 6:00 A.M. the judicial party was back in Ohio.[20]

The firing of Governor Mason ended the Toledo War but not Michigan's quest to become a state. On 5 October 1835, despite the federal government's refusal to recognize Michigan as a state, Michigan voters chose a congressman (Isaac Crary), a state legislature, elected Mason governor of the state of Michigan, and overwhelmingly approved the state constitution. In his 1 November inaugural address, Governor Mason promised cooperation with existing territorial officials and urged all Michiganians "to await with patience the final recognition of our equal sovereignty" by the Congress. To minimize conflict, the legislature, after choosing Lucius Lyon and John Norvell as the state's first United States senators, disbanded after meeting for only two weeks; it would reconvene in February.[21]

Less than a month after Mason was fired as acting territorial governor, his replacement, John S. Horner of Virginia, arrived in Detroit, boasting that he would discharge his duties "under all circumstances." However, rallies denouncing Horner, who was described by critics as "immensely fat" and "sour-faced," minimized his chances for success. Two thousand people gathered to censure him at Monroe, while Detroiters resolved that Horner should "relinquish the duties of his office, and return to the land of his nativity."[22]

Horner worsened his public relations when he pardoned the Ohioans who had violated the Pains and Penalties Act. The new territorial governor recognized that the pardons would be "unsavory to some extent," but he failed to realize the extent of their unpopularity. From Monroe he noted:

> I placed pardons . . . amidst a wild and dangerous population, without any aid, a friend, servant or bed to sleep in, in the midst of a mob excited by . . . *bad men*, I could not enlist a friend, or an officer of the Territory. . . . The district attorney had the effrontery and timidity to say, "that, if he acted, the mob would throw him and myself in the river." Threats were made, and communications in writing, insulting and menacing in the extreme, were received.

Horner concluded, "There never was a government in Christendom with such officers." As a final indignity, the governor stopped in Ypsilanti on his way back to Detroit, and a mob barraged his room with horse dung. Horner remained in Detroit until April 1836, but he was generally ignored. He then moved the seat of his government to the westernmost part of the Territory, in what is now Wisconsin.[23]

During the winter of 1835–36, Michigan's efforts to join the Union were focused on Congress. Ohio re-marked the boundary line according to its interpretation without further incident; and when Congress convened in December 1835, Michigan's congressional delegation—

Senators Norvell and Lyon and Representative Crary—prepared to take their seats. They would have a long wait.

For six months Congress debated Michigan's admission. The most vocal opponents included the Whigs, who disliked Michigan's strong Democratic ties; Ohio congressmen, who feared the loss of Toledo; and Indiana and Illinois legislators, who worried that if Michigan retained Toledo, their states would have to pull their northern boundaries southward and lose their ports on Lake Michigan.

Some critics suggested that Michigan begin the whole process of applying for admission all over again. Mississippi Sen. Jefferson Davis commented:

> I do not like the mode in which Michigan has conducted this business. She has assumed rights that all agree are not well founded, and the consequence is, that she stands in an embarrassing posture. She claimed to be a State before she could be one.[24]

Other congressmen expressed different concerns. According to one New York legislator, a Michigan constitutional provision that enfranchised all twenty-one-year-old males who lived in Michigan at the time of the signing of the 1835 constitution proved that illegal aliens, especially the Irish, were trying to take over the United States and make it a "Catholic Country."[25]

Michigan also had defenders. Massachusetts Rep. John Quincy Adams, known by his fellow congressmen as "Old Man Eloquent," believed Michigan deserved the Toledo Strip "by every law, human and divine." The former president concluded that "never" in the course of his life had he known of a controversy in which "all the right was so clear on one side and all the power so overwhelmingly on the other."[26] One of Michigan's staunchest supporters was Sen. John M. Niles of Connecticut. Opposed to any suggestion that Michigan be asked to retrace its steps, Niles warned:

> There is a point beyond which a free people cannot be driven. Why are the people of Michigan to be vexed and harassed in this way? They feel that they are treated harshly; that great injustice is done them. They have been opposed and resisted in every course they have pursued to obtain admission into the Union; and you have now divided their territory. . . . Do you wish to drive that people to desperation to force them into acts of violence?[27]

On 15 June 1836, the House of Representatives concurred with an earlier Senate decision and passed the Northern Ohio Boundary Bill. The act gave the Toledo Strip to Ohio and offered Michigan the western Upper Peninsula and immediate statehood. It also required Michigan to hold a convention to approve, or "assent," to the compromise measure.[28]

The Northern Ohio Boundary Bill asserted Congress's claim that no measure, including the Northwest Ordinance, could prevent it from altering the boundaries of a territory. The Congress also contended that it was "expedient" to give Ohio the mouth of the Maumee River to guarantee the completion of the canal connecting Lake Erie with the Ohio River. But beneath this logic was one fact: 1836 was a presidential election year. Giving Toledo to Michigan would offend three states— Ohio, Indiana, and Illinois—states with a total of thirty-five electoral votes. Michigan had only three electoral votes. Though President Jackson was not seeking reelection, he had handpicked his successor, Vice Pres. Martin Van Buren, and he wanted a Democratic party victory that autumn.

Most Michiganians were appalled at the Northern Ohio Boundary Bill. They expressed their discontent by holding meetings and passing memorials. Monroe citizens described Congress's actions as "oppressive, unconstitutional and dangerous to the permanency of our Republican Institutions." As for the offer of the western Upper Peninsula, one thousand Detroiters signed a petition rejecting the gift of "the sterile region on the shores of Lake Superior, destined by soil and climate to remain forever a Wilderness."[29]

Senator Lyon, who had once described the western Upper Peninsula as a place "where we can . . . supply ourselves now and then with a little bear meat," offered a different opinion. Acknowledging that Michigan had been treated unfairly, Lyon argued, "We are wholly without the means of redress." Instead, Lyon saw the western Upper Peninsula— approximately twenty thousand square miles—as land that "may at some future time be esteemed very valuable." The Michigan senator added:

> A considerable tract of country between Lake Michigan and Lake Superior is known to be fertile and this with the fisheries on Lake Superior and the copper mines supposed to exist there may hereafter be worth to us millions of dollars. At any rate, it can do us no harm and I am in favor of getting it while we can, for at best, if we are cut down in the south, as we certainly shall be, our State will be quite poor and small enough.[30]

Governor Mason appeared equally resigned to Michigan's fate. Declaring that Congress's decision violated "every principle of justice," Mason observed that Michigan's alternatives were "resistance or unqualified submission." Mason acknowledged that his "first impulse" was to resist Congress's demands, but such resistance offered "so little hope of gain but the certainty of permanent loss and lasting injury to ourselves and the nation."[31]

On 25 July 1836, after "a great diversity of opinion," the state legislature agreed to hold a convention of assent. On the second Monday of September, fifty delegates from across the state would be chosen on the basis of the distribution of population. On the fourth Monday of September, the delegates would convene at the Washtenaw County Courthouse in Ann Arbor.[32]

The election of delegates to the convention of assent was heated. The *Detroit Free Press,* the state's largest newspaper, argued that continuing the struggle for Toledo would involve Michigan "in heavy expense, in loss of character, [and] in dangers and sufferings not to be calculated until they have happened."[33]

The *Constantine Republican* added:

> The boundary line is . . . fixed and established, irrevocably . . . the assent required by Congress . . . is nothing more than assenting to be a state in the Union, with certain privileges as a condition, or refusing assent, deprived of those privileges.[34]

Monroe Democrats, on the other hand, believed that the Toledo Strip was more valuable than "the whole of Wisconsin." Comparing Congress's request for assent to a robber who "forces the traveler . . . to give up his purse," the *Monroe Sentinel* suggested, "Michigan ought now to attend to her own affairs; to go on with her state government, unless stopped by the general government; and if stopped, relinquish no rights, but to submit to superior power."[35] On the other side of the state, Cass County Democrats resolved that they would "never sign the bond of our disgrace, whereby we are to be compelled to surrender our honor, as well as our rights."[36]

On 28 September 1836, forty-nine elected delegates (no delegate from Michilimackinac County attended) gathered in Ann Arbor. After several days of intense debate, the delegates rejected the congressional compromise by a vote of 28 to 21. The victors argued that Congress had no power "to dispose of the territory in contest between Ohio and Michigan, upon the mere grounds of expediency."[37]

As the impact of the September convention became evident, some dissenters began to question what Michigan had gained by its continued recalcitrance. A primary reason for this reconsideration was the estimated $500,000 Michigan could receive as its share of the federal treasury surplus that was to be divided among the states. These funds would be forfeited if Michigan was not a state by 1 January 1837. Equally important was the 5 percent of all public land sales that was returned to the states. (Michigan public land sales in 1836 had exceeded 4.2 million acres.) Lesser concerns included the fact that, as a state, Michigan would have more power to seek legal redress regarding jurisdiction over the Toledo Strip. Some dissenters, responding to Michigan's nascent antislavery movement, also believed Michigan needed to be admitted into the Union immediately to restore the free/slave state balance in the United States Senate, which had been disrupted by the admission of Arkansas the previous June.[38]

On 29 October, Wayne County Democrats called on Governor Mason to seek another convention for the "immediate acquiescence in the preferred terms of admission." Mason also received "numerously signed petitions" requesting that another convention be called.[39] In mid-November, the governor acknowledged the importance of assent but noted that it was too late to convene the legislature to call for elections to choose delegates for another convention. Instead, he suggested that if the September proceedings stemmed from the "distorted representations of designing men," then the people had "an inherent and indefeasible right . . . to reverse acts of their agents they found prejudicial to their interests." Mason recommended that the assenters "take the measure with their own hands" and form a convention "for the purposes contemplated by Congress."[40]

The day after the governor's pronouncement, a committee of Wayne County Democrats issued a circular that declared that since the "people" represented the state's "highest authority," qualified voters would hold an election on 5 and 6 December 1836. Each county would elect twice as many delegates as it had representatives in the state house. These delegates would meet in Ann Arbor on 14 December to reassess the compromise offered by Congress.[41]

The call for another convention was controversial, but the election was held in most counties. Opponents of the election, especially the Whigs, did not participate. On 14 December, eighty-two delegates gathered in Ann Arbor. Because of the unusually cold temperatures, critics labeled the gathering the "Frostbitten Convention." After a short debate, the delegates approved the compromise that would allow Michigan to enter the Union.[42]

On 27 December 1836, Pres. Andrew Jackson sent the proceedings of both the September and the December conventions to Congress. Jackson noted that he thought the results of the latter convention fulfilled the assent requirement and that Michigan should be admitted into the Union.[43]

Throughout January, Congress again immersed itself in debate over Michigan's admission. The primary concern was the extralegal nature of the December convention. Because that gathering had not received the sanction of the state legislature, the results, especially the forfeiture of the Toledo Strip, might not withstand legal scrutiny at a later date. Several congressmen even suggested that Michigan begin the process of admission all over again.[44]

Nevertheless, on 5 January 1837 the Senate voted 25 to 10 to recognize the December election results and admit Michigan into the Union. Twenty days later, the House concurred by a margin of 132 to 43. On 26 January, without ceremony, President Jackson signed the bill making Michigan the nation's twenty-sixth state.[45]

At a ceremony in Detroit on 9 February, congratulations were generously offered, especially to Governor Mason. As the evening's festivities came to a close, an unidentified spectator offered a toast to the new state of Michigan:

> Nature has done her work, may her sons put the polish on; that education and internal improvements be our motto; let no sister state outdo us—if they undertake it, may they find themselves barking up the wrong tree.[46]

Michigan's quest for statehood had achieved its goal.

Michigan State Archives

Stevens T. Mason, territorial governor and first governor of the state of Michigan.

NOTES

1. George Fuller, ed., *Messages of the Governors of Michigan*, 4 vols. (Lansing: Michigan Historical Commission, 1926), 1:129–39; Lawton T. Hemans, *The Life and Times of Stevens T. Mason* (Lansing: Michigan Historical Commission, 1930), 136–38; House of Representatives, *Report of Committees, Report 380* 24th Cong., 1st sess., 25–27 (hereafter cited as *House Report 380*).

2. Hemans, *Mason*, 106–25; Claude S. Larzelere, "The Boundaries of Michigan," *Michigan Pioneer and Historical Collections* 30 (1905): 1–20; Anna May Soule, "The Southern and Western Boundaries of Michigan," *Michigan Pioneer and Historical Collections* 27 (1890): 346–60; *House Report 380*, 1–19, 61–62, 73–76.

3. Hemans, *Mason*, 138–40; *House Report 380*, 84–90.

4. *U.S. Senate Documents, Document 6*, 24th Cong., 1st sess., 22–24, 30–37 (hereafter cited as *Senate Document 6*).

5. Ibid., 4–13.

6. Ibid., 61–65.

7. William D. Hoyt, Jr., ed., "Benjamin C. Howard and the 'Toledo War': Some Letters of a Federal Commissioner," *Ohio State Archaeological and Historical Quarterly* 60 (1951): 304.

8. *House Report 380*, 103–4.

9. U.S. House of Representatives, *Executive Documents, Document 7* 24th Congress, 1st sess., 212–13 (hereafter cited as *Executive Document 7*).

10. "The Battle of Phillips Corners," *Michigan Pioneer and Historical Collections* 12 (1887): 409–14; *Senate Document 6*, 57–61, 145–46; *House Report 380*, 90–91; *Executive Document 7*, 59–61, 220–21.

11. Ibid.

12. Hemans, *Mason*, 156–63; *Senate Document 6*, 2–15; Harold M. Dorr, ed., *The Michigan Constitutional Conventions of 1835–36* (Ann Arbor: University of Michigan Press, 1940), 55–419, 462–539 (hereafter cited as *Conventions*).

13. Willard Way, *The Facts and Historical Events of the Toledo War of 1835* (Toledo: Commercial Steam Book and Job Printing, 1869), 26–28; Sister Mary Karl George, *The Rise and Fall of Toledo, Michigan . . . The Toledo War!* (Lansing: Michigan Historical Commission, 1971), 49–50, 106–9; *Executive Document 7*, 166–72, 281–85.

14. *Senate Document 6*, 69–74.

15. George, *The Rise and Fall of Toledo*, 53.

16. *House Report 380*, 112–16.

17. Ibid., 116–17.

18. J. Wilkie Moore, "How They Fought: Personal Recollections of the Contest with Ohio Fifty Years Ago," *Michigan Pioneer and Historical Collections* 7 (1884): 70.

19. Hemans, *Mason*, 170–72.

20. Way, *Toledo War*, 42–45.

21. Hemans, *Mason*, 183–89; Fuller, *Messages*, 1:253–56.

22. Clarence Edwin Carter, comp., *The Territorial Papers of the United States: Territory of Michigan, 1827–1837* (Washington, D.C.: Government Printing Office, 1945), 12:984–86; *House Report 380*, 98, 102–3.

23. *House Report 380*, 124–27.

24. *Register of Debates in Congress* (Washington, D.C.: Gales and Seaton, 1836), 12:1019–20.

25. Ibid., 4253–58.

26. Willis Dunbar and George May, *Michigan: A History of the Wolverine State* (Grand Rapids: Eerdmans, 1980), 257.

27. *Register of Debates*, 12:1017–18.

28. Ibid., 1050–52; Hemans, *Mason*, 198–200.

29. Carter, *Territorial Papers*, 12:1149–67, 1177–79; *Detroit Democratic Free Press*, 23 March 1836.

30. George W. Thayer, ed., "Letters of Lucius Lyon," *Michigan Pioneer and Historical Collections* 27 (1896): 478–80.

31. Fuller, *Messages*, 1:177–78.

32. Alec R. Gilpin, *The Territory of Michigan* (East Lansing: Michigan State University Press, 1970), 189; Hemans, *Mason*, 231.

33. *Detroit Democratic Free Press*, 10 August 1836, 3.

34. *Constantine Republican*, 24 August 1836.

35. *Monroe Sentinel*, 9 July, 4 August 1836.

36. *Niles Gazette*, 7 September 1836.

37. Door, *Conventions*, 421–41, 540–67, 591–92.

38. *Detroit Democratic Free Press*, 9, 16 November, 3 December 1836; Hemans, *Mason*, 243–44; George, *The Rise and Fall of Toledo*, 72.

39. *Detroit Democratic Free Press*, 2, 16 November 1836; Hemans, *Mason*, 244.

40. Dorr, *Conventions*, 568–72; *Detroit Democratic Free Press*, 16 November 1836.

41. Dorr, *Conventions*, 572–74; *Detroit Democratic Free Press*, 16 November 1836.

42. Dorr, *Conventions*, 442–58, 575–78.

43. Hemans, *Mason*, 249; *Congressional Globe*, 24th Cong., 2d sess., 1836–37, 4:54.

44. *Register of Debates*, 13:204–325.

45. Ibid., 325; *Detroit Democratic Free Press*, 8 February 1837.

46. *Detroit Democratic Free Press*, 15 February 1837.

---◆---

SUGGESTED READINGS

Secondary sources to consult for additional information on Michigan's efforts to become a state include Lawton T. Hemans, *The Life and Times of Stevens T. Mason* (1930); Willard Way, *The Facts and Historical Events of the Toledo War of 1835* (1869); Sister Mary Karl George, *The Rise and Fall of Toledo, Michigan . . . The Toledo War!* (1971); and Claude S. Larzelere, "The Boundaries of Michigan," *Michigan Pioneer and Historical Collections* 30 (1905): 1–20. The discussions and debates of Michigan's first two constitutional conventions can be found in *The Michigan Constitutional Conventions of 1835–36* (1940), edited by Harold M. Dorr.

The many primary documents chronicling Michigan's struggle can be found in the U.S. Congress, House, *Report of Committees,* 24th Cong., 1st sess., 1836, Report 380; U.S. Congress, House, *Executive Documents,* 24th Cong., 1st sess., 1836, H. Doc. 7; and U.S. Congress, Senate, *Document 6,* 24th Cong., 1st sess., 1836. The extensive debates in Congress can be found in the *Register of Debates in Congress* (1836).

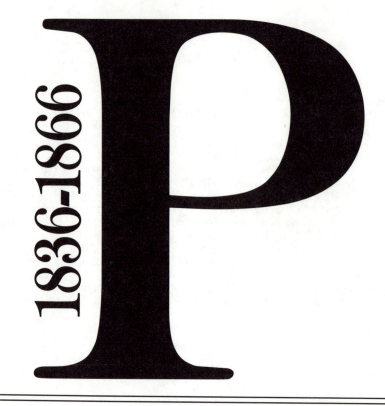

1836-1866

P

LARRY B. MASSIE

Larry Massie is a freelance historian specializing in Michigan history, antiquarian books, and archival management. He received his bachelor's and master's degrees from Western Michigan University, where he served from 1978–1983 as assistant director of the Archives and Regional History Collections. Mr. Massie is a prolific author of articles and books such as *From Frontier Folk to Factory Smoke: Michigan's First Century of Historical Fiction* and *Voyages into Michigan's Past.*

lows, Ships & Shovels:

Economic Development in Michigan

Throughout the summer of 1836, an army of land hunters, several thousand strong, thronged the dusty streets of the frontier boom town newly renamed Kalamazoo. Every house became a hostelry where men gladly paid for a spot on the floor. Others found shelter amid the sea of white canvas tents that billowed over vacant downtown lots. They had journeyed by canal boat, Lake Erie steamer, stage coach, horseback, and on foot to Kalamazoo, the site of the territory's western branch of the federal land office, to purchase tracts of Michigan's virgin wilderness at one dollar and twenty-five cents an acre. Anxious land seekers queued up in long lines before the register's office to learn if their desired claims were still on the market, sometimes waiting for weeks to get an answer.

Most were Yankees from Connecticut, Massachusetts, Vermont, and other New England states or sons of those who had pioneered western New York state a generation before. They brought with them the Yankee penchant for whittling; and their penknives had such an effect on Register Abraham Edward's picket fence, window sills, and other wooden objects that to save his property he supplied a free load of shingles. Local culinary entrepreneurs earned small fortunes by hawking cakes and pies to the hungry multitude.[1]

Pioneer historian George Torrey remembered Kalamazoo in 1836 as "one great mass convention of men almost raving with land mania."[2] The Kalamazoo land office set a record that year unmatched by any other such facility in the previous history of the United States. Edwards transferred 1,634,511 acres of Michigan soil into private hands at a total cost of $2,043,866.[3] Some of the land went to bona fide settlers anxious to start a new life amidst the territory's rich prairies and parklike oak openings. Speculators, however, grabbed up many choice tracts at the cheap government price, intending to resell to later arrivals at a tidy profit.

"Everybody," wrote Torrey, "was crazy for land, and felt rich and wanted to be crazier and richer still!"[4] The cagiest of the speculators were town site developers. They platted out likely port sites or locations on rivers where water power could be harnessed and hoped to sell lots for hundreds of times their purchase price. Some locations, such as Kalamazoo, Battle Creek, and Grand Rapids, met their founders' expectations and grew lustily into urban centers. But despite elaborate engravings depicting nicely laid out streets and commercial improvements, many others never got beyond the stage of "paper cities."

During the 1830s, Ottawa County alone witnessed the creation of at least five such paper cities, none of which survived the decade. Warren City, platted on the Grand River, won the original designation as county seat, although it never contained more than a couple of log cabins. The most ambitious Ottawa County undertaking, the brainchild of a syndicate of eastern capitalists, sprang into existence in 1836 when a schooner unloaded a quantity of supplies and precut houses at the mouth of Pigeon Creek on Lake Michigan. Company employees proceeded to survey lots, build dwellings, and chop out roads. A twenty-thousand-dollar steam sawmill, the finest in the area, and an opulent hotel with a stately pillared porch soon graced the community of Port Sheldon. By 1838 the city had grown to three hundred inhabitants, nearly all company employees. But the panic of 1837 bankrupted the Port Sheldon Company. The promising settlement was abandoned and soon it and most other paper cities were little more than memories.[5]

Much of the nation had been enjoying boom times during the early 1830s. The availability of cheap labor and reciprocal trade agreements, which opened new world markets, brought huge profits to American manufacturers. Pres. Andrew Jackson's feud with the conservative Bank of the United States resulted in a proliferation of more liberal

state banks. The easy credit they offered encouraged additional speculation. By 1836 the Territory of Michigan contained seventeen banks.[6]

Michigan's General Banking Act, which went into effect on 15 March
1837, made it possible for just about anyone to open a banking institution. The law required a capital stock of fifty thousand dollars, 30 percent of which was to be in gold and silver specie. But many of the
approximately twenty-three additional Michigan banks that rushed into
operation flouted the law. Sufficient specie to meet the requirement was
sometimes shipped from bank to bank just ahead of the examiner. The
beautifully printed, but nearly worthless, bank notes issued by these so-
called "wildcat" banks further fanned the flames of speculation and
inflation.

The inflationary spiral in conjunction with high transportation costs
caused prices to escalate sharply on the Michigan frontier. Government
land, in fact, became one of the few affordable commodities. Wise pioneers carted supplies and tools with them. But the cost of living en
route bit deeply into their meager cash. Mrs. Richard Dye, who emi-
grated with her husband and family from New York State to Ionia in
1837, was shocked to pay five dollars for overnight lodging at the home
of a Dr. Laing. "It was some time," she recorded, "before we took shelter in another home."[7]

In 1837 a severe depression gripped the eastern states, precipitated
in part by President Jackson's Specie Circular of the previous year
which stipulated that government lands be paid for in hard money. "The
Specie Circular," wrote T. S. Atlee, a clerk at the Kalamazoo land office,
"killed the bastard progeny of irresponsible bankers, while the ink upon
their lying 'promises to pay' was yet moist on the fair faces of their
treacherous issue."[8] At first the west remained insulated from the worst
effects of the depression, in part because of the dominant mood of optimism. But by 1839, the rush of new settlers into Michigan had dwindled, and commodity prices came crashing down. Many businesses went
bankrupt, and much of the land bought by speculators was ultimately
lost to back taxes.

In the meantime, however, the state had launched an ambitious plan
to improve its transportation facilities. When Michigan officially
entered the Union on 26 January 1837, a network of primitive roads
linked Detroit with most settlements in the southern peninsula. The
Chicago Military Road traversed the lower tier of counties. The Territorial Road split at Ypsilanti to link Ann Arbor, Jackson, Albion, Marshall, Battle Creek, Kalamazoo, and Benton Harbor. Pontiac, Ionia,
Grand Rapids, and Grand Haven were reached via the Grand River
Road. Other thoroughfares ran from Monroe, Port Huron, and Bay City.

But many of these routes were practically impassable during the wet seasons. Harriet Martineau, a cultured English author who traveled by stage from Detroit to Chicago during the summer of 1836, found the going so deplorable that the driver sometimes left the road for the relative smoothness of the open country. Passengers were frequently required to help push the stage out of sinkholes.[9]

Port cities naturally relied on Great Lakes shipping. Settlements located on navigable rivers utilized rafts and flat-bottomed boats for commercial shipments. Heavy vessels, known as arks, carried thousands of tons of flour, wood products, lard, and other goods from St. Joseph River settlements to St. Joseph, a major Great Lakes shipping center. At Kalamazoo, David Walbridge operated a successful fleet of flatboats that transported grain to the mouth of the Kalamazoo. It offered the only viable method of getting grain to market until the arrival of the first railroad in 1846.[10]

The Kalamazoo and Erie Railroad, the first railroad west of Schenectady, New York, linked Port Lawrence [Toledo, Ohio] with Adrian on 2 November 1836. By the following year, a little steam locomotive capable of making ten miles per hour on the downgrade had supplanted the original horsepower, and lengths of strap iron had been spiked onto the first wooden rails. Frequent derailments and the tendency of the strap iron to curl up like a giant spring, sending a "snake head" crashing through the bottom of the coach, made early train travel perilous. As late as 1841, the thirty-three-mile run between Toledo and Adrian took as long as ten hours.[11]

The Internal Improvements Act passed on 20 March 1837 projected three transpeninsula railroads and a number of canals. The southern route would link Monroe with New Buffalo, the central route would link Detroit with St. Joseph, and the northern route would connect St. Clair with Grand Haven. The legislature authorized Gov. Stevens T. Mason to negotiate a five-million-dollar loan to finance the plan. Despite the deepening depression, he managed to strike a deal with a New York company to sell bonds backed by the faith and credit of the state of Michigan.

By 1 January 1838 all surveys had been completed. Two months later, a locomotive pulling a coach named in the governor's honor chugged into Ypsilanti to be greeted by a gala celebration. The southern route west of Adrian, however, encountered political squabbling. Boomers for the various settlements in Lenawee and Hillsdale counties lobbied to divert the path of the railroad so as to enhance their economic position. The easiest and most direct route to Hillsdale would have passed through Keene, a Lenawee County hamlet. But Lanesville, later renamed Hudson, advocates succeeded in causing the line to be kinked

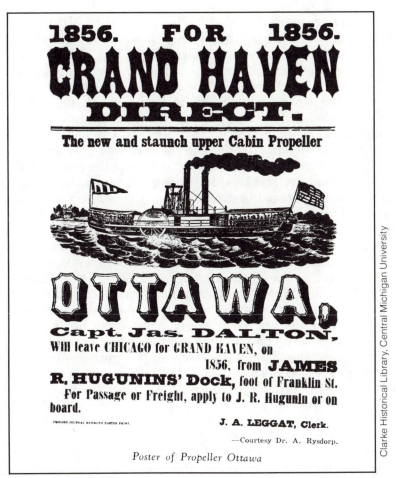

1856. FOR 1856.
GRAND HAVEN
DIRECT.

The new and staunch upper Cabin Propeller

OTTAWA,
Capt. Jas. DALTON,
Will leave CHICAGO for GRAND HAVEN, on
1856, from JAMES
R. HUGUNINS' Dock, foot of Franklin St.
For Passage or Freight, apply to J. R. Hugunin or on
board.

CHICAGO JOURNAL MAMMOTH POSTER PRINT.

J. A. LEGGAT, Clerk.

—Courtesy Dr. A. Rysdorp.

Poster of Propeller Ottawa

Clarke Historical Library, Central Michigan University

The steamboat *Ottawa* provided a means for western Michigan farmers and merchants to ship their goods to Chicago. Printed in Leo C. Lillie, *Historic Grand Haven and Ottawa County* (Grand Haven, 1931), 278.

through three miles of rough terrain to their village. Whereupon, an ambitious Keene businessman jacked up his hotel and had it pulled by oxen to the more promising village of Lanesville.[12]

The projected northern railroad route never progressed beyond the survey stage. A similar fate befell the northern canal, which was to have linked the Saginaw River via the Bad River with the Grand River. The Clinton-Kalamazoo Canal fared only slightly better. On 20 July 1838,

Governor Mason and other dignitaries traveled to Mt. Clemens for a celebration to mark the beginnings of a project that was thought to be second in importance only to the Erie Canal. Col. James L. Conger, in charge of the festivities, carried the first ceremonial load of dirt in a wheelbarrow. In an effort to demonstrate his strength, however, he so overloaded the wheelbarrow that he broke one handle. A spectator remarked, "That failure was emblematical of the fate of that canal." Although a twelve-mile stretch between Mt. Clemens and Rochester was completed, the spectator's statement proved correct.[13]

The first attempt to construct a canal around the rapids at St. Mary's also proved a failure. The Board of Internal Improvements had let bids in April 1838 for a canal that was to be seventy-five feet wide and ten feet deep. Three locks would raise and lower ships the eighteen-foot difference between the foot of the rapids and the level of Lake Superior. In May 1839, contractor Aaron Weeks arrived at the Sault with a ship-load of supplies and workmen. He immediately proceeded to cut across a millrace that had been constructed in 1823 to power the Fort Brady sawmill. An officer from the fort ordered Weeks to stop; he refused, and a contingent of troops drove the workers away at bayonet point. Weeks protested, but not too strongly. Apparently, his firm had bid the job too low, and he was anxious to get out of the contract.[14]

Shortly after the Sault Canal fiasco, the entire internal improvements project fell on hard times. In 1840, the eastern institutions that held Michigan's bonds went bankrupt. Without finances, railroad and canal construction came to a virtual halt. However, proceeds from the sale of a 500,000-acre federal land grant to the state offered some relief. The southern railroad reached Hillsdale in 1843, but the legislature voted to proceed no further. The central line slowly inched west, arriving at Jackson in 1842 and at Marshall two years later. On Sunday, 1 February 1846, Kalamazoo residents emptied churches when they heard the long-awaited whistle of the first train. The state sold its railroad interests to private concerns that year, and in 1852, both lines finally reached Chicago. Access to eastern and western markets proved an economic boon to communities located on the Michigan Central and Michigan Southern railroads.

Settlements not on the railroad lines obviously suffered a considerable economic disadvantage. Some communities campaigned for the construction of spur lines, but few were actually completed prior to the mid-1850s. Plank roads built by private companies served as feeder lines to railheads. Operated as toll roads with gates every few miles, they were constructed of three-inch-thick planks of the abundant hardwood available. Satisfactory at first, most plank roads soon deteriorated. Pioneer poet Asa Stoddard of Cooper, located on the important plank road that linked Grand Rapids with Kalamazoo, described a typical ride on the "plank":

Horses balking, drivers lashing,
Wishing all plank roads in ——
And their owners with them flashing
So it goes upon the Plank.

Wagons creaking, groaning, cracking,
Wrecks bestrewing either bank
Jarring, jolting, jambing, dashing,
This is riding on the Plank.

Crocks and baskets rolling, smashing,
Helpless owners looking blank,
Eggs and butter mixing, mashing,
Cannot help it on the Plank.[15]

As the state's transportation system took form, settlers rapidly tamed the wilderness. The colorful log cabin era lasted but briefly as the frontier pushed north. In Kalamazoo, for example, a number of frame dwellings and stores stood complete within two years after founder Titus Bronson had built his first tamarack pole lean-to. As soon as they could afford to, most pioneers replaced their original log cabins with fashionable Greek revival farmhouses. Water-powered sawmills and gristmills were among the first commercial ventures in most settled townships.

While establishing homesteads, settlers supplemented their meager livelihood by reaping the state's abundant natural resources. While the game lasted some became professional hunters. William Nowlin, for example, who pioneered at the present site of Dearborn in the 1830s, paid off the mortgage on the family farm by deer hunting. He shipped carloads of venison in 1841 to the eager market in Detroit via the rail line.[16] Squirrel, rabbit, wild fowl, and an occasional bear provided welcome relief from the traditional diet of salt pork. Entire communities dropped all other activities to harvest enormous passenger pigeon nestings.

Many townships set bounties on wolves of three dollars to five dollars as one of their first ordinances. The state later enacted a eight dollar bounty on adult wolves and three dollars on whelps. These bounties provided occasional windfalls for hard-pressed pioneer budgets, and wolves were soon eradicated from settled areas.

The pioneer lucky enough to discover a bee tree found a ready market for the surplus honey, and some made a profession of bee hunting. Others learned maple-sugaring techniques from the Indians and sold mococks of sugar and maple syrup. Nearly 2.5 million pounds of maple sugar were produced in 1850 alone.[17] Sugar Island in the St. Mary's River, named because of its famed sugar bush, also abounded in raspberries. Philetus Church settled there in 1845 and soon established a large trade in maple sugar and raspberry jam. By 1861, he was selling five to twelve tons of raspberry jam annually.[18]

Agriculture, however, provided the core of Michigan's economy during the antebellum (pre-Civil War) years. Wheat, corn, and oats were the preferred crops. In 1849, Michigan farmers grew 5.7 million bushels of corn, nearly 5 million bushels of wheat, and 1.8 million bushels of oats.[19] Yet, agricultural technology remained primitive and labor intensive. Hiram Moore and John Hascall of Kalamazoo County patented in 1836 a combination threshing machine and reaper. The huge ungainly contraption, which required twenty horses to pull, never proved practical in Michigan, and most farmers continued to cut grain with a scythe and cradle and thresh with a flail.

By the mid-1840s immigration to Michigan had rebounded from the aftermath of the Panic of 1837. Robert Sears, editor of the *New Pictorial Family Magazine,* observed in 1847 that

> every part of the peninsula wears a new aspect to what it did five years since. The log houses have given way to fine brick and pine dwellings, ornamented with paint, and the windows bedecked with blinds or tasty curtains. The slab sheds are hardly known. Large barns have taken their places. Where the wolf prowled undisturbed, herds of sheep are seen—the bleating of the frolicsome lambs is heard, where the doe had full sway. You can scarcely ride on any road that has been open for five years, that is not lined on either side with grain. The whole country has the appearance of fifty years' settlement. Enterprise and industry are everywhere prevalent.[20]

Sears might well have noted Michigan sheep and lambs. By 1854 the state boasted nearly one million head of sheep, fully one-third more than all other types of livestock combined.[21] The wool industry began in Macomb County in the 1830s. By 1840 the federal census taker counted 89,934 sheep in Michigan. In 1840 and 1841, businessmen from Vermont imported some twenty-five thousand additional sheep into Kalamazoo, Van Buren and Eaton counties for farmers to raise on shares. Others, including the Rev. John D. Pierce, first state superintendent of public instruction, brought into Calhoun County and vicinity blooded breeding stock. Breeders from New York drove hundreds of thousands of merinos and other fancy breeds to Michigan. Pontiac, Ypsilanti, Ann Arbor, Marshall, and Jackson developed large wool factories. The amount of Michigan wool passing through Buffalo to eastern manufacturing mills tripled from 1844 to 1847.[22]

Logging, the industry that would dominate Michigan's economy during much of the nineteenth century, increased steadily during the prewar years. Early settlers, however, wantonly destroyed much choice hardwood because they considered trees an impediment to the establishment of crop lands. Ashes from enormous bonfires of forest giants were converted into "black salts" and lye that brought many pioneers their first cash crop. The Dutch colonists who founded Holland in 1847, for example, sometimes earned enough to pay for their farms by carrying baskets of ashes on their backs to the city for shipment by schooner to Chicago processing plants.[23]

Oak and hemlock bark, rich in tannic acid, formed an early item of commerce which also spurred the development of local leatherworks. The manufacture of shingles, a cottage industry that could be practiced far upstream, offered an economic opportunity for backwoodsmen skilled with the froe and mallet. Raftsmen floated wooden shingles, the dominant roofing material of the time, downstream by the millions.

The harvesting of Michigan's seemingly inexhaustable stands of virgin white pine began in the 1830s. The Saginaw River valley, laced with hundreds of miles of logging streams, witnessed the first commercial cutting for outside markets. On the western side of the state, lumber from the Grand and Muskegon rivers was being shipped to Chicago prior to 1840. Gangs of lumberjacks in red flannel shirts finished axing their way across Maine and moved on to Michigan's high timber. They brought specialized tools and techniques, river drives and wanagans, ox sleighs and peavies. By 1850 Ottawa County, which then stretched north to Pentwater, led Michigan in timber production. Its eleven water-powered and thirteen steam sawmills cut fifty million feet of lumber that year, nearly one-sixth of the state's entire annual production.[24]

As some eastern investors staked their fortunes on Michigan's "green gold," others saw bright prospects in the state's subterranean resources. Rumors of huge native copper nuggets in the Upper Peninsula had circulated for nearly two centuries. But it took documented reports by Michigan's first state geologist, Douglas Houghton, in 1841—and the publicity caused by the exhibition of the Ontonagon boulder (a mass of copper ore) in 1843—to focus the nation's attention on the Keweenaw Copper Country. Thirty-six-year-old Houghton's promising career ended when he drowned in Lake Superior's icy waters near Eagle River in 1845, but not before he had witnessed a frenzied scramble for red metal that rivaled the California gold rush of 1849.

Copper Harbor, Eagle Harbor, Eagle River, Ontonagon, and other boom towns sprang up to accommodate the hordes who left comfortable homes down below to seek fortunes in the Keweenaw wilderness. Most

BIRDS EYE VIEW OF COPPER HARBOUR.

Clarke Historical Library, Central Michigan University

View of Copper Harbor, 1847. Miners and speculators rushed to the area to make their fortunes in copper ore. Printed in Charles T. Jackson, *Report of the Geological and Mineralogical Survey of the Mineral Lands of Michigan* (Washington, 1849), part III, between 896 and 897.

knew little or nothing about prospecting; but as they hacked their way through the dense forests and splashed through the many swamps, they often found masses of native copper. Practically unique to Michigan's Copper Country, those large masses, in fact, were the only copper considered worth looking for in the early days.

A lively trade also developed in the selling of claims and government mineral lease permits. Some speculators made small fortunes without lifting a shovel. Charles Lanman, who visited the region in 1846, estimated there were over five hundred men, predominantly permit speculators, in Copper Harbor alone.[25] When Pres. James K. Polk suspended the government leasing system in 1846, and it appeared that existing leases might not be legally secure, the copper bubble burst. By 1847 most speculators had left the Keweenaw area, poorer but wiser men.

Despite some spectacular finds such as the Cliff Mine, few prospectors discovered enough copper to make a profit over and above the steep transportation costs, which included unloading at the Sault for a trip around the rapids on the horse-drawn railway. Robert C. Clarke, an eastern journalist who visited the region during July 1852, marveled at the huge chunks of solid copper, fifty tons in all, laying about the dock at the Sault awaiting shipment to Detroit.[26]

The month after Clarke made his observations, the United States Congress finally acted to relieve the shipping bottleneck at the Sault. The Sault Canal Bill, approved on 26 August 1852, provided 750,000 acres of federal land by way of financing. Charles T. Harvey, an employee of the Fairbanks Scale Company of Vermont, was recuperating at the Sault from an illness when he learned of the act. Realizing that the projected canal would open to the world the mineral resource of the Upper Peninsula in which his firm had invested heavily, Harvey convinced his employers that he should devote his time to promoting the project.

Harvey, in conjunction with officials of the Michigan Central Railroad, succeeded in pushing a bill authorizing the canal through the state legislature on 5 February 1853. The St. Mary's Falls Ship's Canal Company, made up of Fairbanks, Detroit railroad officials, and other investors, won the contract for construction of the canal. Harvey imported an army of workers, constructed housing and a hospital for their use, and supervised the construction of the 5,400-foot-long canal with two locks. On 18 June 1855, the steamer *Illinois* became the first vessel to lock through the Sault.

The Sault Canal also made feasible the development of the Upper Peninsula's rich iron ore deposits that had been discovered near Negaunee in 1844 when surveyor William A. Burt noticed the erratic fluctuation of his magnetic compass. The Jackson Mining Company established a forge there and in 1848 began smelting iron. Shipments of iron ore increased from 1,449 tons in 1855 to more than 36,000 tons the following year.[27] Smelting iron ore in the Upper Peninsula, however, proved relatively unprofitable. Prior to the Civil War, most Upper Peninsula iron ore found its way to processing centers outside Michigan. But the opening of the Sault Canal inspired Detroit shipping magnate Eber Ward to acquire control of a pioneer ironworks located at Wyandotte. He ultimately developed an extensive industrial complex there and in 1864 produced the first Bessemer-type steel made in the United States.[28]

Michigan's first efforts at producing iron, however, came from deposits in the Lower Peninsula. In 1850, for example, the federal census taker listed 2,700 tons of iron raised in Branch County, 1,890 tons in Kalamazoo County, and none in the Upper Peninsula.[29] The southern Michigan product came from bog iron or "kidney iron," a sedementary deposit left by iron-rich water. A blast furnace went into operation at Union City in 1847 that reputedly produced the first pig iron made in Michigan. The furnace continued in operation for several years and ultimately evolved into the Nye Manufacturing Company, producer of the Nye chilled plow.[30]

A similar deposit of bog iron occurred near a riverbank north of Kalamazoo. After the arrival of the Michigan Central Railroad made transportation of pig iron feasible, Ezra Wilder, an entrepreneur from New York State, in 1848, constructed a blast furnace in Kalamazoo. It produced 120 tons its first year of operation. The availability of pig iron also spurred the development of several foundries and machine shops in

The Sault Canal, ca. 1865. A west view shows three ships locking through, with the superintendent's office and dwelling on the left, and Indian huts on the right.

Kalamazoo that manufactured stoves, steam engines and agricultural implements.[31]

Southern Michigan's bituminous coal deposits had been first exploited in the Jackson vicinity in 1835. Shortly thereafter, other mines were opened in Eaton County. During the Civil War, additional mines went into production at Jackson, Corunna, Shiawassee City, and Williamston. Michigan coal, however, proved to be a poor grade containing sulfur. Its unpleasant smell while burning rendered it fit only for industrial purposes.

Discovery of gypsum deposits near Grand Rapids inspired Daniel Ball to pioneer in the mining of that mineral in 1842. Seven years later, Richard E. Butterworth installed a mill that ground gypsum for wall plaster and fertilizer. By the Civil War era, three plaster mills operated in Grand Rapids. The most notable, the Grand Rapids Plaster Company, mined gypsum, ground it into powder, and merchandised the plaster in barrel containers.[32]

Michigan's salt production, which eventually led the nation, began in a small way in the Saginaw Valley in 1860. The previous year, the state legislature had voted a bounty of ten cents per bushel on salt

Clarke Historical Library, Central Michigan University

production. The East Saginaw Salt Manufacturing Company promptly bored a deep well, began pumping brine, and evaporated four thousand bushels of salt in 1860. Cordwood, originally used as fuel, proved too expensive after the state eliminated salt bounty payments that were eating heavily into the treasury. Proprietors, therefore, moved their operations near the sawmills of the region. They used surplus steam from the mills to flush out the wells, and used the waste wood and sawdust for fuel. By the end of the Civil War, Michigan was providing enough salt to satisfy the needs of the entire Midwest and the Mississippi Valley.[33]

In addition to mineral resources, rich agricultural lands, a timber bonanza, and pioneering manufacturing efforts, the Great Lakes exerted a tremendous influence on Michigan's early economy. The sailing vessels and steamboats that plied the great inland seas made possible much commerce. Important shipbuilding industries developed prior to the Civil War at Detroit, St. Clair, St. Joseph, Holland, and other port cities.

As the fur trade diminished during the 1830s, places like Mackinac Island shifted their economy to fishing. The quantities of whitefish and trout caught in northern Michigan and shipped from Mackinac Island increased from sixteen hundred barrels in 1837 to twenty thousand barrels nine years later. At Sault Ste. Marie, twelve thousand barrels were shipped in 1840. In addition to those preserved by salting in barrels, large quantities of fresh fish were boxed in ice for shipment to Detroit, Chicago, and other Great Lakes markets.[34] By 1852, however, one observer noted a decrease in yearly catches at Mackinac caused by commercial fishermen continuing to take large numbers of fish during the spawning seasons. He thought it presented "a state of things which may in time call for legislative provision."[35]

The Michigan tourism industry also traces its roots to the antebellum period. In the 1830s and 1840s, a distinguished list of literary travelers, including Anna Jameson and Frederick Marryat, made their way to the north country for an obligatory stopover at Mackinac Island and Sault Ste. Marie. The travel narratives they penned stimulated other tourists to sample "the fairy island's" scenery and to shoot the Sault rapids in birchbark canoes. By 1855 popular guides to vacation resorts, such as those published by John Disturnell, provided glowing accounts of the fashionable "watering places" at the Sault and Mackinac Island.[36]

The moderating influence of Lake Michigan permitted the development of a fruit-growing district that by the Civil War was already attracting national attention. The first settlers at St. Joseph found mature peach trees that had been planted years earlier by Indian trader

William Burnett. Several followed his example and set out peach and apple seedlings. In 1840 Capt. Curtis Boughton carried peaches in his vessel to Chicago. He found a ready market and sold some for as much as forty-five dollars per barrel. By 1850 he was shipping ten thousand bushels per year to Chicago. News of his enormous profits inspired other local growers to start peach orchards. S. B. Morehouse planted the first peach orchard in South Haven in 1853. Fruit culture spread rapidly throughout southwestern Michigan and along the "fruit strip" to the north, reaching the Grand Traverse region by 1856. A Benton Harbor horticulturist conducted a fruit census in 1865 and found "no less than 207,639 peach trees, 40,957 pear trees, nearly 70,000 apple trees, about 10,000 cherry trees, 2,500 quince trees, 3,000 plum trees, 35,000 grape vines, and more strawberry, blackberry, and raspberry plants than could well be enumerated" growing in his vicinity.[37]

By the Civil War era, the culture of other specialty crops, including celery at Kalamazoo and mint in St. Joseph County, which would bring later fame to those regions, had begun. Loggers had vigorously attacked the state's enormous stands of white pine. Michigan copper, iron, and salt helped win the Civil War. The foundations for Detroit's pharmaceuticals, tobacco products, and heavy industries were in place, as were those of the Grand Rapids furniture industry and the industrial-based economies of many other urban areas. As Michigan left its pioneer period, the imprint of its adolescent years would continue to influence its subsequent economic evolution.

◆

NOTES

1. James J. Thomas, comp., *Kalamazoo County Directory with a History of the County* (Kalamazoo: Stone Brothers, 1869), 55; *Quarter Centennial Celebration of the Settlement of Kalamazoo* (Kalamazoo: Gazette Print, 1855), 50–51.

2. Thomas, 62.

3. Samuel Durant, *History of Kalamazoo County, Michigan* (Philadelphia: Everts & Abbott, 1880), 221.

4. Thomas, 62.

5. See Leo C. Lillie, *Historic Grand Haven and Ottawa County* (Grand Haven, 1931).

6. Willis F. Dunbar, *Michigan: A History of the Wolverine State* (Grand Rapids: William B. Eerdmans Publishing Company, 1965), 324.

7. Mrs. Richard Dye, "Coming to Michigan," *Michigan Pioneer Collections* 8 (1886): 263.

8. *Quarter Centennial Celebration*, 51.

9. Harriet Martineau, *Society in America,* 2 vols. (Paris: A. and W. Galignani and Company, 1837), 1:166.

10. Willis F. Dunbar, *Kalamazoo and How It Grew* (Kalamazoo: Western Michigan University, 1959), 56.

11. Willis F. Dunbar, *All Aboard! A History of Railroads in Michigan* (Grand Rapids: William B. Eerdmans Publishing Company, 1969), 23–24.

12. James J. Hogaboam, *The Bean Creek Valley Incidents of Its Early Settlement* (Hudson: Jas. M. Scarritt, 1876), 57–62; Jerome James Wood, *The Wilderness and the Rose* (Hudson: Wood Book Company, 1890), 96.

13. John N. Ingersoll, "The Clinton and Kalamazoo Canal Celebration," *Michigan Pioneer Collections* 5 (1884): 469; S. C. Woodard, "Reminiscences of the Early Itineracy," *Michigan Pioneer Collections* 14 (1890): 553.

14. Joseph E. Bayliss, Estelle L. Bayliss, and Milo M. Quaife, *River of Destiny, The Saint Mary's* (Detroit: Wayne State University Press, 1955), 102.

15. Asa H. Stoddard, *Miscellaneous Poems* (Kalamazoo: C. G. Townsend, 1880), 8.

16. William Nowlin, *The Bark Covered House* (Detroit: Herald Publishing House, 1876), 156–57.

17. *Census and Statistics of the State of Michigan,* May 1854 (Lansing: Geo. W. Peck, 1854), 393.

18. Bayliss, Bayliss, and Quaife, 164–65; Robert Dodge, "The Great Lakes to St. Paul," *The Continental Monthly* 5 (January–June 1864): 398.

19. *Census and Statistics 1854,* 391.

20. Robert Sears, ed., *The New Pictorial Family Magazine* 4 (1847): 510.

21. *Census and Statistics 1854,* 362.

22. Sears, 506.

23. Henry S. Lucas, *Netherlanders in America* (Ann Arbor: University of Michigan Press, 1955), 98.

24. *Census and Statistics 1854,* 394.

25. Charles Lanman, *A Summer in the Wilderness* (New York: D. Appleton and Company, 1847), 98.

26. Robert C. Clarke, "Notes from the Copper Country," *Harper's New Monthly Magazine* 6 (1853): 439.

27. Lewis Beeson and Victor F. Lemmer, *The Effects of the Civil War on Mining in Michigan* (Lansing: Michigan Civil War Centennial Observance Commission, 1966), 20.

28. Kenneth N. Metcalf and Lewis Beeson, *Effects of the Civil War on Manufacturing in Michigan* (Lansing: Michigan Civil War Centennial Observance Commission, 1966), 27–28.

29. *Statistics of the State of Michigan Compiled from the Census of 1860* (Lansing: John A. Kerr, 1861), 331.

30. Crisfield Johnson, *History of Branch County, Michigan* (Philadelphia: Everts & Abbott, 1879), 210–11.

31. Larry B. Massie and Peter J. Schmitt, *Kalamazoo: The Place behind the Products* (Kalamazoo: Windsor Publications, 1981), 43–44.

32. Franklin Everett, *Memorials of the Grand River Valley* (Chicago: Chicago Legal News Company, 1878), 544–45; Beeson and Lemmer, 31.

33. Beeson and Lemmer, 29–30.

34. Sears, 500–501.

35. Clarke, 437.

36. *Springs, Water Falls, Sea—Bathing Resorts* . . . (New York: J. Disturnell, 1855), 166–79.

37. J. P. Thresher, "History of Benton Harbor," *Second Annual Report of the Michigan State Pomological Society* (Lansing: W. S. George and Company, 1873), 336–38; A. S. Dyckman, "History of Fruit Growing in South Haven," *Second Annual Report of the Michigan State Pomological Society* (Lansing: W. S. George and Company, 1873), 352.

◆

SUGGESTED READINGS

Willis Dunbar's *Michigan: A History of the Wolverine State* (Grand Rapids, 1980), revised and updated by George May, remains the best comprehensive history of the state. Earlier works of enduring value include Henry N. Utley and Byron M. Cutcheon's *Michigan As a Province, Territory and State*, 4 vols. (New York, 1906), and George N. Fuller's *Michigan: A Centennial History*, 5 vols. (Chicago, 1939). Anyone interested in Michigan history owes a deep debt of gratitude to the Michigan Pioneer and Historical Society for the forty volumes of invaluable reminiscences and historical articles published from 1876 to 1929 in the *Michigan Pioneer Collections* and to the Michigan Historical Commission for *Michigan History Magazine*, 1917 to the present, with indexes covering 1917 to 1962.

The monographs published by the Michigan Civil War Centennial Observance Commission, particularly those by Kenneth N. Metcalf and Lewis Beeson on manufacturing, Beeson and Victor Lemmer on mining, and Joseph Marks on farming are particularly useful for the watershed Civil War era.

Dunbar's *All Aboard!* (Grand Rapids, 1969) is a detailed history of Michigan railroads. For the Sault Canal, I recommend Quaife and Bayliss's *St. Mary's River of Destiny* (Detroit, 1955) and *The Saint Mary's Falls Canal Semicentennial Volume* (Detroit, 1907), edited by Charles Moore. Stewart Holbrook's *Holy Old Mackinaw* (New York, 1938) and Irene Hargreaves and Harold Froehl's *The Story of Logging the White Pine in the Saginaw Valley* offer good popular accounts of lumbering. For the copper industry, consult Angus Murdock's *Boom Copper* (New York, 1943) and William Gates's *Michigan Copper and Boston Dollars* (Cambridge, 1951). For iron mining, see Holbrook's *Iron Brew* (New York, 1939) and Harlan Hatcher's *A Century of Iron and Men* (Indianapolis, 1950).

1836-1866

M

JUSTIN L. KESTENBAUM

Justin Kestenbaum is professor of History at Michigan State University where he has taught Michigan history for more than ten years. He received his bachelor's degree from the University of Illinois and his master's and doctorate degrees from Northwestern University. Professor Kestenbaum is the author of numerous articles and books including *Out of a Wilderness: An Illustrated History of Greater Lansing* and the forthcoming *The Making of Michigan: A Pioneer Anthology*.

odernizing Michigan:
Political and Social Trends

In 1835, Edward W. Barber of Vermontville recalled that his father and neighbors in Vermont began talking about the Great Lakes, "about magnificent forests . . . [and] the wonderful richness of the soil, which only needed to be tickled with the hoe to yield a bounteous harvest." His father, Edward H. Barber, made several "land looking" expeditions to Michigan, and in September 1839 the Barber family "bade adieu to the old Vermont home" and set forth for Michigan, never to see many of their loved ones again.[1]

Having succumbed to the "Michigan fever" in 1839, the Barber family joined one of the great population movements of American history.

By 1835 population in the Territory of Michigan sufficed for statehood; it doubled again by 1838. So quickly did Michigan continue to grow, that in 1836 receipts from land sales exceeded one fifth of the land sales for the entire country. The federal census of 1840 showed 212,267 persons, the state census of 1845 counted 302,521, and on the eve of the Civil War Michigan's population stood at 749,113—an increase of 84-fold since 1820.[2]

Diverse origins as well as rapid growth characterized Michigan's population. Many new arrivals came from foreign countries as well as the older states. The early settlers from western New York and New England were followed by Germans, who settled in the Saginaw and Ann Arbor areas. The Dutch came to western Michigan, the Irish to the rolling green territory they named the Irish Hills, and blacks—who remained a small part of the total population until the early twentieth century—settled in Detroit as well as Cass County in western Michigan.

Once in the state, Michigan's pioneers began to create institutions and build a society. Several factors greatly affected the social and political development of Michigan from the time of statehood to the end of the Civil War. The first was the New England-New York origin of most of the settlers—a fact that profoundly shaped their values and lifestyle. Many settlers from western New York State had experienced the wave of religious and moral revivalism that swept that region in the second quarter of the nineteenth century. A second factor was that, as Michigan was being settled, the American people had undergone a political transformation. Property qualifications for voting and holding office had been swept away; a new type of mass political party, based on egalitarianism and organized down to the precinct level, replaced the elitist parties of the early Republic. The Second American party system, centered around the Democrats and Whigs and reflecting a new and more open political process, was coming into being as Michigan became a state. During the 1850s, the conflict over slavery, fugitive slaves, and the Mexican War destroyed the Whigs, gave rise to the Republican party, and brought into being the Third American party system. The wave of humanitarian reform which swept the United States in the second quarter of the nineteenth century also affected Michigan as it did other northern states. Michigan, under the influence of the reform wave, established prisons, insane asylums, abolished the death penalty (the first English-speaking jurisdiction to do so), and experienced the temperance crusade, as well as a surge of religious revivalism.

Michigan's settlers also took great pride in their system of local government. Counties were organized first by the territorial government and then by the state. When the population in a given area began to grow significantly, a county government was organized. In many cases in lower Michigan counties were named and their boundaries were set off before a single settler had arrived. When settlers appeared, the legislature authorized the eligible voters of the area to organize county government and to elect officers. By 1846 thirty-two counties had been organized. The functions of the early county governments were limited to maintaining courts and records; township governments had a more immediate effect on the lives of early settlers. Michigan's system of local government was modeled on that of the New England states, in which the town (or in Michigan, the township) had a unique vitality.

Township governments, unlike counties, were organized by the direct initiative of the settlers. When a surveyed township had a dozen or so families, little time was lost in submitting a petition for organization to the legislature. A legislative enabling act defined the township's boundaries, designated a place and date for the first township meeting, and almost always approved the name proposed in the petition.

Pioneer William A. Dryer was present at the first meeting of Ingham Township in Ingham County, held at the home of Caleb Carr in the spring of 1838. "We felt the need for some proper authority to lay out roads and organize school districts," recalled Dryer. The twenty-five eligible voters at the meeting "had no records, no laws, nothing to guide us." They had come from several different states, each with its own tradition of local government. After an animated discussion, it was agreed to elect the same officers as in Stockbridge Township, which had been organized earlier.

"Now commenced an interesting scene," reported Dryer. The men did not know each other, and "they knew still less of each other's abilities or qualifications." The voters, with some embarrassment, described their respective qualifications, and a slate of candidates was agreed upon. Then arose the question of "who should receive the votes," and someone nominated their host, Caleb Carr. Carr "doffed his hat into which the votes were cast," and when the votes were counted, "we swore each other into office, adjourned, shook hands all around, a happy and contented people with full-fledged government fairly organized."[3]

In the newly-organized townships, there were often as many offices to fill as there were eligible voters. In a township adjoining Ingham, twenty-four voters filled twenty-three offices; there was one case of thirteen voters filling twenty-one offices. The officers generally included a supervisor, town clerk, justices of the peace, constables, "directors of the poor," school inspectors, road commissioners, "fence viewers," and a poundmaster. Fence viewers determined that "lawful fences," at least four and a half feet high, were built; poundmasters cared for stray livestock.

Politics came naturally to these pioneer politicians. For most of the territorial period (1805–1837), party politics had not existed in Michigan. There were elections—and often they were bitterly-fought contests—but not party conflict. In 1835, at the convention which crafted Michigan's first constitution, there occurred the first Democratic-Whig contest along party lines. Patterns of party loyalty were established early and lasted for years. The Democratic party was generally victorious in Michigan from the time of statehood to the 1850s, despite the fact that the voters of the state were fairly evenly divided between the two parties. The fact that the Democrats generally were more skilled politicians than the Whigs largely explains their success at the polls. They had, after all, invented the new political techniques—including organization to the precinct level—and knew how to use them. While economic difficulties and a spirited campaign produced a Whig victory in the Michigan elections of 1839, the Democrats quickly recovered. Between 1841 and 1854, the Democrats won all state elections and controlled all the annually-elected state legislatures. After 1840, the Whigs increasingly became the minority party.[4]

Politics was taken very seriously by Michigan's pioneers. The campaign styles of the era—parades, rallies, singing, floats, wagon trains, and impassioned oratory—reflected the intense partisanship of the voters. A high proportion of straight-ticket voting is further evidence of intense party loyalty. At this time, voters were permitted to bring their own ballots—often printed by newspapers or supplied by parties—to the polling place. Undoubtedly, this also encouraged straight-ticket voting.

Historians do not agree on the issues that divided the Democrats and Whigs in pioneer Michigan. Recent scholars have challenged the traditional view, which depicts the Whigs as conservatives and the Democrats as radicals, and sees Michigan political debate as a mirror image of that going on in Washington. In Michigan, many of the national issues—such as banks, corporations and internal improvements—were hardly issues, since the Michigan parties did not disagree on them. In Michigan, for example, both parties supported internal improvements even though the national parties differed.

The Michigan parties differed on other issues—most fundamentally, some historians now argue, on the kind of society each party wanted Michigan to become and the proper role of government in that society. The Whigs agreed with Ralph Waldo Emerson that "morality is the object of government." The Whigs, therefore, tended to support public policies that would enforce morality, such as temperance legislation and compulsory Sabbath observance. The Democrats, on the other hand, rejected the idea of publicly-enforced morality.

The first important issue on which Whigs and Democrats disagreed was that of the right of aliens to vote. Most Democrats would have allowed aliens—rapidly becoming an important presence in the state— the right to vote after a brief period of residence, while the Whigs favored limiting the vote to citizens. This issue, in fact, brought the Michigan Whig party into being. The Democrats won on the issue of alien voting. The clause in the Michigan Constitution of 1835 granting the vote to aliens was one of the factors, in addition to the dispute over the Toledo Strip, which aroused the opposition of such national Whig leaders as Sen. Henry Clay of Kentucky and helped to delay the admission of Michigan as a state. The same dispute later divided the Democrats and Whigs in three other states (Iowa, Wisconsin, and Illinois).

If there were issues between the Michigan Whigs and Democrats, there were also factions within each party. Among the Democrats, one faction, led by Postmaster John Norvell of Detroit, was composed mostly of federal officeholders. A second faction, led by Lucius Lyon, one of Michigan's first United States senators, favored property qualifications for voting. Kinsley S. Bingham of Livingston County—who would later become Michigan's first Republican governor—echoed the sentiments of Pres. Andrew Jackson in opposing special privileges for banks and corporations. During the 1840s, this faction became increasingly antislavery. A fourth faction, centered around the western part of the state and led by Epaphroditus Ransom of Kalamazoo (who would also serve as governor), believed that the interests of their part of the state were being overlooked. This opposition to Detroit's growing political and economic power led to the move of the state capital to the then wilderness of Lansing in 1847. The Whigs, on their part, were divided into two factions—a conservative faction led by William Woodbridge (Whig governor in 1840 and United States senator) had much in common with the conservative Democrats, while a radical antislavery faction attracted many young lawyers.

Party strife, plus Michigan's unfortunate experience with internal improvements and the depression which followed the panic of 1837, as well as other factors, had an important bearing on the drafting of the Constitution of 1850, the state's second charter of government. The new constitution prohibited state aid for internal improvements and placed a limit on state debt. The constitution's framers, recalling the sharp practices of some unscrupulous bankers, made them personally liable for financial misdeeds. Michigan corporations would be formed under a general law of incorporation, thereby ending the political manipulation that sometimes occurred when the legislature approved corporation charters. Two-year terms replaced the annual election of legislators, but the legislature would meet only once in a two-year period. Since several incumbent governors had been elected to the United States Senate by the legislature, the governor and lieutenant governor were declared ineligible for legislative appointment during their term of office. The constitution also modified the state's court system and once more enfranchised aliens.

The Constitution of 1850 also confirmed the state's earlier role as a leader in education. Perhaps the most enduring and significant legacy of Michigan's pioneer era is the state's exemplary educational system. The Rev. John D. Pierce of Marshall, one of the most respected Michigan public servants in the pioneer era, deserves much of the credit along with Isaac E. Crary for the creation of the state's public educational system. The state Constitution of 1835, whose educational provisions were largely the work of Crary, provided for a superintendent of public instruction. Michigan was the first state to create such an office, and Pierce, the first appointee to the post, was the first superintendent of public instruction in the United States.

A farsighted decision which affected Michigan's educational system had to do with control of the federal grant of Section 16 (one square mile) in every surveyed township. The proceeds from the sale of this section were to support public schools. In Michigan this amounted to over a million acres. Since Crary was a nonvoting member of the United States House of Representatives at the time Michigan was admitted as a state, he persuaded Congress to grant the sixteenth sections in Michigan to the state rather than to the townships in which they were located. As a result of Crary's foresight, the state was able to place the land-sales proceeds in a fund for the support of education.

Pierce and Crary were also largely responsible for the education provisions of Michigan's Constitution of 1835. Pierce later recalled that he and Crary had read, and were strongly influenced by, Victor Cousin's report to the French minister of education on the Prussian system of education. "Sitting one pleasant afternoon upon a log," Pierce recalled later, "General Crary and myself discussed for a long time the fundamental principles which were deemed important for the [constitutional] convention to adopt in laying the foundations of our State." Education, they felt, was of particular importance. The two men agreed that "if possible, that it should make a distinct branch of government, and that the constitution ought to provide for an officer who should have this whole matter in charge and thus keep its importance perpetually before the public mind."

In 1836, Pierce was appointed superintendent, even before Congress admitted Michigan to the Union. The legislature also passed an act requiring the superintendent to submit plans for organizing and supporting primary schools, for a university with branches, and for the sale of the university and primary school land grants.

Pierce spent five months preparing his plans, which he submitted to the legislature in January 1837. He conferred with educational leaders in the older states. "It was a day," Pierce wrote, "when all was astir with activity and life . . . [and] the watchword was progress and improvement." There were, however, problems. While "there were no old institutions and deep-rooted prejudices to be encountered and removed," Michigan was largely undeveloped: "We were less than 100,000, all was wild, and the people were comparatively poor." But despite these problems, "the people then here came mostly from the region of schoolhouses, and were anxious for schools. I may add, also, that the early movement in this direction aided materially in the settlement of the country."

Michigan law required that "every township containing fifty inhabitants or householders shall employ a schoolmaster of good morals to teach children to read and write . . . as well as arithmetic, orthography [spelling], and decent behavior." The settlers hardly needed prodding by the authorities; pioneer accounts reveal that after meeting the physical needs of their families, the "greatest solicitude" was for "a suitable educational training" for their children, who had been suddenly withdrawn from schools and other sources of culture. All over the state, township residents built log cabin schools and hired teachers.[5]

The log schoolhouse, immortalized in the paintings of Winslow Homer and in the poetry of John Greenleaf Whittier has a secure place in American folklore. As a source of virtue and dispenser of the pristine values of American civilization, it was believed to have no peer. In creating log schools, the pioneers of Michigan were, despite primitive conditions and cultural isolation, participants in one of the great humanitarian crusades of the time.

The interior of a log school was as spare as the log houses in which the pupils lived. There was usually one door and one window; the door swung on wooden hinges and was secured by a wooden latch. A fireplace took up one whole side of the room, usually opposite the door. Against the log walls were desks or planks supported by pegs. In the early days books were scarce; blackboards were uncommon and even the school bell was unknown. School was "called" by rapping a book on the window sash. In the evening and during the long winter season, log cabin schools served as community centers for adult education as well.[6]

Colleges, both public and private, also proliferated in Michigan. Olivet, Albion, and Hillsdale were established in the 1840s, and Michigan Agricultural College (now Michigan State University) in 1855. But The University of Michigan stood at the apex of the state's comprehensive educational system. The university was established in 1817 and remained in Detroit until 1837, moving to Ann Arbor when residents of that community offered forty acres of land; the new campus opened formally in 1841. The university's first decade in Ann Arbor was difficult. For a time, its future was threatened by disputes over the role of religion in the institution, the proper mission of a state university, and the degree of legislative control. During the 1850s, however, the university came into its own under the leadership of Henry Philip Tappan, a scholar who admired German ideas about what a university ought to be. Tappan ignored religion in making faculty appointments and stressed academic excellence and professional competence. By 1860, under his leadership, the university had earned its reputation as one of the best American state universities. But Tappan made enemies. He thought of Michigan as an uncouth primitive state and offended members of the state legislature by his preference for the German idea of a university. The *Detroit Free Press,* a Democratic paper, ridiculed him while reformers regretted his opposition to the admission of women. In 1863 Tappan, a controversial figure, was forced to resign.[7]

The role of blacks in Michigan created an even greater series of challenges in the pioneer era as the antislavery movement began to affect the state. The proportion of blacks in Michigan was small in the pioneer period; most were concentrated in the Detroit area, with black enclaves in other places—most notably Cass County. In Michigan, the overriding

UNIVERSITY OF MICHIGAN, 1857

The University of Michigan, 1857. Printed in Henry M. Utley, *Michigan as a Province Territory and State,* 3 (New York: Publishing Society of Michigan, 1906), facing 242.

Clarke Historical Library, Central Michigan University

issue for blacks in the antebellum period was the denial of their right to vote. The antislavery movement had a powerful hold on Michigan, a fact that appears to have energized some blacks and their white allies (including Austin Blair, who would become governor of Michigan during the Civil War) to demand full rights of citizenship for blacks. The fact that Pennsylvania granted blacks such rights in 1838, and that there was strong support for a similar step in New York, appears to have been a powerful example for Michigan blacks, who demanded the same from their state. They suffered as well from other legal disabilities: they could not serve on juries, attend white schools, or use public facilities. While some Michigan abolitionists, including those who published the Ann Arbor *Signal of Liberty,* an antislavery newspaper of the period, supported the black vote, many did not. It is an anomaly of American history that many whites were antislavery and, at the same time, were racists, unwilling to extend civil rights to blacks.

In 1842, Detroit blacks formed a Colored Vigilance Committee to wage "moral and political warfare" for civil rights. A year later, black leaders held a national convention, which was followed by a convention of Michigan blacks in October 1843. The convention, which was led by ministers and small-business proprietors, objected to denial of educational opportunity but placed greatest stress on denial of the right to vote. A ballot proposition granting Michigan's blacks the right to vote accompanied the referendum on the Constitution of 1850; it was defeated 32,026 to 12,840.[8]

While there were a few fugitive slaves in their midst, recent research has shown that most of the blacks of Cass County were not runaway slaves but free Negroes from North Carolina—people who had been free, in fact, for more than a century. When Cass County was established in 1829, it had not a single black inhabitant; by 1840, there were 3,305. The blacks in Cass County lived near a large Quaker settlement located on Young's Prairie, close to the center of Cass County in Calvin Township. A few miles from the Birch Lake Monthly Meeting House, a Quaker place of worship, was the largest concentration of Cass County blacks.

It was well known that Quakers helped slaves to freedom by participating in the secret activities of the Underground Railroad. Two Michigan women, the Quaker Laura Smith Haviland and Sojourner Truth, were active in the Underground Railroad and abolition movements. Haviland, from the Adrian area, in addition to her efforts to aid escaped slaves, founded the Raisin Institute in 1836. This manual labor school was open to boys and girls, and black, as well as white, children. Truth, a former slave and eloquent advocate of black and women's rights, moved to Battle Creek in 1858, where she lived for the remainder of her life.

Slaveholders sent spies into southern Michigan to ascertain the

THE SLAVEHOLDERS' ASSAULT.

Laura Haviland confronting slave catchers on the train between Toledo and Adrian, 1840. Printed in Laura Haviland, *A Woman's Life Work* (Chicago: S. B. Shaw, 1902), 76.

Clarke Historical Library, Central Michigan University

names and whereabouts of runaway slaves. In August 1847, a group of about a dozen Kentuckians—including the sheriff of Bourbon County—set up headquarters in Battle Creek. The townspeople, discovering their purpose, forced them to flee to Bristol, Indiana, about an hour from Cass County. On the night of 16 August 1847, a heavily-armed party of Kentuckians descended on Calvin Township with the plan of seizing black persons on Young's Prairie and restoring them to slavery. Word of the danger quickly spread, a large crowd gathered, and the plans of the Kentuckians came to naught.[9] Foiling the "Michigan Raid of 1847" was by no means the only such incident in Michigan. In 1848, one Adam Crosswhite, a fugitive slave who lived near Marshall, was rescued in a similar manner.

Increasingly, the national conflict over slavery in the national territories and other issues in the growing sectional conflict shaped the course of Michigan's politics. In 1840 many abolitionists, who demanded the immediate and unconditional end of slavery, formed the Liberty party, which nominated antislavery leader James Birney for president. Birney, a former slaveholder who had been converted to abolitionism, moved to Bay City. In 1842 he ran for governor on the Liberty party ticket, but polled only a small portion of the vote.

The Mexican War of 1846 to 1848 placed the question of slavery in a new light, especially the debate over slavery in the territories. While a majority of the people of Michigan apparently supported Pres. James K. Polk and the war with Mexico, all did not. Sen. William Woodbridge, the elder statesman of the Michigan Whigs, as well as the editors of many Michigan Whig newspapers, saw the war as part of a plan to acquire additional slave territory.

The war had hardly begun when an obscure antislavery Pennsylvania congressman, David Wilmot, introduced a rider (the Wilmot Proviso) to an appropriation bill that would prohibit slavery in any territory acquired from Mexico as a result of the war. The Wilmot Proviso was defeated. But, when the Mexican War ended in 1848, the question of territorial slavery once again became a national issue. Michigan political leaders played a conspicuous role in the debate. In Michigan, Liberty party abolitionists and Free Soil Democrats organized the Free-Soil party to oppose the extension of slavery into the territories.

Lewis Cass of Michigan, who had been elected United States senator in 1845 after some years of diplomatic service abroad, at first supported the Wilmot Proviso but voted against it when he saw how divisive the issue of territorial slavery had become. In order to obtain the support of southern Democrats for his presidential bid, Cass argued that Congress had no constitutional authority to ban slavery in the territories. Instead, he urged, territorial settlers should decide this question for themselves. Cass's position, which became known as popular sovereignty, enabled him to win the Democratic presidential nomination in 1848. He lost the general election in a close race to Zachary Taylor, a hero of the Mexican War.

Despite his defeat in the presidential election, Cass was determined to play a continuing part in national politics. In January 1849, he was reelected by the Michigan legislature to the seat in the United States Senate, from which he had resigned to accept the presidential nomination. The legislature instructed Cass and his Senate colleague, former Gov. Alpheus Felch, to support the Wilmot Proviso. When Cass arrived in Washington in December 1849, Congress was in the throes of the crisis caused by the issue of territorial slavery and the petition of California for admission as a free state. Admitting California would give the free states a majority in both houses of Congress and would in effect set aside the Missouri Compromise of 1820, under which there was an equal number of free and slave states.

Congress debated these issues in an atmosphere laden with crisis. Southerners, angry at the activities of the Underground Railroad, demanded a more effective fugitive slave law; northern antislavery spokesmen demanded an end not merely to slavery in the territories but also prohibition of the slave trade in the District of Columbia. On the issue of territorial slavery, Cass, who participated actively in the debates, fought hard for the compromise position of popular sovereignty he had advocated during the presidential election.

The crisis alarmed the nation, and Congress began to feel the pressure of moderates. The Michigan legislature, responding to this mood, rescinded its instructions to Cass and Felch, and Congress adopted a series of compromise measures proposed by Henry Clay. California was to be admitted as a free state, a new and more stringent fugitive slave law was passed, and the residents of new territories to be carved out of the Mexican cession would decide the question of slavery for themselves. Cass voted for all the compromise measures except the fugitive slave law, which he opposed because it did not allow a trial by jury.

At first most Michiganians supported the Compromise of 1850; state conventions of both parties endorsed its features in September 1850. The Michigan Whigs, however, opposed some features of the Fugitive Slave Law, and, for a brief time, agitated against it. But by the summer of 1851, agitation against the law abated considerably.

The introduction of the Kansas-Nebraska Act of 1854 changed everything and brought about a political realignment in Michigan and the nation. The act, that organized Kansas as a territory without excluding slavery, aroused fears of a conspiracy which sought not merely to extend slavery into the new territories but to impose it on free states as well. Almost spontaneously in the North, fusionist or anti-Nebraska rallies were held, including one at Jackson on 6 July 1854. This meeting, held at the call of ten thousand persons, was the first to officially adopt the name Republican. The new party drew its members from the Free-Soil party, antislavery Whigs, and antislavery Democrats.

The new party gained strength as the sectional crisis revived and deepened. In the elections of 1854, the Michigan Republican party won all state offices and a two-thirds majority in the state legislature. Such national events as the outbreak of armed violence in Kansas, the caning of Sen. Charles Sumner of Massachusetts on the Senate floor, and the Supreme Court's Dred Scott decision of March 1857, heightened antisouthernism in Michigan and added to the ranks of the party's supporters. In 1855 and 1859, the Michigan legislature passed personal liberty laws, which conflicted with the federal Fugitive Slave Law. Under Michigan's statutes, no

Michigan resident could be surrendered as a fugitive without a jury trial and the kidnapping of a fugitive slave was outlawed.

The year 1860 saw the culmination of a decade of intense sectional and party strife. Michigan Republicans had favored Sen. William H. Seward of New York for the presidency but loyally supported the party's nominee, Abraham Lincoln of Illinois. Seward, who would become Lincoln's secretary of state, made a campaign tour in Michigan; his appearance in Lansing attracted the largest crowd in the history of the capital city. National Democratic party leaders, including standard-bearer Stephen A. Douglas, also campaigned in Michigan but had little chance of carrying the state, which went heavily for Lincoln and the Republican ticket. On 20 December, South Carolina and other states of the Deep South made good their threat to secede from the Union if a "black Republican" were elected. The seceding states seized federal forts, arsenals, and custom houses. By February 1861, seven states had formed the Confederate States of America, with Jefferson Davis as provisional president. Lincoln's attempt in April to relieve Fort Sumter, one of two southern military installations still in federal hands, led to the firing on Fort Sumter by South Carolina and the secession of yet more states. It had really come to war—the war so many had predicted but so few had believed would happen.

Michigan State Archives

Austin Blair, Michigan's Civil War governor, was an uncompromising foe of slavery who rallied Michigan troops to the Union cause.

Michigan State Archives

Corp. Kinchen Artis enlisted in Company H, First Michigan Colored Infantry, 19 December 1863 at Battle Creek. He mustered out 30 Sept. 1865. The First Colored Infantry began service with an enrollment of 895 officers and soldiers, and eventually totaled 1,673 troops.

Austin Blair, Michigan's Civil War governor, took office on 2 January 1861, within days of the secession of South Carolina. Blair, one of Michigan's most remembered governors, would have preferred a seat in the United States Senate, but that distinction went to Zachariah Chandler of Detroit. Blair, in his inaugural, affirmed Michigan's loyalty "to the Union, the Constitution, to the Laws, and will defend them to the uttermost," and assured the president that "the whole military power of the State" was at his disposal. The legislature, dominated by Republicans, supported the governor in joint resolutions. When Fort Sumter fell to Confederate guns on 13 April, a wave of anger spread across Michigan. The war department in Washington began raising troops and sent Blair a message asking that Michigan provide one infantry regiment. Since the legislature was not in session, Blair went to Detroit, where private citizens agreed to advance the necessary funds against a legislative appropriation. Blair called a special legislative session to meet on 7 May; his ringing address to the legislators deplored the action taken by the seceding states and pledged all-out support of the war by the people of Michigan. "In this sacred war," Blair observed, "the people of Michigan desire to do their whole duty, and it is for us, their chosen representatives, to provide the means and lead the way." Unlike other Northern political leaders, who underestimated the determination of the southern states, Blair predicted that the war would be a protracted and bloody conflict. "This is to be no six-weeks campaign," he told the legislators. "I do not under-estimate the gallantry of Southern men."[10]

About ninety thousand Michigan men (about 23 percent of the male population of 1860), served in the Union army and navy, including about sixteen hundred blacks. Michigan men served in all of the theaters of the war and fought in more than eight hundred battles and skirmishes. They played a pivotal role in some of the key battles of the war, including Gettysburg, where the Twenty-Fourth Michigan Infantry fought off a major Confederate attack and sustained 80 percent casualties. Michigan men also fought hard in such engagements as the Battles of Antietam, Shiloh, Vicksburg, and in Gen. William T. Sherman's march through Georgia, which brought the war home to the Confederacy. During the war, Blair and Chandler, Michigan's major political leaders, brought pressure to bear on the Lincoln administration not only for a more vigorous prosecution of the war but also for an end to slavery. An important legacy of the war was the Fifteenth Amendment to the Constitution of the United States, which finally assured all black males in the United States the right to vote.

◆

NOTES

1. Edward W. Barber, "The Vermontville Colony: Its Genesis and History, with Personal Sketches of the Colonists," *Michigan Pioneer and Historical Collections*, vol. 28 (Lansing: Robert Smith Printing Company, 1900), 197–265.

2. Willis F. Dunbar and George S. May, *Michigan: A History of the Wolverine State* (Grand Rapids: William B. Eerdmans Publishing Company, 1980), 195.

3. Mrs. Franc L. Adams, *Pioneer History of Ingham County* (Lansing: Wynkoop, Hallenbeck, and Crawford Company, 1923), 398–99.

4. See Ronald P. Formisano, *The Birth of Mass Political Parties: Michigan, 1827–1861* (Princeton: Princeton University Press, 1971).

5. This account (and all quotations) of the framing of Michigan's educational system is drawn largely from John D. Pierce, "Origin and Progress of the Michigan School System," *Michigan Pioneer and Historical Collections,* vol. 1 (Lansing: W. S. George & Company, 1877), 37–45.

6. A. D. P. Van Buren, "The Log Schoolhouse Era in Michigan," *Michigan Pioneer and Historical Collections*, 2d ed., vol. 14 (Lansing: Wynkoop, Hallenbeck, and Crawford Company, 1908), 283–402.

7. Willis F. Dunbar, *The Michigan Record in Higher Education* (Detroit: Wayne State University Press, 1963), 63–81.

8. David M. Katzman, *Before the Ghetto: Black Detroit in the Nineteenth Century* (Urbana: University of Illinois Press, 1973), 33ff.

9. See Benjamin Calvin Wilson, "Michigan's Ante-Bellum Black Haven: Cass County, 1835–1870" (Ph.D. diss., Michigan State University, 1975).

10. See Robert Charles Harris, "Austin Blair of Michigan: A Political Biography," (Ph.D. diss., Michigan State University, 1969) for this account of Austin Blair and quotes.

SUGGESTED READINGS

Dunbar, Willis F., and George S. May. *Michigan: A History of the Wolverine State.* Grand Rapids: William B. Eerdmans Publishing Company, 1980.

————. *The Michigan Record in Higher Education.* Detroit: Wayne State University Press, 1963.

Formisano, Ronald P. *The Birth of Mass Political Parties: Michigan, 1827–1861.* Princeton: Princeton University Press, 1972.

Harris, Robert Charles. "Austin Blair of Michigan: A Political Biography." Ph.D. diss., Michigan State University, 1969.

Katzman, David P. *Before the Ghetto: Black Detroit in the Nineteenth Century.* Urbana: University of Illinois Press, 1973.

Wilson, Benjamin Calvin. "Michigan's Ante-Bellum Black Haven: Cass County, 1835–1870." Ph.D. diss., Michigan State University, 1975.

1866-1900s

BRUCE A. RUBENSTEIN AND
LAWRENCE E. ZIEWACZ

Bruce Rubenstein, professor of history at The University of Michigan-Flint, is a native of Port Huron, Michigan, and received his bachelor's, master's and doctorate degrees from Michigan State University. Professor Rubenstein has co-authored, with Lawrence E. Ziewacz, *Michigan: A History of the Great Lakes State* and *Three Bullets Sealed His Lips*. In addition, he has written numerous articles and presented papers on both Michigan's political history and American Indian-white relations in Michigan.

Lawrence E. Ziewacz, professor of American Thought and Language at Michigan State University, is a native of Sault Ste. Marie, Michigan, and received his bachelor's, master's, and doctorate degrees from Michigan State University. In addition to his publications with Professor Rubenstein, he is co-author of *The Games They Played* and *Sports History*. Dr. Ziewacz has also presented papers and written articles on Michigan's nineteenth century political history, and is co-chair of the sports section for the Popular Culture Association.

ichigan in the Gilded Age:
Politics and Society

In many respects Michigan was a microcosm of the political and social milieu prevalent in the northern United States during the thirty-five years following the American Civil War. Dominated by the Republican party (GOP), Michigan could be relied on to deliver faithfully its votes to the Republican candidates for president, Congress, and state legislators who, in turn, would select members of their party to the United States Senate.[1] In fact, Michigan's reputation as the "most Republican state in the Union" actually kept its native sons from being considered for nomination as president or vice president, since both major parties chose to look toward candidates from swing states whose electoral votes were up for grabs. As the northern "depot" for the Underground Railroad, the birthplace of the Republican party, and one of the foremost abolitionist states prior to the Civil War, Michigan unexpectedly found itself torn by heated exchanges debating the merits of black rights after the war. Closely linked to the question of black rights was that of women's suffrage, which also divided the populace. Despite the growth of industry, Michigan remained predominantly agricultural and engaged in urban/

rural confrontations. Furthermore, in the best traditions of the Northwest Ordinance, Michigan, like most other northern states, continued to battle for expanded, quality educational opportunities for all its residents.

While this so-called 'Gilded Age' correctly may be designated one of transition, it was also for Michigan years of steady, although sometimes reluctant, growth in social and political reform. Michigan not only mirrored the national scene, but also frequently provided stalwart progressive leaders such as Hazen Pingree and Chase Osborn in the later years of the period.

THE REPUBLICAN ERA

Republican strength during the Gilded Age was rooted in several factors. First, Michigan farmers retained their loyalty to the party that had established the Michigan Agricultural College in 1855 and that had enacted a national Homestead Act. Second, businessmen favored Republican advocacy of high protective tariffs. Third, the GOP attracted the best candidates, both conservative and liberal, because it was associated with nearly certain success at the polls. Fourth, workingmen viewed Republicans as an enemy of monopoly and a friend of labor; consequently, they joined their employers in a somewhat ironic allegiance to the self-admitted party of business. Fifth, virtually every Protestant denomination remained Republican, primarily because they considered the Democrats to be the party of Roman Catholics. Finally, Republicans labeled themselves the "Party of Union"—the party that had saved the republic from the grasp of southern Democratic secessionists and their pro-slavery northern fellow party members, as well as emancipating blacks from bondage.

Until 1900, many Republican candidates for public office at all levels of government were guilty of "waving the bloody shirt"—that is, reminding the state's electorate that it was the Democratic party that should be held responsible for the blood shed by their fathers, sons, and brothers during the Civil War—and also of reminding voters that the southern leaders who tried to destroy the nation had all been Democrats who opposed basic human rights for blacks. The attraction of this appeal may be seen in the following editorial from the *Port Huron Daily Times* of 2 November 1874:

> The political contest of tomorrow is one of the most important of recent years. . . . What a restoration of Democratic rule means you all know. It means repudiation of the National obligations, as openly expressed in the Democratic platforms. It means an effort to extort from the people of the

North payment of Southern war claims; a refunding of the cotton tax; payment for emancipated slaves; and even the assumption of the Confederate debt. When Democratic victories are announced, the credit of the Nation declines, and holders of United States bonds in foreign countries, and even at home, begin to sell them. Throughout the world the Democratic party is regarded as a foe to American unity, American liberty, and American honesty. . . . A vote for the Democratic candidates aids in its restoration to power throughout the Nation . . . the rebels of the South, who stand upon the same platform they occupied in 1861 when they opened fire on Fort Sumter. Republicans! Patriotic Democrats! Not one of you can afford to cast such a vote.

Against this broad-based coalition, Democrats had little chance to avoid defeat.

While one-party rule assures victory in the general elections, it also breeds the potential for intraparty strife; and Michigan Republicans savagely ripped into each other in prolonged internal conflicts. Republicans retained the governorship for all but four years during the 1865 to 1900 period; yet, a closer examination reveals that the party triumphed primarily because of factionalism among its opponents. Republicans

Republican campaign rally in Coldwater, 1896.

Michigan State Archives

kept control over the state's congressional delegation by judicious reapportionment and the creation of gerrymandered districts to dilute the ever-increasing Democratic strength in Oakland, Macomb, and Washtenaw counties by dividing them into heavily Republican districts.

GOP partisans, however, squabbled mightily over the money issue. A majority of the state's congressional delegation favored redemption of the paper greenbacks, first issued during the Civil War, with gold and silver, while a minority opposed such a step. The state's prominent Republican United States senators were divided as well, with Thomas W. Ferry on record in support of soft money and Zachariah Chandler claiming to be a hard money man. This battle became even more intense after the Panic of 1873 and the ensuing depression. The rural sector argued for paper money and inflation, while most urban businessmen vociferously took the opposing stance.

Prohibition, one of the cornerstones of the state Republican party since its inception, suddenly became another divisive issue, even though the state had enacted a prohibition law in 1855. Advocacy of prohibition had always been a successful ploy against the so-called whiskey-drinking Irish Catholics who voted Democratic. After the war, however, German immigrants, who had favored the Republicans because of their antislavery stance, began to desert the party because it sought to deprive them of the right to drink beer. In 1875, after much bickering, Republican Gov. John J. Bagley recommended and received legislative repeal of the prohibition statute and institution of taxation and licensing of the state's liquor trade.

The party was split evenly on the question of business regulation. Virtually all of the party leadership were wealthy lumber barons or industrial entrepreneurs; but, after the scandals of the Grant administration involving railroads and corporate swindles, prominent Michigan Republicans found themselves firmly impaled on the horns of a dilemma.[2] If the party came out in favor of stricter regulation of big business, many influential party contributors and officeholders would be alienated. To oppose regulation in the face of burgeoning calls for reform, however, would establish the image of Republicans being controlled by the rich and being insensitive of the need to protect common citizens.

If all these problems were not enough, the Republicans were divided geographically, with party faithful in the Upper Peninsula and western and central portions of the Lower Peninsula complaining that Detroit had an unwarranted political dominance and cared little for its outstate friends. As a result of these internal disputes, the GOP party, despite remaining dominant throughout this period, saw its foundation gradually being eaten away.

Without question, the major Republican force during the early years of the Gilded Age was Zachariah Chandler (Old Zach), who had served in the United States Senate since 1857. During his eighteen years in the Senate, Chandler had earned a reputation for his unyielding Radical Republican positions in support of the abolition of slavery, black rights, harsh reconstruction policies, and impeachment of Pres. Andrew Johnson. A master of machine politics, Chandler used his "Detroit Ring" to seize total control of federal patronage positions. In 1875, a small group of moderate young Republicans, angered by Chandler's extremist beliefs and cronyism, joined with the Democrats to deny the incumbent a fourth term, choosing instead the respected Republican associate justice of the Michigan Supreme Court, Isaac P. Christiancy.

Chandler was furious and vowed revenge. Joining President Grant's cabinet as secretary of the interior, Chandler began to rebuild his political base and, in 1876, he masterminded the disputed election of Rutherford B. Hayes to the presidency. Two years later, as head of the Michigan Republican State Committee, Chandler directed the campaign that resulted in the election of a Republican governor, the entire Republican slate of state officials, and every congressman; even though nationwide, the Republican party underwent dramatic reverses. Once again, "Old Zach" was the unchallenged king of Michigan politics.

Meanwhile, Senator Christiancy, amid widespread rumors of ill health and marital strife caused by his young wife's adulterous misadventures, resigned his seat in January 1879 to accept the post of minister to Peru. Democrats and moderate Republicans immediately cried that the resignation had been orchestrated by Chandler. They claimed that the old Radical had urged President Hayes to pressure Christiancy to step aside, and they hinted that Chandler had gone so far as to bribe Christiancy.[3] With his supporters boasting that it was time to return "the greatest Radical of them all," Chandler was reelected to the Senate in February 1879.

Dreaming of the White House, Chandler embarked on a crusade to warn the nation of the dangers of a Democratic return to national power. In November 1879, after making a lengthy diatribe against southerners and Democrats before a Chicago audience, Chandler suffered a fatal stroke. After his passing, the state GOP fell into disarray, with moderates and conservatives brutalizing each other in a struggle for supremacy.

During the 1880s, the Republican split grew to such proportions that a Republican defeat was assured if their opponents united. This occurred in 1882 when Democrats and Greenbackers joined in a Fusion party and nominated former Republican Cong. Josiah Begole for

governor. Incumbent Gov. David Jerome, a wealthy Saginaw lumberman, was depicted both as a tool of big business and as an enemy of the
working class. The result was the election of a non-Republican governor
for the first time since the party's birth in 1854.

In 1883 Thomas W. Palmer, a wealthy Detroit lumberman and supporter of former Senator Chandler, defeated incumbent Sen. Thomas
W. Ferry, after nearly two months of struggle and eighty-one ballots in
the Republican legislative caucus, primarily because of allegations that
Ferry had been involved in numerous questionable financial dealings.
The following year, Detroit lumber baron Russell Alger recaptured the
governorship for the Republicans and served one undistinguished term
before opting for the role of behind-the-scenes manipulator.

Despite the claims of several pretenders to the throne, the man who
ultimately replaced Chandler as the "King of Michigan Republicans"
was James McMillan. A millionaire Detroit businessman, McMillan had
close ties to railroad and utility companies, the Grand Army of the
Republic Veterans' Association, and Upper Peninsula Republicans.
McMillan's influence was demonstrated best in the 1887 United States
senatorial race. The Detroit boss, anticipating a senate race for himself
to succeed Palmer, knew that the western part of the state would want a
senate seat. Thus, to clear the way for himself in 1889, McMillan
financed the election of enough state legislators pledged to vote for
Francis Stockbridge of Kalamazoo so as to block the reelection bid of
popular incumbent Omar D. Conger of Port Huron.[4]

The 1890s, however, began with a series of devastating defeats for
the Republicans. In 1890, Edward Winans became the first Democratic
governor of Michigan since 1855 and brought with him a Democratic
majority in the state senate. Even worse for the Republican faithful, the
only star on their horizon was Hazen Pingree, the forty-nine-year-old
mayor of Detroit. The mayor was an ardent progressive who battled the
city's vested interests. While this gained for him the adoration of many
of Detroit's working class, it also brought him into direct conflict with
the conservative "old guard" Republicans led by McMillan.

In response to conservative Republicans repeatedly voting to kill legislation creating municipal reforms, Pingree made futile bids for his
party's gubernatorial nomination in 1892 and 1894. However, in 1896
many Republicans, including party chairman Russell Alger, feared that
presidential nominee William McKinley might not be strong enough to
carry depression-ravaged Michigan on his own against Democratic candidate William Jennings Bryan. Consequently, much to the dismay of
McMillan, Pingree was given the gubernatorial nod in the hopes he
would lure the normally Democratic ethnic groups, who had voted for

him as mayor, into voting for the entire Republican ticket. Much to the chagrin of party leadership, after nomination, Pingree ran an independent campaign, going so far as to urge his backers to split their ticket by voting Republican for governor and Democratic for president because Bryan's position on flexible currency was closer to Pingree's own views. Political pundits were astonished when the maverick Republican won by such a margin that McKinley managed a narrow victory in Michigan by riding on Pingree's coattails, despite Pingree's support of Bryan.

As governor, Pingree continued his crusade for liberal reforms such as fair taxation, better wages and working conditions for laborers, and an end to corrupt business practices. However, his efforts were stymied in the state senate by the McMillan bloc, which Pingree dubbed "The Immoral Nineteen." Despite these setbacks, Pingree left a rich political legacy, not merely to the state but also to the nation. By assembling a coalition of reformers, workers, and immigrants, Pingree both paved the way for a new Republican philosophy that would become dominant in the Progressive Era of the twentieth century, and prepared the state for a smoother transition into its new role as a key element in the country's urban, industrial growth.

AGITATION OVER BLACK RIGHTS

Ironically, much of the state's political and social turmoil during the post-Civil War period centered on the question of black suffrage. Michigan long had been in the forefront of the antislavery movement and had earned the hatred of southerners for its advocacy of personal liberty laws and its participation in the Underground Railroad. Yet, in 1850 the state's voters had rejected by a 7 to 1 margin a constitutional amendment granting enfranchisement to blacks. During and immediately following the war, Michigan's two Radical Republican United States senators, Jacob M. Howard and Zachariah Chandler, supported black rights by strongly pleading for passage of the Thirteenth, Fourteenth, and Fifteenth amendments to the federal Constitution. Yet, in 1867, Michiganians voted down their proposed new state constitution, which included a provision for black suffrage, by nearly forty thousand votes.

Black suffrage was an emotional issue. Democrats and moderate Republicans argued that blacks were neither competent to cast an intelligent vote nor to be elevated to the status of being considered the electoral equal of a white man. Moreover, these critics ominously warned of a possible black migration to the state should the constitutional provision pass. In rebuttal, Chandler and other prominent Radicals asserted that it was hypocritical and irrational for state residents to favor imposing black suffrage on the South while denying it in their own districts. For their appeals to reason, advocates of black suffrage were derisively referred to as "Africanists" or "Sambo's Best Friends."[5]

In 1870, by a narrow margin of 54,105 to 50,598, voters in Michigan approved a constitutional amendment eliminating racial qualifications for voting; but in the fifteen counties with the largest black population, the sentiment at the polls was overwhelmingly in opposition to the measure. Cynics observed that the results did not signify a change in racial attitudes but rather a weak vote of acceptance for the newly ratified Fifteenth Amendment to the United States Constitution, which had already eliminated white-only suffrage qualifications.

Once black enfranchisement was secured, Democrats earnestly sought to win the new voters to their party. Their effort proved futile, however, as Republicans offered blacks representation at political conventions, gave blacks patronage positions, ran black candidates for office, supported additional civil rights legislation, and constantly reminded blacks that Democrats had been violently opposed to racial equality in the state and nation.

The seriousness with which blacks assumed their newly-gained right and responsibility quickly earned the respect of many whites. In 1876 a black was elected coroner of Wayne County; two years later, Detroit hired its first black policeman; and, by the early 1880s, black attorneys began to appear regularly in Detroit courtrooms. In 1893 William W. Ferguson, a native of Detroit and a graduate of that city's college of law, became the first black member of the Michigan legislature; and three years later, Joseph Dickerson was elected to the first of his two terms in the state House of Representatives.

Black leaders emphasized education as the key to success; and, in Detroit, Robert and Benjamin Pelham gained national influence through the editorial opinions expressed in their newspaper, the *Plaindealer*. In 1884 the Pelhams urged the assembling of a third Colored Men's State Convention in Battle Creek. Unlike the two prior meetings held in 1860 and 1865, which sought black suffrage, this body passed a resolution requesting the state GOP to select black Detroit physician Samuel C. Watson as a delegate to the national party convention in Chicago. As word of the conference spread, the Pelhams were viewed as spokesmen for black rights throughout the country. Once again Michigan had achieved leadership in the struggle for racial equality.

Michigan State Archives

Rep. William W. Ferguson of Detroit, Michigan's first black state legislator, was elected in 1893, and reelected in 1895.

WOMEN'S SUFFRAGE

Another recurrent—and divisive—political ember which supporters in Michigan often fanned into a roaring blaze was women's suffrage. The Democratic-dominated 1850 constitutional convention had decisively rejected a provision for female voting, though it granted that right to American Indian males who renounced their tribal loyalties. Seventeen years later, another constitutional convention, this time controlled by Republicans, grappled with the issue; but it became entwined with the heated debate over black rights. Thus, a proposal to strike the word "male" from state voting qualifications was defeated resoundingly when opponents reminded delegates that it would enfranchise "Indian squaws and colored mammies" as well as white women.[6]

During the three years after the defeat of the 1867 constitutional revision, women managed to gain the right to cast ballots in school elections, but nothing more. In 1870, however, the Michigan Suffrage Association and the Northwestern Association were established. Because of their efforts, in March 1874 the state legislature put forth for a public referendum a constitutional amendment granting suffrage to women. From March until the November ratification vote, angry discussions raged between friends and foes of the proposal. Supporters predicted success because Michigan possessed a large, progressive populace, many of whom had roots in New York and New England where women's suffrage had its origins.

Despite the fact that it had been a Republican legislature that passed the suffrage amendment, party leaders, including Governor Bagley and Senators Ferry and Chandler, found themselves enmeshed in a political embarrassment. In 1872 the Republican National Convention had embraced women's suffrage as a party commitment throughout the country. Two years later, however, the state's two largest and most influential Republican newspapers, the *Detroit Advertiser and Tribune* and the *Detroit Daily Post* (the latter of which was partially owned by Senator Chandler), joined the Democratic *Detroit Free Press* in denouncing the action of the state legislature. The ensuing intraparty furor culminated in August 1874 when the state Republican convention refused to endorse ratification of the suffrage ballot proposal.

Having lost their major political ally, suffragists encouraged petition drives and brought in speakers. Nationally-known figures, such as Elizabeth Cady Stanton and Susan B. Anthony, visited Michigan but did more harm than good by speaking against the tyranny of the state's male population for denying women their rights and treating them as downtrodden slaves. Immediately, a bipartisan reaction sprang forth in newspapers, including those favoring female suffrage, decrying the "importation of foreigners" to demean Michigan males.[7]

On election day, the amendment was crushed 135,957 to 40,077. Susan B. Anthony placed much of the blame for the outcome on the state's liquor interests having convinced voters that if women got the right to vote, prohibition legislation would never be rescinded. Anthony said dejectedly that "every whiskey maker, vendor, drinker, gambler, and besotted man [in Michigan] was against us."[8] A more objective observation came from the *Detroit Free Press*, which offered sage advice to its defeated adversaries: "They must know that for the present, at least, they are in a hopeless minority, and that their only chance for success lies in educating the people to an acceptance of their views."[9]

Stunned by the landslide against them, suffrage advocates lapsed into a decade of virtual inactivity, only to emerge again in 1884 with the founding of the Michigan Equal Suffrage Association. This new organization, with Mary Doe as president and Gov. Josiah Begole as vice president, had the support of United States senators Palmer and Conger but still could not attain its goal.

Undaunted, some Michigan women, such as Sarah E. Van de Vort Emery, courageously continued their crusade for equality and creation of a true system of democracy in the country. A spokesperson for economic and political reform, Emery authored several books on the need for fiscal change, served as a delegate to the National Greenback Labor Party Convention in 1884, was associate editor of the Populist party periodical *New Forum,* and was affiliated with the Union Labor party, Knights of Labor, Farm Alliance, and the Women's Christian Temperance Union. Emery was a constant reminder of how much women, even though denied a basic freedom, could contribute to their state and nation.[10]

A new state constitution, passed in 1908, permitted women taxpayers to vote on bond issues, but continued to deny general suffrage. Only after enactment of the Nineteenth Amendment to the United States Constitution in 1920 did Michigan insert a long-awaited amendment to the state constitution granting general suffrage to the state's female residents.

THE PATRONS OF HUSBANDRY

The Civil War brought major changes to Michigan's farm community. A labor shortage, created by large numbers of men enlisting in the Union military, was temporarily eased by having children, women, and the elderly work the fields, but only increased mechanization could offer a permanent solution. Purchases of farm machinery reached such a level that in 1864, a Pontiac farmer wrote to *Country Gentleman* magazine that in Michigan "men are of no account now except to vote."[11] While that was an obvious exaggeration, it did reflect how far Michigan had gone since 1861 toward modern farm techniques.

Investment in equipment was made possible by the increase in farm revenue caused by the war. The huge amounts of food required by the Union goverment for its soldiers resulted in soaring crop prices. For example, the price of red wheat, a major Michigan commodity, rose from eighty-four cents a bushel in 1861 to two dollars and twenty-five cents per bushel in 1865. Farm income was also bolstered by soldiers' wages.

Threshers on a Michigan farm, ca. 1880.

Michigan State University Archives and Historical Collections

Increased prosperity brought an accompanying rise in rural standards of living. After the war many farm families moved from log cabins into more spacious frame dwellings, furnished with so-called luxury items such as real furniture, carpeting, books, bathtubs, and screen doors. With the advent of labor-saving devices, some of the drudgery associated with traditional rural life in Michigan disappeared, and by 1870, modern commercial agriculture was firmly established.

During the Gilded Age several organizations for farmers emerged, the best known being the Patrons of Husbandry, or Grange. Originally founded in New York as a social, cultural, and educational group for farm men and women, the Grange opened its first Michigan chapter in 1872, and by the end of the year six more chapters had been created.

The depression of 1873 caused the Grange to shift from social to political and economic interests. Railroads, big business, and banks were targets of Grange outrage; and in 1874, Michigan Grangers demanded legislative action to control and regulate all railroad freight rates. Grangers also set up the first large-scale cooperative movement in the nation's history. Across the Midwest, farmers established their own stores, grain elevators, warehouses, factories, and insurance companies. Michigan Grangers were more conservative than most. They operated their cooperatives by county councils and local agencies as well as employing a state agent to negotiate contracts with manufacturers and dealers. By the late 1870s, state Grangers recognized that they lacked the business acumen to make their ventures profitable, so they hired firms in Detroit and Chicago to market their products while they returned to the business of agriculture.

With the restoration of prosperity in the late 1870s, membership in the Michigan Grange, which had peaked in 1875 with 605 chapters and 33,196 members, rapidly declined. A revival was attempted in 1881; but, with its failure, the Grange never again sought political and

144

economic power, opting instead to revert to its original intent of being a social body.

EDUCATIONAL ACHIEVEMENTS

Michigan always prided itself on being a leader in educational development, and, during the Gilded Age, the state continued in that tradition. Public education for Michigan's children was mandated by the original 1836 state constitution. The Constitution of 1850 stated that primary instruction had to be made available at no cost. However, the legislature did not act on that stipulation for nearly two decades.

In 1869 rate bills (tuition charges) for common schools were finally abolished, thereby fulfilling the constitutional directive. Two years later, over Democratic objections, Michigan became one of the first states to pass a compulsory education law requiring children between the ages of eight and fourteen to attend school for a minimum of twelve weeks a year. In 1883, due in part to lobbying efforts by the Knights of Labor, the minimum was raised to sixteen weeks, and the legislature included a proviso that no child could be employed until his or her educational requirement had been met. However, since Michigan did not provide truant officers to enforce the attendance laws until 1905, many parents and children ignored them at their convenience. High school education received a boost in 1874 when the Michigan Supreme Court ruled unanimously that a city had the legal right to levy taxes to finance postprimary education. Unfortunately, until legislative action remedied the inequity, farm children living outside of a defined school district continued to have to pay tuition to receive an education beyond the eighth grade.

Higher education also underwent changes during the postwar era. In 1867 the state legislature, for the first time, allocated limited tax dollars (equaling one-twentieth of a mill on all property in the state) for The University of Michigan. Previously, The University of Michigan, Michigan Agricultural College, and the Normal School (teachers' college) at Ypsilanti had been funded primarily by income obtained from their original federal land grants.

State support for higher education resulted from a compromise between proponents of the university and those of the agricultural college. Each agreed to vote for state funding of the other. The university, however, reneged on the deal; it not only opposed money for the rival agricultural college but attempted to take it over to acquire its land grant. Only after the legislature appropriated significant monies for program development and a dormitory to the college in 1869 did The

University of Michigan grudgingly accept the fact that the college would remain a separate entity.

Administrators of the university were faced with other pressures as well. Sensitive to a rising sentiment for female suffrage, many legislators urged that the university open its doors to women. As a further prod, several bills calling for the establishment of all-female colleges were introduced. Already angered by having to share financing and students with the agricultural college, university officials could not risk additional potential rivals and, in 1871, reluctantly capitulated and admitted its first woman student, Madelon Stockwell of Kalamazoo.

Due in part to the success of the agricultural college, a demand arose for vocational and technical courses to be added to the university curriculum. In 1875, under pressure from Governor Bagley, the legislature established within The University of Michigan professorships in architecture and design and dental surgery, as well as a school of mines. Ten years later, the Michigan School of Mines was created at Houghton to train experts for work in the iron and copper mining industries of the Upper Peninsula. Moreover, between 1895 and 1904 additional Normal schools were opened at Mount Pleasant, Marquette, and Kalamazoo.[12] Thus, by the early years of the twentieth century, Michigan was well on

Michigan Agricultural College in 1884 (now Michigan State University). Students playing lawn tennis in front of the chemistry laboratory.

Michigan State University Archives and Historical Collections its way to meeting its obligation to furnish educated farmers, mechanics, engineers, and teachers, as well as traditional liberal arts scholars.

Another important element of the state's higher education structure dated back to the territorial period. With the opening of Kalamazoo College in 1833, private schools, usually church sponsored, began to attract students, and, by 1860, there were colleges at Kalamazoo, Albion, Adrian, Olivet, and Hillsdale. Initially, these colleges were handicapped by an inability to award state certified diplomas, but that barrier was removed in the late 1850s when the legislature passed a general college bill establishing uniform degree requirements for all colleges and universities. Following enactment of that measure, private institutions of higher education embarked on a course of steady expansion during the Gilded Age which carried into the twentieth century.

SUMMARY

During the later years of the nineteenth century, despite severe political factionalism, economic distress, and unwillingness to change long-standing views on the roles of blacks and women, Michigan moved cautiously forward along the path of progressivism. Whenever the siren call of retrenchment was heard, offering the state's citizens the safe course of complacency that could only be gained by closing their eyes to the sufferings and injustices endured by their neighbors, Michiganians, for the most part, resisted the temptation and continued to walk the more difficult, and sometimes rocky, path of social justice. Often, the citizens were forced to show their political leaders the real meaning of democracy, and they accepted the challenge. Clearly, without the hard-fought victories gained during the Gilded Age, Michigan would have found itself totally out of step with the progressive mood of much of the country as it entered the twentieth century.

NOTES

1. During the years 1865 to 1900, Michigan voted Democratic for president only once—in 1884. In that span, every United States senator, all but eleven congressmen, and nine of the state's eleven governors were Republicans.

2. Republican governors Henry H. Crapo (1865–1869), David H. Jerome (1881–1883), and Russell Alger (1885–1887) were lumber barons, as was Fusionist Josiah

Begole, who had been a Republican congressman before bolting the party. Govs. Henry P. Baldwin (1869–1873), John J. Bagley (1873–1877), Charles Croswell (1877–1881), and Hazen Pingree (1897–1901) were wealthy merchants. Cyrus Luce (1887–1891) and John T. Rich (1893–1897) made their fortunes in agriculture. United States Sens. Thomas W. Ferry (1871–1883), Thomas W. Palmer (1883–1889), and Francis B. Stockbridge (1887–1899) were lumbermen. Zachariah Chandler (1857–1875, 1879) and James McMillan (1889–1901) were businessmen, while Jacob M. Howard (1862–1871), Isaac P. Christiancy (1875–1879), and Omar D. Conger (1881–1887) were practicing attorneys.

3. *New York Times,* 19 March 1880. This purported deal, which was denied by partisans of both Chandler and Christiancy, was detailed during the divorce proceedings, that were headlined nationally as "The Christiancy Scandal."

4. Bruce A. Rubenstein, "Omar D. Conger: Michigan's Forgotten Favorite Son," *Michigan History* (September/October 1982): 38–39.

5. Ibid., 35; *Detroit Free Press,* 4, 11, 23 August 1868; Bruce A. Rubenstein and Lawrence E. Ziewacz, *Michigan: A History of the Great Lakes State* (Arlington Heights, Ill.: Forum Press, 1981), 108.

6. *Detroit Free Press,* 23, 31 May 1867; 24 July 1867.

7. Lawrence E. Ziewacz, "The Progress of Woman Suffrage in Nineteenth Century Michigan," *The Journal of the Great Lakes History Conference* 2 (1979): 33.

8. As quoted in Alma Lutz, *Susan B. Anthony: Rebel, Christian Crusader, Humanitarian* (Boston: Beacon Press, 1960), 217.

9. Ibid., 34; *Detroit Free Press,* 6 November 1874.

10. Pauline Adams and Emma S. Thornton, *A Populist Assault: Sarah E. Van de Vort Emery on American Democracy, 1862–1895* (Bowling Green: Bowling Green State University Popular Press, 1982), 10, 11, 31.

11. As quoted in Rubenstein and Ziewacz, 131, 132.

12. These normal schools became Eastern Michigan University (Ypsilanti), Central Michigan University (Mount Pleasant), Northern Michigan University (Marquette), and Western Michigan University (Kalamazoo). Michigan School of Mines is now Michigan Technological University and, of course, Michigan Agricultural College is now Michigan State University.

SUGGESTED READINGS

Although no single-volume comprehensive overview of the Gilded Age in Michigan exists, anthologies such as those by Robert M. Warner and C. Warren Vander Hill, *A Michigan Reader: 1865 to the Present* (Grand Rapids: William B. Eerdmans Publishing Company, 1974) and Alan S. Brown, John T. Houdek, and John H. Yzenbaard, *Michigan Perspectives: People, Events, and Issues* (Dubuque, Iowa: Kendall/Hunt Publishing Company, 1974) provide a variety of articles concerning the period. Two excellent examinations of the political scene are those by George M. Blackburn, "Michigan: Quickening Government in a Developing State," in *Radical Republicans in the North: State Politics During Reconstruction,* ed. James C. Mohr (Baltimore: Johns Hopkins University Press, 1976) and C. Warren Vander Hill, "Representative from Holland: Gerritt John Diekema," *Michigan History* (Winter 1967). Shedding important light on the Greenback movement and its impact on state politics are Richard M. Doolen, "The National Greenback Party in Michigan Politics," *Michigan History* (June 1963) and Donald Swift and Lawrence E. Ziewacz, "The Election of 1882: A Republican Analysis," *The Journal of the Great Lakes History Conference* (1976).

Insight into the political machinations of the Republican party is provided by Bruce A. Rubenstein, "Omar D. Conger: Michigan's Forgotten Favorite Son," *Michigan History* (September/October 1982) and Lawrence E. Ziewacz, "The Eighty-First Ballot: The Senatorial Struggle of 1883," *Michigan History* (September 1972). Sister Mary Karl George, *Zachariah Chandler: A Political Biography* (East Lansing: Michigan State University Press, 1969) is a flawed, yet significant, work on Michigan's famous senator. Melvin Holli, *Reform in Detroit: Hazen S. Pingree and Urban Politics* (New York: Oxford University Press, 1969) not only resurrects the reputation of one of Michigan's "forgotten eagles," but also sets forth a brilliant, concise analysis of the politics of the time.

A wide-ranging study of the women's rights movement is presented in Lawrence E. Ziewacz, "The Progress of Woman Suffrage in Nineteenth Century Michigan," *The Journal of the Great Lakes History Conference* (1979), while Pauline Adams and Emma S. Thornton, *A Populist Assault: Sarah E. Van de Vort Emery on American Democracy, 1862–1895* (Bowling Green: Bowling Green State University Popular Press, 1982) looks at an often ignored, but important female activist in Michigan. Reginald Larrie, *Black Experiences in Michigan History* (Lansing: Michigan Department of State, 1975) offers a well-written, comprehensive summary of black achievements before, during, and after the Gilded Age.

Background on the state Grange may be found in Ford Trump, *The Grange in Michigan* (Grand Rapids: Dean Hicks Company, 1963), while the growth of public education is discussed in Martha Bigelow, *Michigan: Pioneer in Education*, Bulletin no. 7, Michigan Historical Collections (Ann Arbor: The University of Michigan, 1955); Charles R. Starring and James O. Knauss, *Michigan's Search for Educational Standards* (Lansing: Michigan Historical Commission, 1969); and Willis F. Dunbar, *The Michigan Record in Higher Education* (Detroit: Wayne State University Press, 1963).

FRANCIS X. BLOUIN, JR.

Francis Blouin is currently at The University of Michigan–Ann Arbor where he serves as director of the Bentley Historical Library and as associate professor of History and Library Studies. He did his undergraduate work at the University of Notre Dame and received master's and doctorate degrees from the University of Minnesota. Dr. Blouin has authored or edited books and articles on the history of Michigan, and, in 1987, was elected president of the Historical Society of Michigan. He has lectured on the problems and issues relating to historical archives throughout the United States and Canada.

ot Just Automobiles:
Contributions of Michigan to the National Economy

By 1920, Michigan was one of the great industrial centers of the world. Though the automobile is the critical factor in this reputation, there were other industries as well. To understand the emergence of these other industries is to understand the process that ultimately led to the development of the auto industry in the state. The story of industrialization in Michigan during the period 1850 to 1920 is an important part of the story of industrialization in the nation as a whole. While much of the credit for the growth of business firms in industries such as furniture, food products, and others goes to the vision, determination, and hard work of a small group of entrepreneurs and a dedicated labor force, the scale and profits of these enterprises reflect larger forces in the institutional development and infrastructure of the national economy. This chapter sets the story of industrialization in Michigan within the context of these larger forces in the nation in an attempt to explain the history of specific non-automotive industries in the state—most notably furniture, food products, and, to a lesser extent, mining, lumbering, and retailing. Firms engaged in these industries operated on a large scale;

and, thus, are particularly relevant to the point of this chapter. Michigan also was the location of a multitude of small-scale manufacturers and other industries. These firms were the backbone of the state's economy for most of the nineteenth century. However, since this chapter focuses on the role of Michigan in the transformation of the national economy, examples of the larger-scale industries are emphasized.

The period of intense industrialization in Michigan, 1880 to 1920, coincides with a period of intense industrialization in the nation as a whole. During this period, the nation moved from being a primarily rural/agricultural-based population to primarily an urban/industrial-based population. This transformation was based on the development of manufacturing and other industries in the United States with notable impact on population figures for select counties in the state of Michigan. For example, in Houghton County, center of the mining industry, the population in 1870 was 13,881; by 1910 it had reached 88,098. Shortly thereafter, the population began to decline toward 47,631 by 1940. These figures represent the boom and bust of the mining industry. In Kent County, center of the furniture industry, the population rose from 50,410 in 1870 to 240,511 in 1930. Most dramatic, of course, was the growth of Wayne County with a population of 119,054 in 1870 and 1,888,946 in 1930. Such was the impact of the automobile in Wayne County.[1]

This scale of population growth was made possible by the emergence of large-scale manufacturing in the late nineteenth century. The Berkey and Gay Furniture Company in Grand Rapids or the W. K. Kellogg Company in Battle Creek are examples. These companies were producing products on a scale previously unseen in the world. As a result, they employed large numbers of workers, giving rise to a new urban and industrial culture in the state. What were the factors that led to the emergence of this kind of enterprise in Michigan?

Large-scale industry was possible in the United States only as a result of certain changes within the economic infrastructure of the country. Of critical importance were changes in transportation and communication. Alfred Chandler, upon whose work the framework for this analysis is based, has argued that "the railroad and the telegraph provided the fast, regular, and dependable transportation and communication so essential to high-volume production and distribution—the hallmark of large modern manufacturing or marketing enterprises."[2]

Only in the 1840s did the country begin to see the development of rail lines in earnest. In Michigan, the Erie and Kalamazoo and other lines began to provide rail-based transport to the agricultural marketing centers of the southern part of the state. In the decade of the 1850s, "when more canals were abandoned than built, over 21,000 miles of railroad were constructed laying down the basic overland transportation network east of the Mississippi River."[3] The success of the railroad was based on its speed, dependability and cost per ton mile compared to canals and inland waterways. The time for freight to travel from Detroit to New York fell from two weeks in 1830 to just over twenty-eight hours in 1857 in all but the very worst weather.

Moreover, the steam locomotive lowered the per unit cost of transport. Because of speed, regularity and dependability of travel, the railroad utilized equipment more intensively. Even by 1840, one historian notes, "railroads could provide at least three times as much freight service as canals for an equivalent resource cost—and probably more nearly five times as much."[4] The point for Michigan is that certainly by the 1860s, manufacturers and industrialists had swift, efficient, dependable access to the major markets of the eastern half of the country and very soon thereafter to those of the nation as a whole. This revolution in transportation had an immediate impact on the cost of transport and the scale of an enterprise. At the same time, the availability of this quality of transport opened the possibility of a national market.

This revolution in transportation was accompanied by a revolution of similar proportion in communication. Chandler notes that "the railroad permitted a rapid increase in the speed and decrease in the cost of long-distance, written communication, while the invention of the telegraph created an even greater transformation by making possible almost instantaneous communication at great distances. The railroad and the telegraph marched across the continent in unison."[5] Later, of course, this was augmented by the telephone. For Michigan as for many locations in the nation, this meant an entrepreneur had more direct access to markets and market information which permitted more control over a geographically scattered operation.

Chandler goes on to argue that the completion of these new networks opened opportunities for a scale of production and distribution hitherto unseen. Technological innovations in machinery and processing tools made possible production on a very large scale. The availability of more efficient transport and communication made possible distribution on a national scale. Those business enterprises that were able to fuse mass production techniques with a mass distribution system quickly came to dominate segments of an industry or whole industries, as in the case of cigarette manufacturing and food processing. This phenomenon marked a transformation in the institutional infrastructure of the American economy and in the process made Grand Rapids and Battle Creek household words across the nation.

To what extent does the furniture industry and the breakfast food industry fit this national pattern? In 1855, Battle Creek was known only as a small farming community and the newly established headquarters of a sect of Adventists, which in 1860 formally adopted the name Seventh-Day Adventists. In 1863, as a result of a vision of the denomination's founder, the sect began to emphasize good diet and proper health care with a focus on vegetarianism.[6] Shortly thereafter, the Adventists established the Western Reform Health Institute at Battle Creek, a sanitarium where their ideas could be put into practice. In 1876, Dr. John Harvey Kellogg, elder brother of W. K. Kellogg, returned from New York to the Battle Creek of his youth to head the sanitarium. A man of boundless energy and drive, John Harvey Kellogg set about to make the 'San,' as it came to be known, "the greatest in the world" and to spread the notion of biologic living to all corners of the globe.[7]

One phase of work at the San focused on the production of natural grain-based foods, which were served to the patients and residents. Fresh air, mineral baths, and vegetarian foods constituted Kellogg's basic formula for clean, healthy living. In 1894, W. K. Kellogg, who worked on the staff of the San in the shadow of his increasingly-famous brother, experimented with various grain-based foods, searching for a bread substitute. While boiling wheat and letting it temper, he noticed it hardened and flaked. W. K. convinced John Harvey to serve this new product he called granose. It proved popular and with John Harvey's nod, W. K. set about packaging and distributing the product on a modest scale through the San Food Company. John Harvey's own ethics prohibited use of his name on any product. He also prohibited any advertising for the product except in the San's own publications.[8]

Despite all attempts at secrecy, the process for making the flaked cereal began to leak out. Between 1902 and 1904, forty-two companies were organized in Calhoun County to manufacture cereal foods and beverages. Of these, C. W. Post, through his Postum Company located in Battle Creek, was the most successful. By 1903, with intensive use of advertising, Post was the first to realize the possibilities of distributing grain-based foods on a national scale.[9]

Meanwhile, W. K. Kellogg was approaching middle age, tired of his subservient role at the San and very much aware of the commercial possibilities of the foods he had developed. Given the success of Post and others, Kellogg, who had broken from his brother in 1901, established his own company in 1906 to market one product, which was still relatively new—the corn flake. While most other manufacturers were content to distribute by mail order, Kellogg wanted to "sell those corn flakes by the carload." His dream was of "modern factory buildings humming with activity twenty-four hours a day, with switch engines busily backing in freight cars of raw materials and strings of 'empties,' and these hauling away loaded cars for many destinations."[10] This was precisely the sort of vision that only became possible in the late nineteenth century. Kellogg realized it in Battle Creek.

The railroad assured a steady flow of raw material (wheat, corn, and barley) to the factory. During the first fifteen years of Kellogg Company history, W. K. built his factory capacity to produce forty-two hundred cases of corn flakes a day, a clear example of mass production of food products. But, in order to achieve the maximum throughput implied in his vision, Kellogg required a system for mass distribution. He quickly signed on a network of jobbers, who took charge of regional distribution of the product. Orders were sent via telegraph and telephone to Battle Creek, and shipments were rapidly sent out in response via rail.

However, despite the real popularity of his product, Kellogg was not content to sit and wait for orders to arrive. Kellogg set about to create, through advertising, the steady demand required to sustain his capacity for the mass production of breakfast food products. C. W. Post had utilized advertising to create his market for products in the Postum Company. The size and sustained dominance of these two companies in the natural foods processing industries can be attributed not only to obvious economies of scale achieved in production, but also to steady investment in advertising.[11]

Kellogg's advertising strategy emphasized the product as a delicious breakfast food, not simply as a health-related product. He then set out to recruit customers nationwide. Though a frugal man, he spent huge sums obtaining full-page ads in *Ladies Home Journal* and others of the principal, nationally distributed periodicals oriented to the home. Kellogg asked readers to demand that grocers stock his product. At the same time, he took care to see that willing grocers always had free samples to distribute. The then daring (because it contained a picture of a woman winking) advertising campaign of 1906—"Wink on Wednesday and see what you get . . . a free sample"—was so successful in New York City that sales increased from two carloads monthly to a carload daily. There were many, many other advertising campaigns to follow—most notably, the ever-familiar "Sweetheart of Corn" image of a country girl clutching an ear of corn. In 1910, using a "Funny Jungleland Moving Picture" inside the boxes, the company began distributing premiums for children. After the great crash of 1929, Kellogg directed his staff to double the advertising budget. "Again his intuition was correct, Kellogg Company sales continued to accelerate, affected scarcely, if at all, by the Depression."[12]

Bentley Historical Library, Michigan Historical Collections, The University of Michigan

Advertisement for Kellogg's Corn Flakes, 1907. Printed in Horace B. Powell, *W. K. Kellogg* (Englewood Cliffs, N.J.: Prentice Hall, Inc., 1956), 135.

The Kellogg and Postum companies, by concentrating on a specific niche in the food products industry, were able to succeed, first, by finding a new product and, second, by achieving a scale of production and level of demand that carried the overhead of a national distribution network.[13] Once these companies had achieved this level of production and distribution, they created formidable barriers to entry into the industry by competitors. Thus, the W. K. Kellogg Company and the Post Cereal Company (amalgamated into the General Foods Corporation in 1925) dominate the industry even today. The success of the Kellogg Company speaks to the vision and energy of an entrepreneur in turn-of-the-century Battle Creek. It points further, though, to the changes in the structure of the national economy brought about by technological innovations in transport and communications. Kellogg saw this and, along with the Post Company, was able to make Battle Creek a name synonymous with breakfast cereals throughout the world.

The success of the furniture industry in Grand Rapids follows similar lines. Though the industry was never dominated by a few companies in the way that Kellogg and Post came to dominate breakfast foods, Grand Rapids did, in the late nineteenth century, come to be known as a world center for quality, mass-produced furniture. As in the case of the breakfast foods industry, the success of furniture manufacturing in Grand Rapids depended as much on the availability of reliable transport and communication as on the cleverness of the furniture makers to seize on opportunities afforded by these changes.

The presence of furniture making in Grand Rapids reputedly began with the 1836 arrival of William Haldane. He and several other cabinet-makers are noted in the early histories of the city. The easy availability of wood from the great forests of the state was a critical factor in sustaining the craft during these early years. In 1849, E. M. Ball, a recent arrival from New Hampshire, entered in partnership with William Powers, a local craftsman. Together, they established the first real mechanized factory capable of supplying quantities of chairs well beyond the demand of the local market. Relying principally on water transport, they began to search for markets along the Lake Michigan shore, primarily Chicago, later expanding to New York and Ohio via the Great Lakes and Erie Canal.[14]

The early history of Ball's company reflects the vicissitudes of business prior to the era of the railroad. Most raw materials had to be received via water. Barges were subject to problems caused by the weather. The canals were not exceptionally well constructed. Even in good weather they could be damaged, causing unpredictable delays in the receipt of raw materials as well as delays in the shipment of goods. Despite the challenge of water transport, the Ball company turned sufficient profit to encourage others to consider Grand Rapids as the location for furniture manufacturing to serve the demands of the region.[15]

With the growth in the number of firms seeking to establish sales on a regional basis, water transport became more reliable, except in winter months. Several steamship lines were established with regular service to the Grand Rapids area. However, the coming of the railroad in 1857 opened obvious possibilities for manufacturers to begin thinking of national markets. The period 1860 to 1870 marks the first major spurt in the growth of the industry. By 1868 Grand Rapids was served by four rail lines. Three years later, the newly formed Berkey Brothers and Gay Company was shipping furniture to most large states east of the Mississippi and west into Colorado.[16]

Firms like Berkey and Gay, the Widdicomb Company and the Nelson and Matter Company were large, capitalized firms geared toward the mass production of furniture. Like Kellogg and Post, these particular Grand Rapids furniture companies emphasized throughput for maximum return on capital investment. They received large quantities of lumber, manufactured large quantities of chairs, tables, and other furniture, then sought to distribute them widely. By the 1860s, some companies had opened stores in key locations such as St. Louis, Milwaukee and Chicago.[17] Others utilized private railroad cars containing samples and a salesman to take orders. If a sample could not be provided, sketchbooks, and later photographs, were used. These traveling salesmen structured the distribution system for these companies and were salaried employees, not independent jobbers.

The year 1876 is usually considered a turning point for the industry in Grand Rapids. At the great Centennial Exposition in Philadelphia, the Nelson and Matter Company exhibited a large and ornate bed that captured the attention of the public. Containing niches with statues of Washington, Columbia, Columbus and Guttenberg, and surmounted with an eagle with wings full spread, the bed won a medal. The exposition created such interest in Grand Rapids that Nelson and Matter quickly opened a New York showroom. Berkey and Gay and the Phoenix Company, who also won medals at the exhibition, soon followed with showrooms in New York.[18]

Given the new-found prominence of Grand Rapids furniture and the general recovery of the national economy after the Panic of 1873, the city's major industry was positioned to expand rapidly. In the decade following 1880, the number of furniture factories nearly doubled. Charles R. Sligh, for example, once a salesman for Berkey and Gay, began a firm of his own in 1880. By the turn of the century, furniture had made Grand Rapids a household word synonymous with quality factory-made furniture. The city had a nationwide reputation.

Given the volume of furniture produced by 1900 (see Table 1), furniture makers needed streamlined organizations that would bring in quantities of raw materials and distribute products of different designs to accommodate a variety of tastes. According to one source, the industry used over fifty million board feet of domestic lumber per year by 1890.[19] The companies frequently formed subordinate or independent land companies to hold timber reserves. In the later years of the nineteenth century, these companies focused on Michigan lands. However, as the lumber resources of Michigan approached exhaustion due to heavy demand and lack of proper conservation measures, Grand Rapids furniture manufacturers began to look elsewhere for resources. Charles R. Sligh, for example, in his constant search for exotic woods, traveled to Honduras in 1883 to find sources of mahogany. Shortly thereafter, he created the Honduras Mahogany Company. In 1902 he established his first timber company, and one year later, he organized the Grand Rapids Timber Company, a separate entity. Then, in 1907, Sligh established a third company, the Clark-Sligh Timber Company. All this was

TABLE 1

Furniture Production in Grand Rapids, 1860–1920

Census Year	1860	1870	1880	1890	1900	1910	1920
No. of firms	9	8	15	31	34	54	71
No. of employees	53	281	2,279	4,437	6,236	7,250	9,372
Wages	$14.8	$131	$ 720	$2,000	$2,582	$ 3,903	$10,594
Capital	$31.2	$329	$1,636	$5,500	$8,362	$13,322	$27,453
Cost of Material	$ 6.9	$117	$ 908	$2,225	$3,300	$ 4,937	$13,563
Value of product	$32.3	$348	$2,016	$5,639	$7,495	$12,630	$34,962
Value added by manufacturer					$4,150	$ 7,693	$21,079

Source: Frank E. Ransom, *The City Built on Wood* (privately printed, 1955), 13, 52.

done to ensure a steady flow of raw materials to his factories. This vertical integration of activities, which enabled his firm to exert greater control over the pace and flow of production, became common practice among large firms.[20]

Marketing, too, was a factor in the integration of activities within firms. Furniture companies tried several approaches to sales. Some had a salaried sales force, others used commissioned salesmen who represented a variety of firms. Still other firms utilized a system of exclusive franchises with specific retailers. The use of a salaried sales force marked the integration of the sales function within the structure of the firms. The other arrangements were equally, if not more, effective but were less controlled by the firm itself.

In the case of Grand Rapids furniture, marketing was done somewhat on an industry-wide basis through the establishment of a furniture market. The precise origin of the market is difficult to pinpoint. However, by 1897 it was institutionalized in the form of the Furniture Exhibition

Factory 1892

The Sligh Furniture Company's Grand Rapids factory in 1892. Printed in Francis X. Blouin and Thomas E. Powers, *A Furniture Family, The Slighs of Michigan*, Bulletin no. 29 (Ann Arbor: Bentley Historical Library, Michigan Historical Collections, The University of Michigan, 1980), 6.

Bentley Historical Library, Michigan Historical Collections, The University of Michigan

Building in Grand Rapids and by the fixed tradition of a market in winter and a market in summer. From 1890 to 1920 the Grand Rapids market was the dominant furniture event in the nation, bringing retailers and wholesalers together with manufacturers. The market not only served Grand Rapids firms but also included furniture manufacturers from New York, Pennsylvania, Ohio, Illinois, Wisconsin, and North Carolina. The presence of the market in Grand Rapids attested to the dominant position of the city in the industry.[21]

Dominant though it was, Grand Rapids never achieved the position in furniture that Battle Creek achieved with breakfast foods or Detroit would achieve with automobiles. The furniture industry remained much more of a craft enterprise than cereal or automobiles. Because of the need to respond to a myriad of tastes, styles, and fabrics, the furniture industry could never realize the economies of scale seen in more mechanized industries. As a result, despite the growth and eventual size of firms such as the Widdicomb Company, Berkey and Gay, and Sligh Furniture Company, the barriers for entry into the industry were never formidable. The Grand Rapids furniture manufacturers were always facing stiff competition. Moreover, because furniture was not a necessity, price and demand varied greatly. The industry was among the first to be hard-hit by the depression in the late 1920s.

Because of this volatile environment, the major firms in Grand Rapids formed the Grand Rapids Furniture Manufacturers Association in 1881. Organized initially to promote the furniture industry in Grand Rapids, it later worked in an oligopolistic fashion to insulate the local industry from pressures resulting from labor, on the one hand, and competition on the other.

The story of the growth of the furniture industry in Michigan is very different from that of breakfast foods. More firms were involved and none ever achieved a lasting dominance. Where cereal was important for its use of advertising and mechanization of production, furniture is important for its use of vertical integration, particularly on the supply side. In the cases of both furniture and cereal, however, the scale of production enabled a Michigan product to become essentially a household word. Kellogg could envision a box of corn flakes on every breakfast table in America and could price his product to be within reach of the average consumer. Grand Rapids furniture, while not within the economic means of every home, was within reach of the rapidly-expanding urban middle classes who had choices among a range of designs and products not conceivable two generations before.

Other industries in Michigan tell bits and pieces of the larger story of the industrial transformation of the American economy. The vast urban

Francis X. Blouin, Jr.

and industrial expansion of the nation created new demands for buildings and housing. This in turn created demand for raw material. Michigan, in the mid-nineteenth century, was well forested, primarily with pine—most notably white pine. Saginaw became the first major commercial center for the export of lumber products to the eastern states via the Erie Canal. By the mid-1870s, the railroad began to play an important role in the industry, providing access to timbered land some distance from water routes and allowing efficient transport of lumber nationwide in all seasons of the year. In 1888, production of sawed lumber in the state peaked at 4.2 billion board feet. The success of the lumber industry created a whole new class of wealth in the state. These lumber barons, as they were called, provided a notable source of investment capital for future industrial expansion in the state.[22]

As the trees on top of the land were gradually lumbered, the mineral resources below ground were discovered and extracted. Though some

Bentley Historical Library, Michigan Historical Collections, The University of Michigan

Engine of the Code and Moore Railroad of Lake City, Lima Construction No. 22, and log train crossing the Clam River on a bed of ice near Falmouth, circa 1885. Printed in May Davis Hill, *Telltale Photographs: The Stoner Railroad Collection*, Bulletin no. 30 (Ann Arbor: Bentley Historical Library, Michigan Historical Collections, The University of Michigan), 21.

silver, gold, salt, coal, limestone, and gypsum were successfully mined, the principal discoveries were the iron and copper reserves of the Upper Peninsula. By 1884, the copper region of the Keweenaw Peninsula was linked to Chicago by rail and to the other four Great Lakes via the Sault Canal. Combined with the application of a more advanced technology for extracting copper, access to efficient transport opened the possibility of shipping huge quantities of copper to a national, even world, market. Production grew from 72,000,000 pounds in 1872 to an all-time high of 266,839,000 in 1916. Unlike lumber, most capital for copper mining originated from sources along the Atlantic coast. Thus, most of the profits and return on investment immediately left the state.[23]

Similarly, the iron resources of the Upper Peninsula were developed in response to the growing iron and steel industries. Access to rail lines and the shipping lanes of the Great Lakes made mining in northern Michigan a profitable enterprise. By the end of the nineteenth century, Michigan, shipping out nine million tons per year, became the principal source of iron for the entire nation. The spectacular growth of these extractive industries is notable because of the huge quantity of output. More important, the scale of the business firms that organized these industries underscores the increased demand for raw materials by a nation undergoing a fundamental economic transformation. The copper and iron firms helped assure a dependable, steady flow of raw materials. The flow of iron, for example, was essential to large steel mills, which represented enormous capital investment and required substantial and steady production to realize what was then considered an appropriate rate of return.[24]

The large mining and lumber firms in Michigan were examples of firms that specialized in the efficient supply of raw materials to various manufacturing enterprises. In later years, after the exhaustion of Michigan resources, these functions were usually integrated into the firm, as in the case of furniture entrepreneurs who formed subsidiary land companies to insure the flow of timber to their factories. At the same time that specialized firms were established to insure supply of materials, others emerged that specialized in the distribution of goods. In Michigan, the most notable example is the S. S. Kresge Company.

The S. S. Kresge Company, founded with one store in Detroit in 1899, was a late arrival in an industry dominated by the F. W. Woolworth Company. But Kresge saw the impact of the automobile industry on the economies of Michigan and other midwestern states. He located his stores in Michigan, Ohio, and Pennsylvania, and later throughout the northeastern states. In 1912 the company had 85 stores and sales of ten million dollars annually; in 1917, it had 164 stores and thirty million

Kresge store number one, corner of State and Woodward in Detroit, 1909.

dollars in sales. The sales philosophy was simple: identify goods that would sell quickly, keep the price low (usually five or ten cents in those days), and anticipate profit based on volume of sales. Mass marketers like Kresge depended on rapid stock turnover, which required a steady supply of finished products from a variety of manufacturers. Kresge would assume costs for advertising and promotion, which focused as much on the concept of the store as on individual products. For manufacturers, obtaining a Kresge account opened the possibility of efficient distribution to a substantial market. As the lumber barons and mining entrepreneurs specialized in supply, Kresge specialized in distribution.[25]

The story of industrialization in Michigan is a complex one. Focusing on the experience of a few firms, this chapter has suggested how patterns of industrialization in Michigan fit patterns of industrialization at the national level. The transformation of the infrastructure of the national economy, through a network of rail and communication lines, opened possibilities for production and distribution on a scale inconceivable decades earlier. The mining and lumber industries in the state produced raw materials in enormous quantities. The Kresge company distributed finished goods in large quantities at reasonable prices. Most important were those firms whose sales volume could sustain large capital investment, fully integrating production and distribution through an efficient organizational structure. Of all the examples cited in this chapter, the Kellogg Company comes closest to achieving this model of full integration of production and distribution on a mass scale. However, it was with the automobile, and particularly Henry Ford's operation, that the model would achieve its finest expression in the state's economy.

◆

NOTES

1. *United States Census of Population, Michigan,* 1910 and 1930.
2. Alfred D. Chandler, *The Visible Hand, The Managerial Revolution in American Business* (Cambridge: Harvard University Press, 1977), 79.
3. Ibid., 83.
4. Stanley Legerbott, "United States Transport and Extermalities," *Journal of Economic History* 26 (December 1966): 444–46 (quoted in Chandler, 82).
5. Chandler, 195.
6. Willis F. Dunbar and George S. May, *Michigan: A History of the Wolverine State* (Grand Rapids: William B. Eerdmans Publishing Company, 1980), 463.
7. Horace B. Powell, *The Original Has His Signature—W. K. Kellogg* (Englewood Cliffs, N.J.: Prentice-Hall, Inc., 1956), 57.
8. "I'll Invest My Money in People," a history of the Kellogg Company (Battle Creek: Kellogg Company, n.d.), 6.
9. Powell, 100.
10. Ibid., 107, 111.
11. Ibid., 134–35.
12. Ibid., 144.

13. Chandler, 299.

14. Dunbar and May, 466.

15. Frank E. Ransom, *The City Built on Wood* (privately printed, 1955), 5.

16. Ibid., 15.

17. Ibid., 19.

18. Ibid., 17.

19. Ibid., 24.

20. Francis X. Blouin and Thomas E. Powers, "A Furniture Family: The Slighs of Michigan," Bulletin no. 29 of the Michigan Historical Collections (Ann Arbor, 1980), 7.

21. Ransom, 7.

22. Dunbar and May, 396–401, 409.

23. Dunbar and May, 417; see also William B. Gates, Jr., *Michigan Copper and Boston Dollars* (Cambridge: Harvard University Press, 1951).

24. Dunbar and May, 425.

25. Chandler, 235; "A Brief History of the S. S. Kresge Company" (Battle Creek: S. S. Kresge Company, n.d.), 5.

SUGGESTED READINGS

In addition to the books cited in the preceding notes, the following books are suggested:

Dorin, Patrick C. *The Grand Trunk Railroad.* Seattle: Superior Co., 1977.

Havighurst, Walter. *Vein of Iron.* New York: World Publishing Co., 1958.

Miller, Raymond C. *Kilowatts at Work. A History of the Detroit Edison Company.* Detroit: Wayne State University Press, 1957.

Whitehead, Don. *The Dow Story.* New York: McGraw Hill Co., 1968.

Woodford, Arthur M. *Detroit and Its Banks.* Detroit: Wayne State University Press, 1974.

1880s-1945

GEORGE S. MAY

Born in Ironwood, Michigan, George May did most of his undergraduate and graduate work at The University of Michigan where he received his doctorate degree. Dr. May's distinguished career includes teaching at Allegheny College, a research associate position at the State Historical Society of Iowa, various positions with the Michigan Historical Commission, and professor of history at Eastern Michigan University from which he retired in 1987. Presently he is a writer and consultant to the Henry Ford Museum. Dr. May has had over fifty articles and books published, including *A Most Unique Machine: The Michigan Origins of the Automobile Industry.*

utting the Nation on Wheels:

The Michigan Automobile Industry to 1945

In the twentieth century, automobiles have been understandably the first thing most people have thought of when Michigan, or especially Detroit, has been mentioned. As early as 1902, the country's largest automobile manufacturer was located in Michigan; and during the next quarter century, three great Detroit-based auto makers gained total dominance of the auto industry, not only in the United States but in the entire world. No other development has had as great an effect on Michigan, and yet it is one whose history is a subject about which many Michiganians are poorly informed.

In spite of what many assume, Henry Ford did not invent the automobile, nor was he an important figure in the auto industry's earliest years. In fact, the ancestors of today's automobiles first appeared not in Michigan or elsewhere in the United States but in Europe. By the latter part of the nineteenth century, European mechanics and engineers had built experimental road vehicles powered by steam, electricity, or gasoline internal-combustion engines. The last type gained the most support; and, by the early 1890s, several French and German companies, including those still making the high-priced Peugeot and Mercedes-Benz automobiles, had become the world's first automobile manufacturers.[1]

Experimenters in the United States, working independently of those across the Atlantic, had also developed steam, electric, and gasoline horseless carriages by the nineties. When the first commercial versions of these vehicles began to appear in the late nineties, the electrics and steamers predominated. However, by 1901 to 1902, the more efficient gasoline-powered cars were gaining increasing popularity. Interest soon declined, never to recover, in the electrics, whose heavy batteries needed recharging every few miles, and in the steamers, which also had a number of disadvantages. By 1902 leadership in the young industry was also shifting from New England, where it was initially centered, to the west, where important companies were springing up in western New York, Ohio, Indiana, and Wisconsin. Moving up fast to become the leader of them all, however, was Michigan.

The Michigan pioneer who blazed the trail for those who followed was Ransom E. Olds, after whom today's Oldsmobiles are named. His initials also supplied the name of another company's vehicles, some of which (the Diamond-Reo trucks) are still seen on the highways, even though the Lansing company that produced them went out of business in 1975. In 1885, when he was twenty-one, Ransom Olds became his father's partner in a small Lansing business that made and repaired steam engines. In 1887, seeking new uses for the engines, Olds built a three-wheeled vehicle powered by a one-horsepower steam engine. He tested it one morning—fortunately before sunrise when hardly anyone was able to see his struggle to make the steamer travel only a short distance. He did, however, encounter a milk wagon drawn by a horse that became frightened and bolted, causing a loss of nine quarts of milk and a quart of buttermilk before the driver and Olds could get the horse under control.[2]

After this inauspicious start to his automotive career, Olds built a second, four-wheeled steamer with increased horsepower. He still was not happy with its performance, although a story about his work that ran in *Scientific American* magazine in 1892 led a buyer in London, England, to purchase the Olds steamer, making it perhaps the first American car to be exported.[3] In the late nineties, Olds also built an electric car, but by then he was already convinced that gasoline engines were the most practical source of power for passenger road vehicles. He and a member of his staff at the family-owned Lansing company developed a gasoline engine in 1895, which they began to manufacture with great success and which Olds used to power his third horseless carriage in 1896. Upon completion of a test run of this vehicle in August 1896, Olds exclaimed, "Eureka!" He expressed satisfaction with his new creation and told the reporter who rode with him that he would begin to manufacture the motorized carriage.[4]

Olds's experience in these years provides one clue as to why Michigan came to be the headquarters of the auto industry. While others elsewhere were trying to perfect steamers or electrics, Olds and nearly all of the other Michigan pioneers concentrated their attention on developing good gasoline cars, getting a jump on much of the rest of the country when it came time to get this type of car on the market.

Finding the money that was needed to begin producing these cars leads to a second clue to Michigan's success. Ransom Olds did not feel that the Olds engine company had sufficient resources to finance the production of his new gasoline horseless carriage; and so, in 1897, he obtained the backing of outside investors who formed the Olds Motor Vehicle Company. The ten thousand dollars they invested, however, was far too little to enable Olds to produce more than a half dozen horseless carriages; and he soon went looking for more financial help.

In the spring of 1899, he got it from Samuel L. Smith of Detroit, who came up with two hundred thousand dollars, to finance the Olds Motor Works, a new company growing out of the merger of the Olds engine and motor vehicle companies. Smith had made a fortune in some of the mining and lumbering activities that had prospered in Michigan since the middle of the century. By the late nineties, however, the boom days were coming to an end, and men like Samuel Smith were looking for something new that would bring the kind of return on their investment they had gotten out of Michigan's copper, iron ore, and white pine. In other areas of the Midwest and East, much of the big money was tied up in economic activities such as steel and oil which were still growing and prospering. The fact that Michigan's future economic development was uncertain made wealthy men like Smith willing to take a chance on the new auto companies that sprang up in the state, providing the money these companies needed to survive the fierce competition of the early years.

With ample financial backing and a new factory in Detroit where the Olds automobile operations were now located, Ransom Olds had to decide what kind of car to build. In 1896 he had declared that his goal was a vehicle that would meet the needs of the average person, one that would be lightweight, relatively inexpensive, and would have enough power to get you to where you were going.[5] In other words, the vehicle had to be what ad writers in later years would call good, basic transportation. For several years Olds strayed from this goal, tinkering with

171

bigger and more expensive models that attracted little interest. In the summer of 1900, however, he returned to his original idea with a little six-hundred-pound, one-horsepower runabout. It was so called because, like nearly all the early American car manufacturers, Olds took one of the standard carriage models—in this case one called the runabout—and replaced the horse with a gasoline engine as the source of its propulsion. Thus, these early cars were literally horseless carriages until about 1905, when Americans began to follow the example of the Europeans. They had created a shape that was unique to this new means of transportation with the engine out in front and under a hood, instead of being hidden underneath the carriage body as the Americans had done.

The Olds runabout, the first of his cars to bear the famous Oldsmobile name, began to be sold at the beginning of 1901. Although a fire that destroyed the Detroit factory in March halted production for several weeks, his company's strong financial backing enabled the factory to be rebuilt and a new plant to be built later that year in Lansing, where Oldsmobile production would be centered in a few years. In 1901 over four hundred Oldsmobile runabouts, with the distinctive curved

Olds Motor Works in Lansing, ca. 1908.

Michigan State Archives

dash in front, were produced. Output climbed to around three thousand in 1902 and went still higher in 1903 and 1904.[6] By later standards, these would have been disastrous figures for an auto company; but, in this period, they made the Olds Motor Works the industry's volume leader, a distinction that has been held since that time by Michigan companies.

These first Oldsmobiles sold for six hundred dollars to six hundred fifty dollars, about half the asking price of the earlier models Olds had tried to sell. It was not the cheapest car available, and, at a time when relatively few working men made that much money in an entire year, it was far too expensive for most people to consider buying. Nevertheless, the Oldsmobile's price was well below that of many of the bigger models emphasized by numerous manufacturers. Also, the profits the Olds company earned from the sales of this early version of a subcompact encouraged others to jump on the bandwagon and come out with similar cars. This influence was felt most strongly in Michigan, especially in the Detroit area, where men who had worked for Olds or who were the owners of companies that made parts for the curved-dash runabout founded their own auto companies. Many of them failed, as would be the case with nearly all of the estimated fifteen hundred or more American auto companies that have been established since the start of the industry in the mid-nineties. But among the survivors, Chrysler, Dodge, Cadillac, and Ford—all in varying degrees—had their beginnings with the interest generated by Ransom Olds and his runabout.

Olds did not stay with the Olds Motor Works, being forced out in 1904 during a dispute with his financial backers. He used his reputation to gain support for a new company, Reo. For some time the company enjoyed success with its cars and its Reo Speedwagons, the first of the truck models that would eventually be all the company produced. After a few years, however, Olds lost interest in Reo's day-to-day operations and was content to enjoy his wealth and to recede to an increasingly minor role in the industry's later development. But in that earlier period, Olds had shown that there was a large market for a reasonably priced car. While manufacturers in other parts of the country continued to favor production of big, high-powered, fancy models that only the rich could afford, the lesson they learned from the success of the Olds runabout led Michigan auto makers to place their emphasis on low-priced cars that gave them control of the mass market and, in turn, dominance of the auto industry.

Credit for really capitalizing on Ransom Olds's idea of a car that would satisfy the ordinary person's needs must go to Henry Ford. A farm boy born and raised in what is now Dearborn, site of the huge manufacturing empire he would establish, Ford left the farm as a teen-ager at the end of the 1870s to seek opportunities in Detroit. There his natural mechanical abilities enabled him, in 1893, to become the chief engineer for the Edison Illuminating Company (today's Detroit Edison). By this time, however, his growing interest in horseless car-riages was making it unlikely he would devote his life to a career in the electric power industry.

In the predawn hours of 4 June 1896, Ford climbed into his first car—a gasoline-powered vehicle he called a quadricycle because he had built it using the materials and methods of the bicycle maker—and drove it for a few blocks near his rented home on Detroit's Bagley Avenue. This was two months before Ransom Olds tested his first gasoline carriage in Lansing. It was not until July 1903, however, that any significant number of Ford-designed cars could be purchased, two years after Olds-mobiles were becoming the most popular cars on the market.

The fact that it took Henry Ford seven years to move from the experi-mental to the production stage of automobile development was largely his own fault. Lack of money was no problem, for by 1897 some of Detroit's wealthiest and most prominent citizens were becoming inter-ested in Ford and were supplying the money he needed to continue his experiments. Later, in 1899 and again in 1901, they formed companies to produce Ford's cars, furnishing him with ample resources and the authority to direct the manufacturing of these cars. But Ford failed to come through for them. He kept insisting that he needed more time to work out the bugs in the mechanisms of his cars, even though his back-ers declared, quite correctly, that the cars he had built were probably as good as most of those other manufacturers were selling.

In the summer of 1901, Ford turned from passenger car development to build a racing car, nicknamed "Sweepstakes," which he entered in Michigan's first auto races, held on 10 October 1901 at a dirt track in Grosse Pointe. To the surprise of nearly everyone, Ford, who had never driven in a race before, won the featured event, defeating Alexander Winton of Cleveland, the most successful race driver of that time. Winton's car was plagued by mechanical problems that slowed it to a crawl halfway through the race. After the race, Ford said that he "was scared to death" by the experience; but he now started work on what he said would be the most powerful racing car ever built.[7] His impatient backers, finally deciding that Ford was never going to settle down to develop an acceptable passenger car, told him early in 1902 to take his racing car and leave. Later that year, they formed the Cadillac Automo-bile Company, which at last brought them the return on their invest-ment they had not gotten with Ford.

Ford Motor Company; Michigan State Archives

Henry Ford in his first car, the 1896 quadricycle.

Meanwhile, Ford completed his monstrous racing car, dubbed the "999," and saw it driven to victory in the fall of 1902 by the legendary Barney Oldfield. Again Ford had received national publicity for his racing achievements. A new group of investors was attracted who established the Ford Motor Company on 16 June 1903. Within a month, the Ford runabouts were ready to be shipped, but Henry Ford found some mechanical problems that he said would have to be corrected. He was overruled by James Couzens, who had charge of the company finances. Couzens pointed out that, unless they got money from the sale of the cars, the company, with a bank balance of only $223.65, would be out of business. The Ford runabouts, defects and all, were sold, and the Ford Motor Company was soon on solid financial ground.

By 1906, when he gained control of a majority of the Ford Motor Company stock, Henry Ford had become president of the company; and until 1979, either he or his son or grandson always held the top job in the business that bore the family name. Ford used his new power to push through programs that revolutionized the industry and made Ford number one for two decades. Ford sought what he called the "universal car" which would have the strength the runabout models had lacked to stand up to the wear and tear exacted by America's notoriously bad roads while, at the same time, would not sacrifice the runabout's low price. After he and his staff had developed a number of experimental models, Ford decided that they had found what he had been looking for when they got to the one they labeled "Model T."

This new model was first sold late in 1908, and it remained in production until May 1927. With total sales of more than fifteen million, the car affectionately known as "Tin Lizzie" set a record for sales of a single, basically unchanged model that would not be surpassed until the 1970s, when the equally famous Volkswagen Beetle set the new record.[8] The Model T was a sturdy, reliable car that was for most Americans in the early decades of the twentieth century the first car they owned. By the early 1920s, the Model T accounted for half the cars sold in the United States and could be bought new for as little as $290. The fact that it was produced in the Detroit area solidified the dominance that city and Michigan had begun to assert with the Oldsmobile runabout.

It was not the Model T, however, but the methods he used to produce it that made Henry Ford the century's most influential industrial figure. In order to increase annual production from the few thousand cars reached by the methods used by Ransom Olds to the two million Model Ts that Ford turned out each year by the twenties, he and his staff (these business leaders did not work alone) concentrated on finding ways of cutting the time it took to assemble the car. Where the typical auto worker had been involved in putting together the entire car, Ford workers were now assigned to perform only one particular task as the car being assembled passed in front of them. A large new factory was opened in 1910 at Highland Park where greatly increased floor space enabled the work flow to be organized more efficiently. Finally, in 1913–1914, the moving assembly line was instituted, mechanically moving the car through the various stages of assembly and dramatically reducing the time it took to finish the job.[9]

The Ford staff borrowed techniques that others had employed in earlier manufacturing operations. But the resulting combination seemed strikingly new, and around the world Ford's name became synonymous with mass production. Not only were the production methods completely changed; so too was the work force. Highly trained, skilled workers were not needed to carry out the minute tasks assigned to each worker along the assembly line. These jobs could be taken by immigrants from Europe and whites and blacks from the rural American South who had had no experience in factories, but who could be quickly taught the task they had to perform. In addition, when Ford announced in 1914 that he would begin paying most of his employees five dollars a day—twice the going factory wage—workers flocked to Michigan for jobs at the Ford plant and at the plants of other Michigan auto companies who soon had to follow Ford's lead.

For years Ford rode the crest of a continually rising tide of demand for one car, but by the mid-twenties that demand began tapering off. The Model T was looking out-of-date. Improved roads no longer made the Model T's sturdy qualities so important. As the growing use of installment buying no longer made it necessary to pay cash, more buyers began turning from the cheap Model T to some of the fancier, more comfortable cars offered by other companies. These cars had higher price tags but could be purchased for so much down and the remainder of the cost spread over twelve monthly payments. Taking advantage of these new conditions was General Motors Company (GM), which in the twenties supplanted Ford as the industry's number one producer.

GM owed its beginnings to the third of the trio of pioneers responsible for making Michigan the world's automobile center—William C. Durant. Unlike Olds and Ford, Durant knew little about the automobile's mechanical workings, but he was a genius at selling and promoting a product. He grew up in Flint, and it was there that GM had its origins. In the late 1880s, Durant formed a company to manufacture horse-drawn vehicles. Within a few years he had built it into one of the biggest companies of its type, helping to bring Flint the nickname "The Vehicle City" long before Buicks and Chevrolets were the vehicles for which that city was famous.

In 1903 another one of Flint's carriage companies, wishing to protect itself against the time when carriage sales would be depressed by the growing sales of horseless carriages, acquired control of a small Detroit firm, the Buick Motor Company, and moved it to Flint. Although the car he had developed was one of the more advanced models of its day, David D. Buick proved as incapable of managing the company in Flint as he had earlier in Detroit. In the summer of 1904, the Flint carriage manufacturers appealed to Durant to use his promotional skills to save their investment. Durant was ready for a new challenge. His highly successful carriage company no longer needed his full attention. So late in 1904, he took over the management of Buick and, within three years, had built it into the chief competitor with Ford for the honor of being the leading producer of cars.

Durant was not content with the control of just one company. Foreseeing an enormous increase in the demand for automobiles during the next ten years, Durant felt that if he could gain control of several companies, he could offer the customer not one but a number of different models and thereby be in a better position to get a larger share of those increased sales. After the collapse of a plan to merge Buick, Ford, Reo, and Maxwell (a company that had been formed by a former Olds employee and a former supplier of sheet metal parts for the Oldsmobile), Durant went ahead on his own to form the General Motors Company in September 1908. GM acquired control of Durant's own Buick company and then quickly added control of the Olds Motor Works, Cadillac, the company that eventually became GM's Pontiac division, and nearly two dozen other companies that made cars or car parts.

Durant's weakness for getting any company that was available led him to overextend GM's resources. The resulting financial crisis in 1910 led to his losing control to a bankers' group who loaned GM the money needed to weather the storm but insisted that Durant step aside in favor of a more conservative management team. Durant then proceeded to organize the Chevrolet Company and use its successful low-priced car as the means by which he was able to regain control of GM in 1915–1916.

During the second Durant regime, new acquisitions were brought into the GM fold, including such well-known names as Delco, Fisher Body, Frigidaire, and, of course, Chevrolet. Finally, in 1918, a reorganization led to the company becoming the present General Motors Corporation. But Durant's inability to recognize the need for a complete management overhaul of this vast business empire led to renewed problems in 1920, when the country slid into a post-World War I depression and GM again found itself on the brink of financial collapse. For the second and last time, Durant was forced out. He was succeeded by a new management team headed by Alfred P. Sloan, Jr., a managerial genius who proceeded to institute new ways of running the corporation that, from then on, would be a model for big corporations. It was also Sloan who instituted new sales techniques that established each of GM's car divisions in a particular price bracket. This enticed customers who owned a Chevrolet, for example, to move up to one of GM's somewhat higher-priced models, thus gaining the added prestige such a model conferred

Michigan State Archives

Chevrolet assembly line in Flint, ca. 1924.

on its owner. Sloan also encouraged people to trade in their old cars for new ones by making the annual models look different from those of the preceding year, even though the difference was a meaningless change in outer appearance and did not reflect any significant mechanical improvement.[10]

By 1927 Sloan's new ideas were proving so successful that Henry Ford was forced to end production of the unchanging, old reliable Model T and to come out a half-year later with a new model that included some of the flashier features that customers now seemed to prefer. The new Ford "Model A," as it was called, put Ford sales back out ahead of Chevrolet's in the low-priced category; but it was only temporary. Henry Ford's unwillingness to see that he could only compete successfully with GM if he adopted Sloan's managerial reforms, as well as Sloan's new emphasis on changing model styles, led to a continued decline in the company's fortunes until Henry Ford II replaced his grandfather after World War II and modernized Ford's management.

In the later twenties, Ford's number two position in the industry was being threatened by the sudden rise of the Chrysler Corporation. Its founder was Walter P. Chrysler, a graduate of the GM organization who took over the management of the Maxwell company and used it as a

George S. May

base from which he created the Chrysler Corporation in 1925. Following the GM approach of offering the customer a diversity of models, Chrysler acquired the Dodge Company in 1928, adding that well-known car name to a roster that soon included the low-priced Plymouth, the medium-priced DeSoto, and the more expensive Chrysler and Imperial models.

By the end of the 1920s, GM, Ford, and Chrysler constituted the Big Three of the auto industry. The three Detroit-based firms produced and sold 75 percent of all cars. During the following decade, when the country suffered through the Great Depression, the three giants increased their share of the market to 90 percent, as most of the smaller companies dropped by the wayside. The depression interrupted the steady pattern of growth in auto sales and registrations characteristic of the century's first three decades; and, with the outbreak of World War II, auto production was halted entirely as auto plants were converted to the production of war materiel. With the return of peace in the summer of 1945, however, the auto industry looked for a resumption of the boom days it had enjoyed before the thirties. Michigan's Big Three were now run by a new generation of leaders, fully prepared to capitalize on the positions of strength they had inherited from their founders.

◆

NOTES

1. For excellent insights into the European origins of the automobile, about which Americans know so little, see James M. Laux, *In First Gear: The French Automobile Industry to 1914* (Montreal, 1976); and *The Automobile Revolution: The Impact of an Industry* (Chapel Hill, 1982), written by Laux and three French automotive historians.

2. Details regarding Olds's test of his first self-propelled vehicle vary considerably in the accounts he provided in later years. The earliest and probably most accurate is one in a talk on "The Horseless Carriage," which Olds presented ten years later and which is in the *Michigan Engineers' Annual, Containing the Proceedings of the Michigan Engineering Society for 1898* (Battle Creek, 1898), 92–93. For other versions, see B. C. Forbes and O. D. Foster, *Automotive Giants of America* (New York, 1926), 225; and, the most unreliable of all sources on Olds, Duane Yarnell, *Auto Pioneering: A Remarkable Story of Ransom E. Olds, Father of Oldsmobile and Reo* (Lansing, 1949), 19–23, a work based on Olds's recollections at a time when his memory of events was clearly fading.

3. *Scientific American* 66 (21 May 1892): 329. The story was reprinted later that summer in *The Hub* 34 (July 1892): 145.

4. Lansing *State Republican,* 12 August 1896.

5. See Olds's specifications for his motor carriage reprinted in James T. Allen, *Digest of United States Automobile Patents from 1789 to July 1, 1899* (Washington, 1900), 501.

6. Automobile production figures in these early years are not as exact as they became in later years. The figures for Oldsmobile production are, at best, estimates, the accuracy of which it is not possible to determine.

7. Although the vast number of books that have been written about Henry Ford would make it appear that every detail of his life had been covered, it is still possible to turn up an occasional new piece of information. Such is the case with the coverage of this race that appeared in the *Detroit News,* 10 October 1901; the *Detroit Free Press,* 11 October 1901, and *Motor Age* 5 (17 October 1901).

8. Worldwide sales of the Volkswagen Beetle passed the earlier Model T totals in the early 1970s, and before the Beetle ceased to be produced in the mid-eighties, the figures were over twenty-two million. However, it should be pointed out that the Model T record was achieved in a period of eighteen and one-half years, while the Volkswagen "Bug," which began production in 1938, took over thirty years to surpass Ford's output.

9. Although Ford did not invent mass production, David A. Hounshell, in his study *From the American System to Mass Production: The Development of Manufacturing Technology in the United States 1800–1932* (Baltimore, 1984), demonstrates that Ford and his staff are entitled to be credited with developing the methods by which an unchanging model such as the Ford Model T could be produced in huge volume.

10. Sloan did not invent the annual model idea, although many writers credit him with having done so. Since the beginning of the industry, most auto companies had sought to create interest in their cars by displaying models that were different from the previous year at the annual automobile shows. Differences in these early years had centered on technical improvements. By the 1920s, however, few changes along such lines were possible, and Sloan can be credited with being one of the first to emphasize cosmetic changes in a car's outward look as a means of distinguishing the new models from the old ones.

───────────── ◆ ─────────────

SUGGESTED READINGS

In recent years there has been a great increase in the amount of information in print on all aspects of the American auto industry and on the impact the automobile has had in the country and in Michigan. A good, brief account of the subject remains John B. Rae, *The American Automobile* (Chicago, 1965). Rae's updating of this work, *The American Automobile Industry,* published in 1984, is excellent but is not as widely found in libraries as is the earlier work. For the early development of the auto industry in Michigan, see George S. May, *A Most Unique Machine: The Michigan Origins of the American Automobile Industry* (Grand Rapids, 1975). For Ransom Olds see George S. May, *R. E. Olds: Auto Industry Pioneer* (Grand Rapids, 1977). The best biography of William C. Durant is Bernard Weisberger, *The Dream Maker: William C. Durant, Founder of General Motors* (Boston, 1979). There is a staggering amount of material available on Henry Ford. A good starting point would be Roger Burlingame, *Henry Ford: A Great Life in Brief* (New York, 1955), one of the most balanced treatments.

Those who have the chance are urged to explore the fascinating exhibit on "The Automobile in American Life" that was opened at the Henry Ford Museum in Dearborn, Michigan, in November 1987. Due out in 1989 is a companion book on the same subject by George S. May. Also coming out in 1988 is *The Automobile Age*, by James J. Flink, the most thorough discussion of the development of the automobile, not only in the United States but in the entire world.

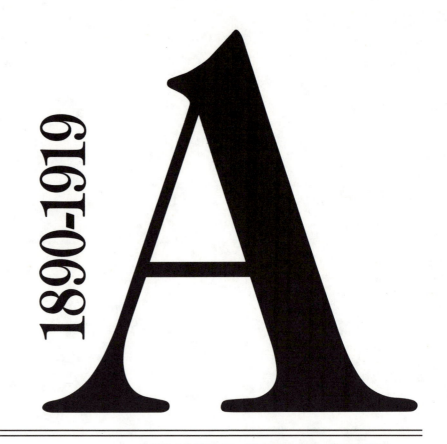

1890-1919

SARALEE R. HOWARD-FILLER

Saralee Howard-Filler is currently Associate Editor of *Michigan History* magazine for the Bureau of History, Michigan Department of State. She is the author of numerous articles relating to Michigan history. Prior to joining the Bureau of History, she was a graduate assistant at the Michigan State University Archives where she authored a guide to their collections. Ms. Howard-Filler received her bachelor's degree from Antioch College and a master's degree from Michigan State University.

Better Life for All:
Political and Social Reform in Michigan

The state was Michigan. The year was 1890. A young man of twenty-seven years of age by the name of Henry Ford was living with his new wife, Clara, on forty acres of farmland in Dearborn next to the farm of his parents. But young Ford described farming as "too much work" and instead tinkered with steam engines and sawed up the trees on his farm for cordwood. By 1890 he had begun to sketch out on paper his ideas for a "mechanical buggy." By September of the following year, Ford moved to Detroit where he soon became chief engineer for the Edison Illuminating Company, and ultimately the preeminent American industrialist of the twentieth century.[1]

That same year, 1890, an adventuresome and energetic thirty-year-old Chase Salmon Osborn, a native of Indiana, became postmaster of Sault Ste. Marie. Osborn had already carved out careers as crusading journalist in both Michigan and Wisconsin, iron prospector, and active political man. Of Michigan's Upper Peninsula he wrote: "I loved the wild new country. It brought into play everything that a soul and mind and body possesses. Nearly all the pioneers were young. The pace demanded youth."[2] In 1911 he became Michigan's outstanding Progressive Era governor.

Youthful pace was not what the First Unitarian Church of Kalamazoo was expecting in 1889 when its members hired newly-ordained minister Caroline Bartlett Crane, mainly to conduct funerals.[3] But by 1890, this thirty-two-year-old native of Hudson, Wisconsin, was rapidly making alive her idea of serving the social and educational needs for an entire community. In the Progressive Era, she would earn the title of "America's housekeeper."[4]

While Crane took to the pulpit, Horatio Earle was taking to the roads—the unpaved, rutted, often impassable roads of Michigan. By 1890 Earle had left his native state of Vermont and was making and repairing small machines and bicycles in Detroit. Bicycles were the great sport and growth industry of the 1890s in Michigan. The 1889–90 *Michigan State Gazetteer and Business Directory* lists under bicycles a mere two entries. But by 1893–94 the *Directory* listed four bicycle enamelers, one bicycle plater, six individual repairers, ten bicycle repair businesses, three firms selling bicycle sundries, seven selling tricycles and tricycle supplies, and sixty-one firms selling bicycles and supplies.[5] Right in the middle of this growing rage for bicycles was Earle, who preached that good roads were necessary for social reform and progress. Begun for bicycles, carriages, and wagons, the Good Roads movement accelerated rapidly.[6] For, on 6 March 1896, Charles Brady King guided a horseless carriage of his own design onto the streets of Detroit and drove away with the honor of being the first in Michigan to operate a gasoline-powered automobile.[7] Better-known auto makers, including Henry Ford and Ransom Olds, would soon follow, and by 1904 Michigan would lead the nation in auto production—a distinction it would continue to hold. The building of suitable roads became of vital importance in the early twentieth century, and Earle became Michigan's first highway commissioner.

Back in the 1890s, however, there were no auto-related dilemmas for John Dancy, a two-year-old black child, who was toddling about in North Carolina. His memories of youth were "mostly pleasant ones, of good friends, and games, and adventuresome trips. . . . But there are painful memories . . . as being bundled into a horse-drawn carriage by my stepmother to flee from a rioting mob."[8]

Dancy came to Detroit in 1916 and for forty years directed the Detroit Urban League. Dancy would lead a crusade for education and the rights of blacks at a tumultuous time in Michigan's history. He was particularly helpful to the large number of blacks who migrated to Michigan to work in the auto industry. In 1890, Michigan's black population stood at 15,816. That number had only doubled in the thirty years since 1860. But by 1920, there were 60,082 blacks in Michigan, most living in the Detroit area.

> The automobile, which was to change all America, wrought its first profound changes in Detroit. . . . Here was a new frontier; a new frontier coming into existence long after the physical frontier had been conquered. Detroit grew as mining towns grow—fast, impulsive, and indifferent to the superficial niceties of life . . . .[9]

But if Detroit had extraordinary challenges, the city also had an extraordinary mayor. Hazen S. Pingree, who, though lacking education and having limited party support, served four terms (1890–1897) as mayor of Detroit and two terms (1897–1901) as Michigan's governor. Born in 1840, Pingree moved to Detroit after serving in the Union Army during the Civil War. He obtained wealth as a shoe manufacturer, who, though keen in business, treated his seven hundred employees with

Brian and Ann Kastman, Kalamazoo; Kresge Art Center, Michigan State University

"Popcorn Vendor, Detroit 1911." Oil on canvas by Roy C. Gamble. This painting by a noted Michigan artist portrays the spirit of turn-of-the-century urban life in Detroit.

equity and respect. In a city dominated by the Democratic party, Pingree ran as a Republican with a rather unusual platform; he simply capitalized on the city's disgust with a patently corrupt government. Asked by a reporter if he had any special qualifications, he replied: "I know I'm honest, and I don't think I'm a damn fool."[10]

As Pingree revived the political life of Michigan, Mary Chase Perry Stratton molded the state's cultural landscape. By 1890, Stratton, born in 1867, had left her native Hancock, Michigan, come to Ann Arbor, and left again for art training at the Art Academy in Cincinnati, Ohio. Continuing her childhood obsession with color and clay, Stratton moved to Detroit in 1893, where she established a ceramics studio and sold a brand of potter's oven called the Revelation Kiln. During the first two decades of the twentieth century she created an extraordinarily successful ceramics and pottery business which she called Pewabic Pottery.[11] In 1906 she was a founding member of the Detroit Arts and Crafts Society, which encouraged "good and beautiful work as applied to useful service."[12] With the huge growth of industry, Michigan buildings were often constructed rapidly with little thought to decoration. Machine-turned decorations were often applied with little care. Stratton and her arts and crafts movement helped to counteract this trend toward mechanization. Throughout Detroit, buildings still stand with Pewabic tile and designs that are tribute to her goal of making art a vital part of public buildings. These include the Guardian Building, the Detroit Institute of Arts, and Christ Church Cranbrook.[13]

Ford, Osborn, Pingree, Crane, Earle, Dancy, and Stratton were still young and relatively unknown in 1890. These seven—along with thousands of others—would become the movers and shakers of Michigan. All were part of the wind of reform that blew through Michigan—and America—as the nineteenth century became the twentieth. All, despite diverse philosophies, changed Michigan.

Just what did Michigan look like in 1890 on the eve of an era of reform? Its population stood at 2,420,982. Just two years before, in 1888, lumbering peaked in Michigan when the lumbermen, who dominated the latter half of nineteenth-century Michigan with untrammeled economic expansion, cut 4.3 million board feet. The strength of lumbering, however, fell rapidly, particularly in the Lower Peninsula where the once seemingly endless forest was cut quickly with devastating results. Fires caused by cut-over lumber land, ghost towns, and economic decline slowly led Michiganians like Chase Osborn to the realization that natural resources needed protection. [Prior to being elected governor, Osborn, an avid conservationist, was appointed Game and Fish Warden in 1897 by Gov. John T. Rich.]

188

Lumbering, however, had created a complex legacy for Michigan. A diversified manufacturing base, including the famous furniture industries of Grand Rapids and carriage making in Flint, had come from timber, as did a pool of investment capital, an entrepreneurial spirit, and a ready body of young men seeking employment.[14]

The Republican party had dominated Michigan since they had first organized in Jackson in 1854. All Michigan governors since then, save one, had been Republicans. But in 1892, the Democratic and Greenback parties nominated Josiah Begole, who served one term as an advocate of wider distribution of cheaper greenbacks rather than specie. Since 1860 Michigan's electoral votes for president—except in 1884—went to the Republicans. But the era of reform throughout the nation from 1890–1920 challenged both Republicans and Democrats and created a national Progressive party.[15]

It was not just political or economic turmoil that characterized this reform era. The population was also shifting, changing in composition and growing. Once-tiny and struggling hamlets in southern Michigan, often settled by immigrants from New York or New England, had turned into well-appointed villages with neat homes, frequent rail service, social institutions, and manufacturing businesses. The 1884 census listed 2,856 church organizations in the state, with Methodists decisively leading, from thirty different denominations.[16] English, Scots, Canadians, Irish, Dutch and Germans had immigrated to Michigan in large numbers before 1880. After 1880, Poles, Finns, Italians, Austrians, Hungarians and Russians dominated the immigrants coming to Michigan; and Catholic and Lutheran churches swung upward in number. By 1890 over one-fourth of Michigan's population was foreign-born.[17]

Despite the depression of 1893 that flattened farm prices and, at times, farms, the number of farms continued to increase and peaked in 1910; however, the number of people listed as living in rural areas (communities under 2,500) decreased. In 1910 rural dwellers held a slight edge; but by 1920 only 39 percent of Michiganians lived in rural areas.[18] From 1890 to 1910 population increased steadily, though not dramatically. In the decade from 1910 to 1920, however, Michigan's population increase was huge—2,810,173 to 3,668,412—due mainly to jobs provided by the expanding auto industry.

Reform was the single most outstanding response to social dislocation, suffering and moral quandaries as the movement toward cities and industries took place. An extraordinary activist in Detroit, Hazen Pingree worked for asphalt roads (rather than cedar blocks or dirt), electric railroads, and reduction of gas rates. The depression of 1893 hit Detroit hard, and Pingree pushed forcefully for public works and direct relief programs to help the twenty-five thousand unemployed. In 1894 Pingree came up with the idea of having the unemployed plant foodstuffs on the unused patches of Detroit land. He gained national recognition as "Potato Pingree" and a loyal following among Detroit workers who offset the hatred he stirred in streetcar, electric, and gas magnates.[19]

It is a measure of the reform sentiment of the 1890s that Pingree—scorned by the Democrats and shunned more quietly by the Republican regulars—was twice elected to the governor's chair. There he pushed for taxation reform and a statewide scientific appraisal of railway and corporation property for tax purposes. (He appointed Chase Osborn as an activist railroad commissioner.) But his personal passionate temperament, and perhaps his too-easily touched heart, made him a vulnerable target. He left the gubernatorial chair in 1901 amid some public unpopularity and rancor, and died soon after while on a trip abroad. He had hoped to return to Detroit again as its mayor in the near future.[20]

Whether historians label Pingree an "urban populist" or a "pre-Progressive," his political saga signaled the end of complacent optimism.[21] Gone was the smug oratory of the 1885–1887 jubilee of Michigan's statehood. The Populist movement of the 1890s and the Progressive movement of 1900–1917 heralded social criticism, while striving for social progress and betterment. While Michigan's leaders were associated with specific reforms, there was also a general uneasiness about the moral, political and economic underpinnings of this rapidly changing society.

Forrester Washington, who served two years as director of Detroit's Urban League before Dancy took over, touched upon that unease when he said, "Nothing is being done in the way of adjusting these colored strangers to their new environment and assimilating them healthfully. Hence, a situation is being created which, unless proper preventable measures are taken, will present a very difficult problem in the not-too-distant future."[22] And from a very different vantage point, George Booth, who with Mary Chase Perry Stratton and others started the Detroit Arts and Crafts Society, said: "I hope it will be possible to have a society . . . whose members will be zealous to spread the gospel of good work and the higher and saner standards of art in objects of use and ornament."[23] Uneasy or not, Michiganians, with their nineteenth-century tradition of small farms and villages, were plunging into a century dominated by autos and the auto industry.

Chase Salmon Osborn, combining a love of the outdoors with a sensitivity toward urban dilemmas, was Michigan's preeminent Progressive. In 1909 he announced his candidacy for the Republican gubernatorial nomination. Frank Knox, future secretary of the navy during World

Michigan State Archives

Hazen S. Pingree: mayor of Detroit (1890–1897) and governor of Michigan (1897–1901).

War II and editor of what had once been Osborn's *Sault News*, managed the race. The energetic and vibrant candidate conducted a fast-paced campaign while crisscrossing the state during the first Michigan campaign done in an auto. He was running against incumbent three-term Gov. Fred Warner. Osborn recalled: "There was much dissatisfaction with the state of public affairs in Michigan. Higher ideals of government began to be asserted in many places. A man, perhaps worthy enough, but who was regarded as being very ordinary, had been elected governor for a third term."[24]

"Osborn, Harmony and a New Deal" was his slogan; anti-Warnerism and anticorruption were the underlying messages. The stress on harmony can be explained by looking at the gubernatorial campaign of 1908. At that time, Governor Warner, a conservative Republican caught up in the wave of progressive reform, successfully spearheaded the drive mandating primary elections for governor, lieutenant governor, and United States senator. This act enabled Warner to run for an unprecedented third term which he won by a minute margin. The episode, coupled with hints of corruption, caused considerable discord within the Republican party. Osborn, capitalizing on the growing unpopularity of Warner, promised to bring the Republicans together.

Osborn touted a platform of legislative and administrative reforms, including teaching of agriculture in public schools, state aid for county agricultural schools, controls on banks, legal use of convict labor to build roads, road improvement, women's suffrage, creation of a State Department, workmen's compensation, and child and women's labor laws. Most of these reforms were not enacted into law until later.[25]

There were no Michigan enterprises during this period that did not gain directly or indirectly from the work, ideas, and influence of Michigan women—in business as well as in the arts, education, politics, and other pursuits. But Caroline Bartlett Crane, as was the case with these other reformers, carried a moral purpose along with her practical enterprises. Her primary concern was religious; and, in fact, she became a Unitarian minister. Crane's early career took her from Wisconsin to Illinois, Minnesota, and Dakota Territory. In the fall of 1889, she became pastor of the First Unitarian Church in Kalamazoo, giving it life as she had other congregations. She wanted a "seven-day church," somewhat in the mode of Frances Willard's urgings to feminists to "do everything."[26]

In Crane's case, it meant tending to the poor, laborers, women, and others in need. Her career broadened as she led a call to rid Kalamazoo County of an abusive and racist county official. This campaign required her to reach out to a larger number of people in order to exert pressure for his separation from office. She initiated the idea of "municipal housekeeping," which demanded a keen eye on city workings, and held her church open to people of any or no denomination.[27]

At the age of thirty-eight, she surprised friends by announcing her marriage to Dr. Augustus Warren Crane, who was to become a famous radiologist. In 1898 she found herself overworked and resigned her pastorate, but she never gave up her role as preacher, attending and speaking at many churches. But hers was now a "civic ministry" that led her, for example, to lead a group of prominent citizens on an inspection tour of Kalamazoo slaughterhouses. There she found appalling work and unsanitary conditions, such as those Upton Sinclair would soon make notorious in *The Jungle.*[28] Such inspections into medical care, poorhouses, and other institutions became a staple of her career.

Between 1907 and 1916, Crane made no fewer than sixty-two American city inspections of social and sanitary conditions, earning for herself the title of "Minister to Cities." The list of her concerns became legendary, and involved sewers, garbage disposal, milk and meat quality, bakeries, and hospitals. The key to her success was the committees she organized, which gave authority and publicity to her findings. Her investigations were not all self-generated. She was called in by concerned citizens in many places because of the authority she had gained. In 1910, for example, she was given a seventeen-city survey to make in Minnesota where she spoke out, not only regarding specific city issues, but on the larger questions of social inadequacy and racism. Her recommendations fostered the building of

Michigan State Archives

Caroline Bartlett Crane, minister to cities.

hospitals and other large-scale enterprises.[29] During the 1920s, Crane was notable as a housing reformer and served as associate editor of the influential *Woman's Journal*. As a "do everything" reformer, she had succeeded in turning attention from herself as a woman's advocate and suffragist to one who was a peer of anyone, man or woman, to whom civic responsibilities came naturally.[30]

The city and offices of government were not the only focus for Progressive efforts. Improvement of roads, particularly rural roads, was a vital cause for the League of American Wheelmen (LAW) and its Michigan chapter. Bicyclists agitated for good roads for the immediate goal of easier bike riding as well as for a series of social goals, including better transportation that would, they said, give prosperity to farmers, better communication, and even greater mobility for greater happiness. One important early accomplishment of Michigan's LAW was the establishment of a county road system in 1893.[31] This advent of the good roads movement came before the first gas-powered auto was driven in Michigan. But speedily, the auto came to dominate Michigan. The first sight of an auto circa 1901 in the Upper Peninsula's Copper Country would be reversed by 1920 by the unusual sight of a horse-drawn wagon.[32]

The outstanding reformer for roads, Horatio Earle, became chairman of the Michigan Highway Improvement Committee in 1898 and chief consul of Michigan's League of American Wheelmen in 1899. Elected to the state senate in 1901, Earle lobbied for state aid to roads. Gov. Aaron Bliss appointed Earle highway commissioner; immediately, the Michigan attorney general ruled the highway bill (which included Earle's job as commissioner) unconstitutional. But Earle—in a true streak of persistence typifying Progressive reformers motivated by cause rather than salary or position—continued to serve as an "unconstitutional" highway commissioner. He wrote:

> I am loath to fight the state officials, be they good or bad, for I enlisted seven years ago, simply to fight 'Bad Roads,' to whip them and evict them, and install instead, 'Good Roads,' for good citizens to use for profit and pleasure. . . . It may be possible for officials to strain the constitution to the extent of prohibiting the paying of a state highway commissioner his salary and expenses, but the constitution, the statutes, and the officials combined, cannot stop me from going ahead with this work; and go ahead with it I will, until such time as the constitution shall be changed to permit laws to be enacted that will equalize the expense of building permanent good roads, and until we have good roads.[33]

His reward was that, by 1905, the name of Horatio "Good Roads" Earle was known throughout Michigan, and a constitutional amendment to allow state aid for roads was passed by a solid public vote. Then,

was legally appointed highway commissioner. However,
uently with Governor Warner, and was finally removed

and Osborn made efforts to increase social awareness
cipation in a changing Michigan. What was at the heart
ichigan? Let it best be described by a statement given to
rters on the morning of 5 January 1914 from the Ford
offices of Henry Ford:

> Motor Co., the greatest and most successful automobile manu-
> pany in the world, will, on Jan. 12, inaugurate the greatest
> revolution in the matter of rewards for its workers ever known to the indus-
> trial world. At one stroke it will reduce the hours of labor from nine to eight
> and add to every man's pay a share of the profits of the house.[34]

Blaring out in headlines around the world, the news of a five-dollars-a-
day wage galvanized workers and business alike. Some ten thousand men
gathered the very next morning at the Highland Park plant. As impressive
as this number seems, it does not even hint at the huge immigration to
Michigan created by Ford's offer. Two years after Ford made this extraordinary offer to men, he offered the same to women. He was also willing to
hire blacks in the factories and thus created one of the most famous
migrations of people in America from south to north.[35]

Critics have probed Ford's policies without mercy, but they have sometimes gone wrong by failing to compare them with other policies that
ruled the land. His Peace Ship of 1915 was ridiculed for its ineptitude;
but was it less futile than the war it sought to stop? No one defends the
anti-Semitism that disfigured his newspaper, the *Dearborn Independent;*
but it brought it into the open, and he himself, no intellectual but aware of
public opinion, repudiated anti-Semitism in 1927. He saw union seekers
as agitators prone to violence, and met fire with fire. He had fought
would-be monopolists in auto manufacturing and beat them in the
courts. Ford then turned to resist the government when it sought to
reduce his power over workers through its National Labor Relations Act
of 1935. It took World War II to force him to accede to government policy
and, in 1941, to sign a contract with the United Auto Workers. Ford is
often seen as representing the ideals of a bygone era. But, as we often
find it necessary to pay tribute to some of an earlier age's ways of thinking and living and to criticize some of the products of modern life, it
seems best to take Ford as a whole, and keep him in perspective.[36]

Part of the world Henry Ford created was the world inherited by
John Dancy. He saw a Detroit where the black churches and voluntary
organizations were not able to cope with the huge pressures of black

migration. To their aid came the Detroit Urban League. Begun in 1910, the league started a Detroit branch in 1916; two years later, John Dancy became its head, with its activities and impact expanding dramatically. Dancy worked to acclimate largely rural southern blacks to Detroit and its industries. A community center was organized giving education to children. With some nine hundred to one thousand migrants arriving each week, housing was a severe problem. The League worked to ensure that blacks received—and kept—industrial jobs. Even as the Progressive Era ended, Dancy's drive toward social betterment and reform did not.[37]

Many Progressive Era reforms, however, did ebb as the war in Europe began. Ford launched his Peace Ship "to make a dramatic appeal to the war-weary peoples of Europe for a negotiated peace."[38] Later he capitulated and joined the war effort. Crane became president of the Michigan Women's Committee of National Defense; her work and that of other suffragists for the war helped build support for the women's suffrage amendment in 1918.[39] Earle was chosen director of Michigan's United States Boys' Working Reserve.[40] The reform impulse as the dominant urge in society was overcome by the war. Yet some of its goals were achieved. Direct elections, governmental regulation of food and drugs, sanitation in

Detroit Urban League community center, 1919. John Dancy and his wife Maude are at the top of the stairs.

Bentley Historical Library, Michigan Historical Collections, University of Michigan cities, and state aid to keep roads paved and free of ruts became—with an occasional exception—almost second nature to the public's sense of what constituted an acceptable social climate.

While specific goals may be won, reform as a force, however, continues in all eras. A movement for a moral drive and education for urban dwellers would be as helpful today as it was in the time of Crane's Kalamazoo and Dancy's Detroit. Accountability in government is as pressing today as it was when Osborn was governor. Potholes are as jarring today as in the days of Earle. Art for public spaces is as important now as in the days of Mary Chase Perry Stratton's Pewabic tile.

Each of these seven—Ford, Osborn, Pingree, Dancy, Earle, Crane, and Stratton—reflected a public urge toward reform. Each appealed to the Michigan public to perpetuate that drive. The era lifted them up and gave dignity and a social forum to their ideas. Their successes are a reflection of the adage that an army invasion may be resisted but not an idea whose time has come.

◆

NOTES

1. Extensive materials, both primary and secondary, on Henry Ford may be found at the Archives and Library, the Edison Institute, Henry Ford Museum, and Greenfield Village. Among the excellent works on Ford consulted include Allan Nevins, with the collaboration of Frank Hill, *Ford* (New York: Scribners, 1954).

2. Quoted in Saralee R. Howard-Filler, "Chase Salmon Osborn," *Great Lakes Informant* (reprint; Lansing: Michigan History Division, 1986), 1.

3. O'Ryan Rickard, "Caroline Bartlett Crane: Minister to Sick Cities," in *Historic Women of Michigan: A Sesquicentennial Celebration*, ed. Rosalie Riegle Troester (Lansing: Michigan Women's Studies Association, 1987), 10–11. Caroline Bartlett Crane's papers are located at Western Michigan University Archives and Regional History Collections, Kalamazoo, Michigan.

4. Charles Starring, "Caroline Bartlett Crane," in *Notable American Women: A Biographical Dictionary* (Cambridge: Harvard University Press, 1971), 401–2.

5. *Michigan State Gazetteer and Business Directory 1893–1894* (Detroit: R. L. Polk and Company, 1893), 1605–6.

6. Philip P. Mason, "The League of American Wheelmen and the Good Roads Movement, 1880–1905" (Ph.D. diss., The University of Michigan, 1957).

7. Sinclair Powell, "In the Beginning," *Michigan History* 69 (November/December 1985): 6–9.

8. John Campbell Dancy, *Sand Against the Wind* (Detroit: Wayne State University Press, 1966), 60.

9. Michigan Writers' Project, *Michigan: A Guide to the Wolverine State* (New York: Oxford University Press, 1941), 231.

10. Quoted in Charles R. Starring, "Hazen S. Pingree: Another Forgotten Eagle," *Michigan History* 32 (June 1948): 132.

11. For a detailed view of the pottery and its creator, see Lillian Myers Pears, *The Pewabic Pottery* (Des Moines, Iowa: Wallace Homestead, 1976).

12. Joy Hakanson Colby, *Art and a City* (Detroit: Wayne State University Press, 1956), 4.

13. Richard Albyn and Charlene Kull, "Michigan History's Cranbrook Tales," *Michigan History* 66 (March/April 1982): 15–31.

14. For a discussion of the effects of Michigan's lumbering era, see Willis Dunbar and George S. May, *Michigan: A History of the Wolverine State* (Grand Rapids: William B. Eerdmans Publishing Company, 1980), 395–409.

15. See Alice Porter Campbell, "The Bull Moose Movement in Michigan" (Master's thesis, Wayne State University, 1939).

16. Saralee R. Howard-Filler, " 'A Jubilee Shall That Fiftieth Year Be unto You': Michigan Churches in 1884," *Michigan History* 67 (July/August 1983): 18.

17. John Kern, *A Short History of Michigan* (Lansing: Michigan History Division, 1976), 68.

18. For an excellent analysis and compilation of population statistics, see Richard Santer, *Michigan: Heart of the Great Lakes* (Dubuque, Iowa: Kendall/Hunt Publishing Company, 1977).

19. See Melvin G. Holli, *Reform in Detroit: Hazen S. Pingree and Urban Politics* (New York: Oxford University Press, 1969).

20. Starring, 142–49.

21. See Holli.

22. Forrester B. Washington, "Report of the Director," 16 October 1916, Associated Charities of Detroit Collection, Wayne State University Archives of Labor History and Urban Affairs.

23. Arthur Pound, *The Only Thing Worth Finding, The Life and Legacies of George Gough Booth* (Detroit: Wayne State University Press, 1964), 477.

24. Quoted in Howard-Filler, "Chase Salmon Osborn," 3.

25. See Robert M. Warner, "Chase S. Osborn's 1910 Primary Election Campaign," *Michigan History* 43 (September 1959): 349–84.

26. Louis Filler, *Appointment at Armageddon: Muckraking and Progressivism in the American Tradition* (Westport, Conn.: Greenwood Press, 1976), 126.

27. Rickard, 122.

28. Upton Sinclair, *The Jungle* (New York: Doubleday, 1906).

29. Michigan Legislature, *Public Acts 1903*, Act 120.

30. See Stanley Lemons, *The Women Citizens: Social Feminism in the 1920s* (Urbana: University of Illinois Press, 1973).

31. Dunbar and May, 568.

32. S. Josiah Penberthy, Jr., "U.P. Auto Memories," *Michigan History* 69 (November/December 1985): 34.

33. Philip P. Mason, "Horatio S. Earle and the Good Roads Movement in Michigan," *Papers of the Michigan Academy of Science, Arts and Letters* 4 (1958): 274–75.

34. *Detroit Free Press,* 6 January 1914, 1.

35. Richard Thomas, "The Detroit Urban League: 1916–1923," *Michigan History* 60 (Winter 1976): 332.

36. See David Lanier Lewis, *The Public Image of Henry Ford: An American Folk Hero and His Company* (Detroit: Wayne State University Press, 1976).

37. Thomas, 332–38.

38. Carl Wittke, "An Echo from the Ford Peace Ship of 1915," *Michigan History* 32 (September 1948): 287.

39. Rickard, 127.

40. L. B. W., "The United States Boys' Working Reserve: Boy Soldiers of the Soil," *Michigan History* 4 (January 1920): 279–86.

SUGGESTED READINGS

For a national look at the Progressive Movement consult Louis Filler, *The Muckrakers* (University Park: Pennsylvania State University Press, 1976). Melvin Holli's *Reform in Detroit: Hazen S. Pingree and Urban Politics* (New York: Oxford University Press, 1969) is an excellent look at Detroit during this time period. Several gubernatorial collections at the State Archives, Lansing, Michigan, are also useful. The papers of Chase S. Osborn are in the Michigan Historical Collections, Bentley Historical Library, The University of Michigan. Materials on Henry Ford are at the Archives and Library, Edison Institute, Henry Ford Museum and Greenfield Village, Dearborn. Materials on Hazen Pingree may be found at the Burton Historical Collections, Detroit Public Library, Detroit. The papers of Caroline Bartlett Crane are at Western Michigan University Archives and Regional History Collections, Kalamazoo. The Pewabic Pottery, Detroit, is open to the public and features artifacts and papers relating to Mary Chase Perry Stratton. Horatio Earle's diaries and correspondence may be found at the Michigan Historical Collections, Bentley Historical Library, The University of Michigan.

T
1917-1945

NORA FAIRES

Nora Faires is associate professor of history at The University of Michigan-Flint. Her research and writing has focused on ethnic and urban history. She is the author of articles on German and Lebanese immigrants, and essays on Detroit and Pittsburgh. Professor Faires has conducted oral history projects, consulted on photodocumentary and museum studies, and participated in the creation of an original play based on the 1937 sit-down strike in Flint. She received her doctorate degree from the University of Pittsburgh in 1981.

ransition & Turmoil:
Social and Political Development in Michigan

In many ways, Michigan mirrored the nation in the tumultuous years between America's entry into the Great War (or World War I, as it came to be known) and the end of World War II.[1] But, as in other eras, the Michigan experience during these dramatic decades had particular characteristics and peculiar shadings. The Great Lakes state weathered the end of twentieth-century America's 'teen' years, the rip-roaring 1920s, the bitter decade of the depression, and the fierce war years with a style all its own. Michigan's social and political life matured between 1917 and 1945, and the developments in these nearly thirty years set the stage for the state's evolution in the last half of the twentieth century.

GOVERNMENT, POLITICS, AND POWER

Since the inception of the Republican party in 1854, Michigan had been a stronghold of the Grand Old Party. In the years between World War I and 1930, Michigan confirmed its reputation as a Republican bastion. From 1917 to 1933, all four men occupying the governor's chair—

Albert E. Sleeper, Alexander J. Groesbeck, Fred W. Green, and Wilbur M. Brucker—were Republicans; only one Democrat, Kalamazoo attorney Woodbridge N. Ferris, won election to the United States Senate before 1930; and in 1921 and 1925 Republicans occupied all seats in the state legislature. Michigan voters also typically supported the Republicans in presidential elections, turning out with the rest of the nation to bring Warren G. Harding, Calvin Coolidge, and Herbert Hoover to the White House. Then, in the wake of the nation's most severe economic crisis, voters' sentiments began to shift away from the party of Hoover and hard times. On the broad coattails of presidential candidate Franklin Delano Roosevelt, Democrats captured the governorship in 1932, 1936, and 1940. At the local level, many Democrats won contests for mayor and city council for the first time in the century. For Michigan, the depression marked a watershed in state politics, ushering in an era of sustained two-party competition.

Of the notable persons who rose to political prominence in the state during these years, several made an especially enduring impression. Alexander J. Groesbeck, governor from 1921 to 1927, possessed a zeal for administrative efficiency and innovation. Governor Groesbeck oversaw the consolidation of state offices, bringing order and financial stability to the system even as state government was growing rapidly. In particular, Groesbeck pushed forward the expansion of Michigan's road system, fighting for a tax on gasoline sales to help pay for the improvement of more than six thousand miles of dirt and gravel roads and the concrete paving of two thousand more. The widening and improvement of Detroit's main thoroughfare, Woodward Avenue, was the governor's particular joy. On these thousands of miles of new roads, more and more Michigan residents drove ever-increasing numbers of automobiles, the product whose manufacture buoyed the state's economy throughout Groesbeck's years in office.[2]

Another influential governor, former Detroit mayor Frank Murphy, took office in 1937. Governor Murphy inherited a ravaged economy and a depression-weary public. He faced auto workers staging a sit-down strike in a huge Flint General Motors plant. By refusing to send in troops to put down the strike and by encouraging both sides to negotiate, the governor showed how a New Deal Democrat approached economic affairs. His handling of the 'Great Flint Sit-down Strike,' and of other workers' disputes in 1937 and 1938, created a more cordial climate for labor in Michigan.[3]

A less well-known politician of the day also left a mark on the state's history. Eva M. Hamilton of Grand Rapids was the first woman to serve in the state legislature. Her election in 1920 came in the same year the nation adopted the Nineteenth Amendment to the Constitution, which extended voting rights to women. This amendment was hotly debated in Michigan, but in the end, the state ratified woman's suffrage.

Prohibition, enacted nationally under the Eighteenth Amendment to the Constitution, was a different matter. Here Michigan led the way, instituting a state ban on alcoholic sales and production in 1918, a year before the federal government. Yet if the state rushed to embrace Prohibition, it also quickly experienced the drastic consequences of this action. Residents in the southeastern corner of the state suspected that a so-called pipeline ran from a whiskey distillery in Ontario across Lake Huron and into the state. Pipeline or no, throughout the 1920s bootleg liquor streamed into Michigan from Canada; meanwhile, backyard stills in the countryside churned out gallons of illegal spirits, and illicit

Women's rights poster used by the Michigan Equal Suffrage Association in their 1918 campaign.

saloons, called speakeasies and blind pigs, flourished from Detroit to Copper Harbor.

With bootlegging came crime. The state's newspapers frequently blazed headlines of the gruesome gangland slayings, kidnappings, and gambling that accompanied the outlawed liquor trade. Detroit's Purple Gang was the most notorious mob in the state. In 1931, gang members were convicted of murdering three other rum racketeers in what became known as the Collingwood Avenue Massacre. Such violence, accompanied by shrinking tax revenues, prompted Michigan residents to end state Prohibition. In 1932 the state law was repealed, and in 1933 Michigan became the first state to ratify the constitutional amendment ending Prohibition. The state quickly established a Liquor Control Commission and, to boost its dwindling finances, placed a tax on the sale of alcohol.[4]

The Prohibition era also taught Michigan residents that crime was too often linked with political intrigue. In the boom years of the 1920s, some government officials found opportunities for graft in the letting of contracts for bridge, road, and school construction projects that sprang up across the state. In the dark depression years, payments to public officials sometimes greased the wheels of public relief projects. The war years seemed to bring relief from political scandal. Then, in 1943, a lobbyist gave evidence that dozens of state legislators had accepted bribes. More than forty ultimately were convicted of wrongdoing—and more might have been if a state senator who was about to testify in the investigation had not been murdered![5] To be sure, only a minority of Michigan's lawmakers were implicated in such scandals. Their eruption, however, spotlighted the political system, drawing attention to the salience of politics in the decades following World War I. In this era, many economic, social, and cultural battles were fought within the political system, and the political system itself was reshaped according to the new dynamics of power in the state.

Several political controversies of the day demonstrate these conflicts and clarify the fault lines of social strain that fractured during these years. Immediately following World War I, for example, a wave of anti-Communism swept the United States. Michigan joined the crusade to stamp out the perceived Communist threat. On 2 January 1920, as part of the nationwide Palmer raid (named after United States Attorney General A. Mitchell Palmer), Michigan public officials arrested hundreds of suspected reds, jailing many for nearly a week in rude, makeshift prisons. The native-born residents' fear of immigrants and the immigrants' alleged sympathy for unions spurred this 'Red Scare.'[6]

This same fear and animosity fueled an explosion of membership in the Ku Klux Klan (KKK) in the 1920s. Robed and hooded, KKK members marched through Michigan streets proclaiming their "100 percent Americanism"—and their hatred for those whom they believed fell short of this mark: immigrants, nonwhites, Catholics, and Jews. By 1924, the Klan reached its zenith in Michigan. Membership topped thirty-two thousand in Detroit, with large klaverns (as chapters were called) in Flint and other industrial cities in the state. Not content merely to demonstrate, the KKK turned to terrorism, burning crosses on lawns and beating up blacks, union organizers, and others of whom it disapproved. The Klan also turned to politics, fielding its own slate of candidates and securing contacts in local law enforcement agencies.[7]

In this same period, Henry Ford, one of Michigan's—and America's—premier business leaders, also stoked the fires of anti-Semitism through his newspaper, the *Dearborn Independent*. For seven years, the *Independent* blamed the state's political and social ills on what it termed "the Jewish racial problem." Then, in 1927, faced with several libel suits and hurt by slumping auto sales, the head of the Ford Motor Company extended an apology for his newspaper's anti-Semitic writings.[8]

Some of the furor over the foreign-born—many of whom were Jews or Catholics—subsided after the Congressional acts of 1921 and 1924 sharply curtailed immigration from most countries. These acts, however, erected no barriers against immigration from the Western Hemisphere. Michigan, sharing much of its shoreline with the Canadian province of Ontario, received an ongoing stream of migrants from the north. When the state's economy crashed in 1929, some Michigan residents became convinced that Canadians, along with other foreign nationals who posed as Canadians, were taking jobs away from those who had a right to work in the state—Michigan residents, like themselves. These beliefs, along with resurgent anti-Communism, led some prominent state business and labor leaders to push for an alien registration act in 1931. The act was later declared unconstitutional.[9]

The same sentiments, mixed with racial antagonism, bred resentment against Michigan's Mexican population. Enclaves of Mexican immigrants had settled in the state during the labor shortage of the 1920s, but with the onset of the depression, employers no longer needed their labor. Some influential citizens began to decry the so-called Mexican problem. To encourage Mexicans to leave the state, government agencies established a repatriation program. Allegedly, this project transported to Mexico only those state residents who wished to return to their native country. In fact, many of those repatriated were pressured to leave. At its peak in 1932, the state effectively deported thousands of Mexicans a month.[10]

These two governmental initiatives exemplify the deepening social cleavages and heightened social tensions that came with the massive unemployment and hardship of the depression years. Lawmakers in Lansing considered these initiatives in an atmosphere newly charged with class conflict. On 6 March 1930, thousands of the unemployed staged demonstrations in the state's three largest cities—Detroit, Grand Rapids, and Flint—and in smaller Muskegon and Kalamazoo. Some of these jobless workers would later find employment in a government program. One of the most successful was the Civilian Conservation Corps. In Michigan's nearly sixty camps, over one hundred thousand workers planted trees, erected fences, cleared trails, built fish hatcheries, or participated in other projects that improved the state.[11] Many other workers, however, remained unemployed or found work only as the state's economy recovered. But finding jobs for workers was not the only problem government and business faced during these lean years. Consumers, too, vented their anger over the depression's harsh consequences. In 1935, for example, Mary Zuk, from the Polish enclave of Hamtramck, led the Housewives Committee Against the High Standard of Living in a protest against soaring meat prices, threatening to "win the fight on meat and go on to the other necessities of life."[12]

Even the return of good times did not mean the end of social conflict. Rather, the influx of workers, many of them from rural Michigan and even more from the South, reinforced some divisions and introduced new ones. Black migrants from the South had long faced discrimination (as had other nonwhites in the state, including Michigan's original native American inhabitants). Matters worsened tangibly, however, in the 1940s, as the state's industry geared up for war production. Michigan's dramatic surge in population, particularly in the burgeoning cities, produced housing shortages. In numerous communities, government stepped in to provide homes for workers. In the case of Detroit's Sojourner Truth Homes project, built in 1942, government action set off a violent reaction. Whites in the area and from miles around gathered to keep black families out of the housing project. Black residents moved into the project only months later, and then under armed guard.[13] Ethnic, religious, and racial antagonisms flared in other Michigan neighborhoods and housing projects during these years, despite the rigid segregation of whites and blacks that was both policy and practice in these wartime installations. At Willow Run, for example, the housing complex built at the giant bomber plant near Ypsilanti, southern white workers, Catholics, southern and eastern Europeans and, especially, the handful of Japanese immigrants, all faced harassment.[14]

On 20 June 1943, a sizzling summer day, the mounting racial tensions of the war years boiled over on Belle Isle, Detroit's picturesque island park. Fighting broke out between whites and blacks and spread across the city. Federal troops finally quelled the violence, but only after twenty-five blacks and nine whites had died. In addition, the riot left more than seven hundred people injured and hundreds of businesses and homes in flames.

The racial hostility that flared during those hot June days and nights bequeathed a legacy of unresolved conflicts. In the years to come, Michigan's political system would reverberate with demands for racial, economic, and social justice.

SOCIAL LIFE

As World War I drew to a close, many Michigan residents realized that they were entering a new era as the old order seemed to fade away. During these years, Michigan residents from Benton Harbor to Alpena and from Ironwood to Sault Ste. Marie read headlines in their newspapers, listened to news bulletins on their radios, or watched newsreels in movie theatres chronicling the startling events of the day.

International affairs commanded center stage in 1918 with the end of the war in Europe, a war that took the lives of five thousand Michigan residents. Those at home gladly gave up their voluntary meatless and wheatless days and abandoned the victory gardens they had planted to help the war effort, happy to return to what they hoped would be post-war prosperity.

Many did experience good times in the next decade, as a tide of automobile buying swept the nation. With rising auto sales came a boom in Michigan's construction business. Some would-be home buyers in Michigan turned to catalogs to make their dreams of property ownership come true. The Aladdin Company of Bay City shipped more than thirty-six hundred redi-cut, complete homes across the United States in 1926 alone. Potential buyers selected their home plans from a range of styles and prices, assured that the company had received a medal for quality from the Michigan Agricultural Exposition.[15] In Flint, the building of homes could not keep up with the rush of workers arriving in the city to assemble the increasingly-popular Chevrolet and Buick automobiles. Consequently, the General Motors Corporation began constructing houses in the city's Civic Park district. Using assembly line techniques like those employed in its plants, the company put up 4,260 homes between 1921 and 1923. Success in Flint led General Motors to launch similar projects in Pontiac, Lansing, and Detroit.[16]

Not all of Michigan's residents shared in the general prosperity of the 1920s. Many farmers and miners, in particular, were hit by hard times.

Still, all but a handful of Michigan's inhabitants suffered from the economic crisis of the 1930s. Michigan investors took the first blows. They watched exultantly as stock prices skyrocketed until, in October 1929, most saw their paper fortunes plummet. Unemployment rocked the state, and per capita income dropped precipitously, from $793 in 1929 to $349 in 1933.[17] When Michigan's banks closed in 1933, a large number of Michiganians lost their life savings.

Many of the state's residents simply did not have enough to live on, and by 1934, one out of eight Michigan families received governmental support. Men and women witnessed the poverty and despair of hard times. In the cities, hunger stalked the streets, and public officials tried makeshift solutions to ease the unparalleled hardship of their citizens. In Detroit, for example, Mayor Frank Murphy opened up a warehouse to those without shelter. Ironically, many of the urban homeless had left their farms in rural Michigan for jobs in the cities during better times. Some returned to the countryside, but there, too, they found economic devastation. In the Upper Peninsula's Keweenaw County, two-thirds of all families were on the relief rolls in 1934.[18]

The voice of one Michigan religious leader became familiar to radio listeners in these dark days. Father Charles E. Coughlin, a Roman Catholic priest, broadcast weekly radio programs from his parish, the Shrine of the Little Flower in Royal Oak. Calling the depression one of history's "unique tragedies," Coughlin decried the "abundance of foodstuffs, millions of virgin acres, banks loaded with money—alongside idle factories, long bread lines, millions of jobless, and growing discontent."[19] At first the Radio Priest of Royal Oak supported Roosevelt's New Deal policies, but by 1936, his admiration of Roosevelt had turned to loathing and his criticisms of America's banks had become anti-Semitic tirades. To halt the spread of his extremist message, the Catholic hierarchy ended Father Coughlin's broadcasts in 1937. Meanwhile, members of the so-called Black Legion, who considered themselves "real Americans," established a network to "protect" Protestants and their business interests. By 1936, public uproar over the beatings and killings perpetrated by Legion members brought about the dissolution of the society.[20]

In general, the appeal of Michigan's hatemongers waned as Michigan's economy began to recover in 1935. That December, state residents read banner headlines touting the rush of consumer spending that marked the holiday season. This spending reflected a rise in employment and, with it, per capita income. As the recovery began to take hold, many of the state's working people organized, and labor struggles dominated the news in 1937 and 1938.

Throughout these years of turmoil, state residents took time to salute extraordinary achievements or bask in the glory of athletic feats. In 1927 reporters hailed the transatlantic flight of Charles Lindbergh, a Detroit native. In 1935 Detroit the Doomed became Detroit the Dynamic when the Tigers baseball team won the World Series and two other Detroit sports clubs—the Lions football team and the Red Wings hockey team—also emerged as champions. Three years later, Detroit heavyweight fighter Joe Louis knocked out Germany's Max Schmeling in a title bout. Louis, known as the Brown Bomber, was a hero to many in Michigan, particularly to other blacks. Schmeling, in contrast, was the darling of Adolph Hitler. As Schmeling hit the deck, many Michigan residents cheered this knock-out punch to a symbol of Hitler's so-called master race. When the United States later entered the war against Germany and Joe Louis, now a soldier, toured American troop camps in Europe, the far-flung realms of politics, sports, and race relations were joined.

During the war, Michigan's motorists struggled through the mandatory rationing of tires, gasoline, and rubber while Michigan homemakers cooked Food for Victory, using recipes with less sugar in their baking, and collected fat drippings from their holiday turkey dinners for explosives manufacturers. Michigan farmers boosted crop yields, and canneries expanded production, some making use of the labor of German and Italian prisoners of war stationed in the state. Men and, in increasing numbers, women from across the state and the nation poured into Michigan's hastily-built defense plants or into factories that had retooled for war work. At Willow Run alone, they produced over eighty-six hundred B-24 bombers in less than three years, and in Battle Creek, the home of breakfast foods, workers at the Kellogg Company turned out a stream of K rations to feed the troops. In August 1945, the war ended in the Pacific when the United States dropped the world's first atomic bombs on two Japanese cities; components for the bombs were made in Michigan. Tragically, for many the war had ended earlier, with their deaths on battlefields far from their home state. In all, more than six hundred thousand of the state's men and women served in the wartime armed services. Of the many who did so with distinction were two hundred black pilots from Michigan, part of a pioneering aerial unit known as the Tuskegee Airmen. Notably, one of the squadron's bombadier officers was Coleman A. Young, who would become Detroit's first black mayor.[21]

With the dramatic events of these years as a backdrop, unheralded shifts in population caused changes in patterns of social life. From 1920 to 1940 the state's population grew from 3.7 million to 5.3 million.

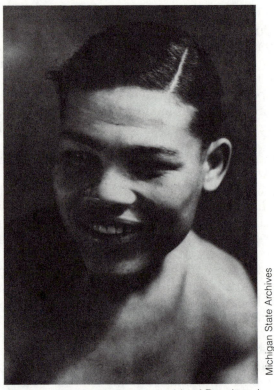

Michigan State Archives

Joe Louis, the 'Brown Bomber,' pride of Detroit and Michigan, was heavyweight boxing champion from 1937 to 1949.

Large cities, like Detroit, Grand Rapids, Flint, Pontiac, and Muskegon grew even larger with the war years, as did educational centers like Ann Arbor and East Lansing. Small settlements and towns on the fringe of larger cities, such as Huntington Woods (near Detroit) and Grand Blanc (near Flint) blossomed into suburbs. In contrast, both rural hamlets and small communities outside of metropolitan areas languished, as did larger settlements in remote regions of the state, such as Houghton and Hancock in the Upper Peninsula's Copper Country. The number of farms and of farm families declined in this period, and life for those who remained in agriculture changed substantially. Some farmers specialized, raising single crops like soybeans or keeping dairy cows; others mechanized, using tractors and automatic milking machines; and still others expanded, acquiring more land for production. Of equal consequence, farm families connected themselves to the urbanizing world beyond through radios, telephones, and automobiles.

Increasingly, children in rural Michigan rode buses to consolidated elementary and secondary schools. The establishment of these schools was one part of the overall expansion of the state's educational system in the interwar years. In the 1920s, and especially in the 1930s, the ranks of Michigan high school, college, and vocational students grew. The University of Michigan in Ann Arbor embarked on a major building program in these years, as did Michigan State College in East Lansing. Meanwhile, in Detroit the board of education combined several existing colleges in 1933, naming the resulting institution Wayne University the following year. Schools such as Ferris Institute in Big Rapids, a vocational center, became part of the state system, and Normal schools, such as Central Michigan in Mt. Pleasant, trained more teachers. Significantly, at the same time another school in Mt. Pleasant lost pupils. In 1934, the federal government, turning away from a policy of native American assimilation through education, sent home the students remaining at the Indian School.

The growth of private colleges paralleled the proliferation of public institutions; examples include Michigan Lutheran College in Detroit, founded in 1936, and Madonna College in Livonia, established ten years

Clarke Historical Library, Central Michigan University

United States Indian School at Mt. Pleasant, 1914.

later. Other sorts of educational institutions were also founded during this period, including the Kalamazoo Institute of Arts in 1924, the Interlochen music camp in 1927, the Cranbrook Academy of Art in 1928, Greenfield Village in 1929, and the Cranbrook Institute of Science in 1931.

Reflecting Michigan's shifting ethnic and racial composition during these years, the state's religious organizations changed as well. Most mainline Protestant denominations, like the Presbyterians, maintained their membership in these decades. In contrast, black churches grew dramatically, and Catholic churches of various rites also flourished. Many Catholic parishoners were immigrants who had settled in the state before the immigration restriction of the early 1920s or, increasingly as the years wore on, their children. The state's enclaves of Poles, Syrians, Lebanese, Bulgarians, Macedonians, Greeks, Belgians, Mexicans, French Canadians, and others worshipped at an array of parishes. Similarly, many of those belonging to Michigan's Jewish congregations were also immigrants or their descendants. Still other immigrants, from the Middle East, brought Islam to Michigan. Meanwhile, some southern white migrants transplanted fundamentalist Christian beliefs to the state. Many of these newcomers joined in the revival of old time religion which spread through Michigan in the 1920s, bringing hundreds of souls into the Nazarene, Assemblies of God, and Baptist churches.

Social organizations of all sorts also proliferated in the interwar years. Service clubs, like Kiwanis International, founded in Michigan in 1915, garnered new members. So did clubs for young people, including the Girl Scouts, which had over six hundred troops in Michigan in 1938. The state's Women's Clubs also grew during these decades, mobilizing women across Michigan for volunteer work. Between 1943 and 1945, for example, the state's thirty thousand clubwomen raised over $2.5 million in war bonds—enough money, they calculated, to build twenty-three airplanes.[22]

Popular culture also changed profoundly between the 1920s and the 1940s. New styles of dress, of music and dance, of dating, and of leisure altered social patterns in Michigan. In the 1920s many Michigan women, sporting short skirts and bobbed hair, took off with young men in cars to go dancing at nightspots like the Walled Lake Pavilion or the Vanity Ballroom in Detroit. Jazz clubs, like Detroit's Graystone, drew both blacks and whites to hear luminaries like Duke Ellington battle with local stars to play the hottest sound. Opera houses closed and repertoire groups shortened their tours, unable to compete with the allure of movies, while radios replaced the piano in many Michigan parlors. In cities and towns, men and women flocked to Y's—the Young Men's (or

Women's) Christian associations—or other newly-built facilities to play volleyball or squash. Some took up golf at one of the state's new public courses.

Others kept up the recreational activities associated with their own culture. Southern white workers in Lansing's Reo Motor Company in the 1920s, for instance, spent their Friday noon hours square dancing, with workers playing a dulcimer and fiddles and calling the sets.[23] The state's other ethnic residents similarly pursued their own pastimes in churches, social clubs, and homes. Blacks, segregated in leisure as in housing, established their own recreational facilities. The Detroit Urban League, for example, founded Camp Green Pastures in 1931, bringing hundreds of black youths annually to Little Pleasant Lake near Jackson for two-week vacations.[24]

Advances in transportation also changed leisure activities. Airplanes became more common after World War I, and Michigan's carnivals and fairs featured the daring of barnstorming pilots. Clem Sohn of Fowler became a sensation for his unique aerial act. As the Human Bat, he thrilled crowds by jumping from a plane, free falling, and then opening up his vespertilian parachute from only a thousand feet off the ground. His career ended tragically, however. While performing at the Paris Air Show in 1937, Sohn's parachutes failed to open, and he fell to his death.[25]

Few of Michigan's residents participated in such daring feats, but a great host of them took up the rage for the automobile. In the early 1920s, auto tourers spent an entire day covering only 150 miles, jolting along on dusty—or muddy—roads with few gasoline stations to be found. These conditions, however, did not quell enthusiasm for the auto. Michigan's love of the road wrought changes throughout the state, boosting tourism in the Upper Peninsula and along the shores of the Great Lakes. But, as the tourist motels and restaurants cropped up along roadsides, they put many old resorts out of business. Bridge construction had the same effect on ferry service.

Characteristically, some of the great achievements in architecture and engineering during these years demonstrate the state's close ties to the automobile. The Ambassador Bridge, constructed in 1929, and the Windsor Tunnel, completed the next year, symbolize this connection. So do several notable buildings of the era, including two designed by renowned architect Albert Kahn: Detroit's Fisher Building, the headquarters of the General Motors Corporation, and the massive Ford River Rouge auto factory in Dearborn. Moreover, one of the state's most famous art works, the "Man and Machine" mural painted in 1933 by Mexican artist Diego Rivera for the Detroit Institute of Arts, portrays the auto assembly process itself.

Founders Society of the Detroit Institute of Arts

Diego Rivera's mural *Detroit Industry* at the Detroit Institute of Arts. Printed in Dorothy McMeekin, *Diego Rivera* (East Lansing: Michigan State University Press, 1985), 15.

Significantly, Rivera's frescoes touched off a furor. Detractors condemned the work as antireligious, Communist, and simply bad art—a "travesty upon the City's life and good name"; admirers hailed the beauty of the frescoes and the "true humanity" they portrayed.[26] As this public outcry demonstrates, Michigan residents knew that Rivera's work said something important about their present and their past. Emblazoned on the walls of one of the state's premier cultural institutions, the murals proved a controversial testimonial to the people and forces that fashioned Michigan's history in the early twentieth century.

Changes in social and political life proceeded unevenly across Michigan's two peninsulas in the years between 1917 and 1945. Yet, many events of the era—war, prosperity, hard times, and war once more—and advances of the age, especially the automobile, brought Michigan's people closer together during these decades. The postwar years would bring new challenges to the state and afford further opportunities for Michigan and its residents to fashion a politics and society even more just, secure, and strong.

———————————◆———————————

NOTES

1. I would like to thank John J. Bukowczyk for his informed and incisive comments on drafts of this essay.

2. Governor Groesbeck's career is profiled in Frank B. Woodford, *Alex J. Groesbeck: Portrait of a Public Man* (Detroit: Wayne State University Press, 1962); on highway improvement, see especially 212–22.

3. On Murphy's early career and rise to political prominence, see Sidney Fine, *Frank Murphy: The Detroit Years* (Ann Arbor: The University of Michigan Press, 1975).

4. For a general account of Michigan's experience with Prohibition see Willis F. Dunbar, *Michigan: The Wolverine State* (Grand Rapids: William B. Eerdmans Publishing Company, 1965), 685–86. For an example of news coverage of gangland slayings see "3 KILLED BY GANG: 5 JAILED," *Detroit Free Press,* 17 September 1931, 1, on the Collingwood Avenue Massacre.

5. Bruce A. Rubenstein and Lawrence E. Ziewacz trace the mystery of the death of state senator Warren G. Hooper in *Three Bullets Sealed His Lips* (East Lansing: Michigan State University Press, 1987).

6. For a good account of the 'Red Scare,' particularly as it unfolded in Detroit, see Steve Babson, with Ron Alpern, Dave Elsila, and John Revitte, *Working Detroit: The Making of a Union Town* (1984; reprint ed., Detroit: Wayne State University Press, 1986), 38–40.

7. On the Ku Klux Klan consult Babson, et al., 44; and Ronald Edsforth, *Class Conflict and Cultural Consensus: The Making of a Mass Consumer Society in Flint, Michigan* (New Brunswick: Rutgers University Press, 1986), 108–10. After 1923, state law forbade Klan members from assembling in masks.

8. Carol P. Bonilla, "The Jewish Reaction to Henry Ford's Anti-Semitic Campaign and 1927 Apology" (Master's thesis, Wayne State University, 1985) explores this issue, including materials on Ford's connection with fascism in the 1930s.

9. The act was aimed at the nearly 250,000 aliens residing in Michigan. Opponents of the law feared that it would be used against any person regarded by state officials as appearing "alien." See Thomas A. Klug, "Labor Market Politics in Detroit: The Case of the 'Spolansky Act' of 1931," *Michigan Historical Review* 14 (Spring 1988): 1–32.

10. See Dennis Nodin Valdés, *El Pueblo Mexicano en Detroit y Michigan: A Social History* (Detroit: College of Education, Wayne State University, 1982), 27–40.

11. See Roger L. Rosentreter, "Roosevelt's Army: The Civilian Conservation Corps in Michigan," *Michigan History* 70 (May/June 1986): 14–23.

12. As quoted in John J. Bukowczyk, *And My Children Did Not Know Me: A History of the Polish-Americans* (Bloomington: Indiana University Press, 1987), 79.

13. Thaddeus C. Radzialowski traces the complex background of discrimination against Poles and of job and housing competition between Poles and blacks that fueled the controversy over the Sojourner Truth housing project. See Radzialowski, "Polish Americans of Detroit," in Frank Renkiewicz, ed., *The Polish Presence in Europe and America* (Toronto: Multicultural History Society of Ontario, 1982), 195–207.

14. Harriette Arnow's novel, *The Dollmaker* (1954; reprint ed., New York: Avon Books, 1972) offers a startlingly-vivid depiction of cultural prejudice in a setting modeled after Willow Run. For an account of the development of the Willow Run community that chronicles much of interest but which omits this important aspect, see Marion F. Wilson, *The Story of Willow Run* (Ann Arbor: The University of Michigan Press, 1956).

15. Robert Schweitzer and Michael Davis, "Aladdin's Magic Catalog," *Michigan History* 84 (January/February 1984): 24–33.

16. See Jay Hicks, "Houses by General Motors: The Flint Housing Crisis and GMC," *Michigan History* 71 (March/April 1987): 32–39.

17. William Haber, Eugene C. McKean, and Harold C. Taylor, *The Michigan Economy: Its Potentials and Its Problems* (Kalamazoo: The W. E. Upjohn Institute for Employment Research, 1959), 141.

18. See Dunbar, 517.

19. As quoted in Babson, et al., 56.

20. For a brief description of the Black Legion's activities, see Bruce A. Rubenstein and Lawrence Ziewacz, *Michigan: The Great Lakes State* (Arlington Heights, Ill.: The Forum Press, 1981), 212–13.

21. See William Phenix, "Eagles Unsung: The Tuskegee Airmen in World War II," *Michigan History* 71 (May/June 1987): 24–30.

22. See Michigan State Federation of Women's Clubs, *A History of the Michigan State Federation of Women's Clubs, 1895–1953* (Ann Arbor: Ann Arbor Press, 1953), 79, 152, 156.

23. Peter Iversen Berg, "Welfare Capitalism at the REO Motor Car Company," *Michigan History* 69 (November/December 1985): 44.

24. See Keri Bancroft, "Snapshots of Heaven: Michigan's Green Pastures Camp," *Michigan History* 69 (September/October 1985): 32–39.

25. Sohn is profiled in "Michigan's Batman," *Michigan History* 67 (September/October 1983): 24–25.

26. See the letters by Henry B. Sullivan, "Museum Leaders Given the Blame," and Milton M. Rose, " 'True Humanity' Traced in Colors," *Detroit Free Press*, 26 March 1933, pt. 1.

---◆---

SUGGESTED READINGS

Harriette Arnow's *The Dollmaker* (1954; reprint ed., New York: Avon Books, 1972) is a vivid and poignant novel of a Kentucky family's life after moving to Michigan in 1943. The novel movingly chronicles the daily existence of the family and their neighbors in the projects set up for war workers.

Charles Denby's autobiography, *Indignant Heart: A Black Worker's Journal* (Boston: South End Press, 1978), traces the author's migration from Alabama to Detroit, first in the 1920s and again in the 1940s, describing life in the auto shops, detailing the discrimination faced by blacks in housing and on the job, and providing a rare inside view of the 1943 race riot.

A fine contemporary account of many aspects of the state's history may be found in *Michigan: A Guide to the Wolverine State,* compiled by the Writer's Program of the Work Projects Administration in the State of Michigan. It was published as part of the American Guide Series and sponsored by the Michigan State Administrative Board (New York: Oxford University Press, 1941).

Another invaluable reference tool of the period is George N. Fuller, et al., eds., *Michigan: A Centennial History of the State and Its People,* 5 vols. (Chicago: The Lewis Publishing Company, 1939).

1917-1945

PHILIP A. KORTH

Educated in American Studies at the University of Minnesota, Dr. Philip Korth directs the Developmental Level Writing Program in the Department of American Thought and Language at Michigan State University. He has published in literary, sporting, and historical journals on topics such as fiction, political movements, business organizations, hunting and fishing, and labor organizations. His recent book, *I Remember Like Today: The Auto-Lite Strike of 1934,* an oral history, recaptures the importance and drama of that event.

oom, Bust & Bombs:

The Michigan Economy

Black Thursday, 24 October 1929, made instant economists of Michiganians who rarely thought about economic principles, and who trusted in conventional wisdom and sought their own pot of gold. Black Thursday forced reassessment of conventional economic wisdom about the role of the community in economic life. The transformation of attitude and action stands clear in the contrast between two demonstrations to demand direct relief and an end to unemployment. On 6 March 1930, such a demonstration in Detroit was dispersed by mounted police wielding clubs. Thirty-one demonstrators were arrested and scores injured.[1] Nine months later, on 24 October 1931, two thousand protesters marched from Grand Circus Park to the city hall where they selected a committee of twelve that conferred with Mayor Frank Murphy for two hours.[2]

The legacy of Black Thursday is with us today. A dramatic fall in the stock market nearly sixty years later, on 19 October 1987, raced through newspapers, radio, and television, repeatedly evoking the frightening memory of the collapse that started the Great Depression.

Philip A. Korth

The collapse of 1929 demonstrated that economics cannot and should not be isolated from social and political life; economics is part and parcel of life itself.

Writing at the beginning of World War II in *The Great Transformation: The Political and Economic Origins of Our Time*, Karl Polanyi asserted: "Nineteenth century civilization has collapsed." He defended that assertion through an economic analysis of political and social institutions of the nineteenth century, a century, he claimed, unlike any before.[3]

> Nineteenth century civilization alone was economic in a different and distinctive sense, for it chose to base itself on a motive only rarely acknowledged as valid in the history of human societies, and certainly never everyday life, namely, gain. The self-regulating market system was uniquely derived from this principle.[4]

Pursuit of self-interest that expresses itself in economic activity may be found in all human communities, Polanyi acknowledged; but in all human history, no civilization had elevated this pursuit to such an honored position. On the contrary, communities had regulated economic activity rather than allow economic activity to regulate itself and, therefore, to control life. Conflicts between self-regulation by the market and community regulation often erupted in the nineteenth century as the community attempted to regulate railroads and interstate commerce and to break up trusts. But the issue became fully joined when self-regulation resulted in the collapse of markets themselves in the 1930s. Michigan became both victim and agent of the resulting transformation.

FROM BOOM TO BUST TO INDUSTRIAL WAR

The central economic question in the decades between World War I and World War II was how to balance a system of private production for personal profit with the public good. World War I demonstrated the need for modest coordination of economic activity to help the country meet emergency demands for war goods. However, the young men from Michigan who marched off to give Kaiser Bill a lesson, like the men and women who remained at home, saw the war as a temporary emergency that would end when the world was made safe for democracy. "The validity of pre-war values was reaffirmed following the war by the rapid speed at which the war demobilization occurred. The temporary disturbance of the war served only to reinforce American commitment to traditional values."[5] Wartime successes validated coordination only as an emergency measure. Michigan shared in the economic stimulation that war production brought. Profits flowed from its contributions in materiel: in trucks, tanks, Liberty engines, guns, and boats—the implements of modern warfare. Michigan's response to wartime emergency drew upon its developing industrial system.

One measure of the "American commitment to traditional values," the 'Red Scare,'[6] followed closely on the heels of war. Federal officials sought, in Detroit and elsewhere, those individuals who questioned traditional economic assumptions, painted them with a red brush, declared them un-American, and harassed, jailed or deported them. The economically conservative 1920s tolerated little dissent from conventional economic wisdom, and committed itself to restoration of a market economy fueled by desire for gain.

The boom of the 1920s, the true "Me" generation, reached into the workshops and living rooms of Michigan as the flivver and flapper became the symbols of prosperity and freedom. Perhaps as a carry-over from the war, Michigan's agricultural production in 1920 eclipsed previous records, setting a mark that would not be reached again for decades. The state's economy continued on the road to industrial growth laid out before the war. Michigan would eventually lead American industrialization.

NORMALCY: PROFIT AND PERIL OF CAPITALISM

The years from World War I to 1929 in Michigan reveal the complexities of Pres. Warren Harding's "Normalcy." Some sectors of the economy grew dramatically (automobiles), some new industries emerged (oil), and some declined (farming). The 1920s brought benefits to many, but not all. The industrial boom in automobile production benefited southern Michigan from Detroit and Flint through Jackson and Lansing, and over to Muskegon. Assembly operations created a demand for parts and supplies, and thus a tier of secondary, small suppliers emerged across the state. By comparison, shipping, which had long contributed to Michigan's economy, responding to demand for ore, and tonnage passing through the waterways surrounding Michigan, rose and fell according to industrial needs. Farming, from its peak production in 1920, suffered continuous decline and depression. Thus, some Michigan communities read about a boom they could not find.

New industries struggled but made their way. Increasing need for oil products fueled drilling and refining, primarily around Saginaw, Muskegon, and Mt. Pleasant. By 1935 Michigan stood eighth among oil-producing states, extracting over fifteen million barrels a year.[7]

Radio station WWJ took to the airwaves on 31 August 1920.[8] Aircraft were built in Detroit, Dearborn, Wayne, Marysville and Northville. Farm tractors and light trucks, most notably Ransom Olds's Reo Speedwagon, improved production and shipment of foodstuffs essential to sustain the sprawl of cities into the countryside. Real estate business in Detroit was stimulated by immigrants and migrants from Michigan farms and the South, who were attracted to jobs in manufacturing. Czechs, Poles, Hungarians, and native black and white southerners filled the cities. Detroit's area grew from 82.55 square miles in 1917 to 140 square miles in 1930.[9] Fields that once produced crops were carved into home lots.

Transportation developments reflected the need for roads to carry Fords, Packards, Pierce-Arrows, Maxwells, and Hupmobiles. In 1919 Michiganians approved a fifty million dollar state bond, which, supplemented by federal and local funds, paid for grading and graveling Michigan roads.[10] Even a few miles of concrete highways replaced worn and rutted roads. Bridges of steel and concrete able to support heavier loads replaced wooden structures. Two engineering triumphs, the Ambassador Bridge and the Windsor Tunnel, linked Michigan's road system to Canada. Trucking companies organized to carry the diverse, new products rolling out of Michigan factories. The state was in the highway business to stay. The pace and distance of movement increased, as goods flowed from point of manufacture to points of distribution.

These developments boosted tourism, for the boom brought leisure, the money to indulge it, and the means to travel—at least for some. Snow trains carried skiers to Grayling, for example, and Idlewild, in west central Michigan, became a nationally famous resort area for blacks. Outdoor recreational opportunities expanded through establishment and growth of state parks, public fishing sites, and hunting lands—all coordinated by the new State Conservation Department formed in 1921.[11]

Bootlegging provided employment that was probably no more hazardous than some jobs in manufacturing, and it certainly paid better. On 1 May 1918, a year ahead of the nation, Michigan became dry, creating an opportunity for quick, though risky, gains. Rival bootleggers fought for profits. Opportunity beckoned from Canadian shores, just a short boat ride away, and improved trucking and roadways aided distribution across the state to Chicago and other inland destinations. Imports met only part of the demand; more liquor was produced in distilleries hidden in warehouses and outbuildings, which sometimes lent peculiar tastes and lethal qualities to the concoctions they produced.

Two economic activities in decline, copper mining and agriculture, had peaked in 1916 and 1920 respectively. Copper declined most dramatically, for production peaked during World War I and fell sharply afterwards. By "1929, only six companies were operating mines: Calumet and Hecla, Copper Range, Mohawk, Seneca, Isle Royale, and Quincy"[12] and these companies employed more machines and fewer workers. Population in Upper Peninsula mining areas plummeted. For example, Houghton County lost nearly twenty thousand people during the decade.

In 1921 agriculture began a long and steady decline that turned Michiganians away from the land to the cities. In 1916, about half of Michigan's residents lived in rural areas; by 1930, fewer than one-third lived there. The decline in the farm economy is reflected statistically in number of farms, farm acreage, and average farm size. From 1920 to 1930, the number of farms fell by 14 percent to one hundred seventy thousand, acreage fell by 10.5 percent to seventeen million, and average farm size increased by 30 percent to one hundred thirty acres.[13] The human anguish such statistics mask can be appreciated with a review of tax delinquency statistics. Not all tax-delinquent land was farmland; but much of it was, particularly in central Michigan. From 1917 to 1928, tax-delinquent acreage increased steadily from nearly five million to a little over nine million *per year*.[14] Michigan was a leader in industrial development during the 1920s, but it was also a "leader" in agricultural decline. "Michigan's agricultural employment declined more sharply than the nation's, -36.2 percent versus -23.9 percent . . ." from 1900 to 1940.[15] The 1920s boom reached much of Michigan but not copper and agriculture.

THE GREAT DEPRESSION:
LAISSEZ FAIRE VS. ECONOMIC COORDINATION

Few Michiganians proved immune to the Great Depression. The search for a cure, or at least for a treatment of its symptoms, emerged in a debate between private versus social production. Economic traditionalists, such as Gov. Wilbur M. Brucker, asserted that the economy would eventually right itself and that the community should not interfere with the market's self-regulation. Joblessness was largely a personal problem, he believed, and should not be solved through unemployment compensation laws or state welfare payments. Reformers sought to treat the illness through temporary solutions to ease the depression's impact on workers, the men and women whose labor was essential to economic life. Socialists asserted that the self-regulating market was a

Philip A. Korth

Henry Walter Armstrong; Michigan State Archives

Farm family in Manistee County during the Great Depression of the 1930s.

dangerous, destructive fiction that threatened to sacrifice the community on the altar of gain. To protect its members, they claimed, the community must intervene, regulate, manage, control—even own—the means of production.

HOOVER AND BRUCKER: TRADITIONALISM

During the first three years of the depression, traditionalists controlled Michigan. The 18 percent unemployment in 1931 grew to 43 percent in 1932 and to 46 percent in 1933. Still, the state refused to intervene. Governor Brucker, echoing President Hoover's fear that moral decay would certainly follow the dole, stolidly refused to use the power of the state to ease the depression's impact on Michigan citizens. Legislative proposals for direct relief, for unemployment insurance, and for aid to the elderly all faced his veto. Brucker became a booster for Michigan products, hoping that this positive approach would stimulate markets, help the economy adjust itself, and set things aright again. In contrast, James Couzens, Michigan's senior senator, tried to engage wealthy Michiganians in direct relief efforts, and encouraged President Hoover to intervene to help the needy.

Hoover instituted the Reconstruction Finance Corporation (RFC) to lend money to solvent banks, railroads, businesses, corporations, and municipalities to help them stabilize their circumstances. He also encouraged public works projects. In the spring of 1931, over $27 million of federal money was slated for Michigan to rebuild highways and post offices, and to dredge rivers.[16] Such efforts saved some businesses from collapse and helped some communities find work for their residents but reached only modest numbers of Michiganians.

ROOSEVELT AND MURPHY: REFORMERS

Hope rose with the new tone Franklin D. Roosevelt set in March 1933 when he became president of the United States. Roosevelt's willingness to revise traditional economic thinking, and to try new, direct approaches to solving economic dilemmas, engendered an enthusiasm that proved infectious and helped him counter despair. "All we have to fear, is fear itself," he asserted, and he promised a New Deal for all Americans.

Michigan found, in a World War I veteran and former Recorders Court judge, a man similarly willing to act, and to try direct solutions to immediate problems. Frank Murphy, who would become Michigan's governor in 1937, was elected mayor of Detroit in 1930, to fill out the term of Charles Bowles. Bowles had been recalled for a number of reasons, including his callous use of mounted police to disperse a demonstration by unemployed workers.[17] In sharp contrast to Governor Brucker, Murphy declared that "no one in this great city of plenty . . . must be allowed to go hungry, or cold, or unhoused, or unclothed."[18] He did not hesitate to use city resources to feed the hungry. He persuaded owners of idle factories to rent buildings to the city to house the homeless.

The task was complex and immense. In April 1931, in an attempt to reduce cost, cash relief in Detroit was changed to food orders; and the weekly allowance was cut from four dollars for man and wife and one dollar per child to one dollar per person. But the issue involved more than money, as the city welfare department's assistant superintendent John S. Ballenger noted.

> Italians will not be at all satisfied with rations which Poles, for instance, would consider splendid. Negroes would not eat what Greeks would buy nor would Greeks stand for a diet designed for native Americans.[19]

Since local resources could not sustain this effort, the state had to provide relief; in 1932, the state spent more than $30 million.[20] Even the state was forced to apply for loans to the RFC; by May 1933, Michigan had received $21 million.[21]

While Governor Brucker reluctantly entered into relief operations, Murphy, in Detroit, struck a bold, new tone. Relief was "the duty of the state. . . not a matter of charity, and [should be provided] not paternally, but as a matter of right."[22] He clearly articulated what would become the underlying principle of the New Deal. However, these efforts ran up a debt in Detroit that forced state support. Since economic traditionalists controlled the state, that help came slowly, reluctantly, as a loan of $1.8 million, which was only enough to cover Detroit's February 1931 relief costs. In 1933, when Roosevelt assumed office, and Democrat William A. Comstock became governor, things began to change.

The New Deal, as Roosevelt's program came to be known, had a dramatic impact on Michigan. The Federal Emergency Relief Act, passed days after Roosevelt's inauguration, quickly pumped money into Michigan. Within the first year, the State Emergency Welfare Commission, created to administer the relief effort, spent $43 million to help the 640,000 Michiganians on relief.[23] In addition, "the Civilian Works Administration [CWA] employed 170,000 Michigan workers during the same period."[24]

During the depression, the federal government became one of the most important economic forces in Michigan. In direct relief alone, the figures are staggering.

> In Detroit (Wayne County), nearly $65 million was spent for public relief during the period from April 1933 to December 1935 . . . 80 percent was spent by the federal government, 10 percent by the state, and 9 percent supplied by the city and county.[25]

In addition, the federal government employed Michigan citizens directly, funded construction projects that employed Michiganians, coordinated efforts to manage the economy, and provided direct relief to the hungry and homeless throughout the state.

Michigan State Archives

Depression spawned relief line in Detroit.

Young, able-bodied men of Michigan, eventually black and native American as well as white, found work and hope through one of the earliest programs of the New Deal. Authorized within the first month of the Roosevelt administration, the Civilian Conservation Corps (CCC) offered food, shelter, and work to dispirited young men wandering unemployed across the land.

The idea for a conservation corps had been introduced the year before in Roosevelt's acceptance speech. Using the United States Army to organize the effort had been proposed by Michigan senator James Couzens even before Roosevelt took office. The CCC mobilized with dramatic swiftness. By mid-June 1933 over thirteen hundred camps had been established nationwide, and in two months, three hundred thousand young men had enrolled.[26] Michigan welcomed the CCC, set up its first camp within five weeks after Roosevelt signed the act, and, during the corps's decade of existence, maintained an average of over fifty camps per year across the state.[27] "CCC boys" planted millions of seedlings, built fire lanes, and fought forest fires. They constructed parks, picnic areas, shelters, fish hatcheries, and reconstructed streams into which they released millions of fry.[28] Two precious resources benefited from this activity: the natural environment and the community's youth—its hope for the future. Over one hundred thousand young Michigan men participated in the program, eighth largest in the nation.

Relief efforts reached across the state. The western Upper Peninsula felt the depression keenly. Iron ore and copper production fell sharply and, consequently, "in 1934 more than a third of the families in Houghton County were on relief, and in Keweenaw County, nearly two thirds."[29] Relief efforts saved many from starvation and despair, but ultimately, these areas could find no way to protect themselves from economic erosion, and population fell sharply.

Early in the depression, banking encountered difficulty, for economic values had been disrupted and public confidence shaken. Branch banks had spread across the state during the 1920s. Centralization, though efficient, also set the stage for an imperiled system, for single bank failures had broad consequences. During the first three years of the depression, over two hundred Michigan banks failed.[30] In Detroit, only six remained; and two, the Guardian Union Company and the Detroit Bankers' Company, were in such deep trouble by February 1933 that their collapse appeared certain. Attempts to secure additional loans from the RFC proved futile, for the RFC tied its approval to commitments by General Motors, Chrysler, and other large depositors to lend the Guardian Union Company money. Despite a direct appeal from President Hoover, Henry Ford refused to support the Guardian Union Company, and, thus, collapse seemed assured.[31] Governor Comstock, only a month in office, recognized at an emergency meeting in Detroit on 12 February that the collapse of the two largest banks in Michigan would create havoc throughout the state. On 14 February, he closed the banks, declaring a bank holiday until 23 February; three weeks later, President Roosevelt declared a national bank holiday. Governor Comstock's decision on Michigan banking saved the state's financial system; Roosevelt's similar decision for the country saved banking from complete disintegration.

Attempts at direct self-defense through organization, so dramatically successful among industrial workers during the depression, occurred in farming as well. Even before the great labor organizing drives of 1936–37, farmers turned to each other for help. Their method, simple and direct, focused on the immediate problem of foreclosure. With little money coming in from crops, farmers found themselves unable to pay taxes or to make mortgage payments. As a result, counties, banks, and other lenders sought court orders to recover their money through sale of farms, often including household belongings as well as farm implements. The sheriff usually conducted the sale. Local farmers gathered on the day of the sale and let it be known that anyone who made competitive bids might be in for a rough time. There is no record of anyone being lynched for doing so, but there are records of farmers' bids.

> In late January [1933] . . . near Howard City in Montcalm County, . . . they offered only a few cents for each item. A grand piano was sold for four cents, a hay loader for eleven. The total proceeds of the sale were $2.40, and the purchasers returned the items to the owner.[32]

Demonstrations occurred at Stanton and Manistee. "In Gratiot County irate farmers . . . bid $3.85 for the property and compelled the receiver to deliver the mortgage . . . ."[33] Doubtlessly, these demonstrations influenced the legislative process, particularly when farmers joined nationally into the Farm Holiday Association. In Michigan the general property tax was replaced by a sales tax. Nationally, in an attempt to bring economic stability to farming, the New Deal enacted programs to support farm prices and regulate planting.

A common reminder of federal programs in Michigan are the forests and wing dams along Michigan's many trout streams. But certainly the most pervasive reminder is three letters stamped into concrete on auditoriums, schools, armories, hospitals, sidewalks, and bridges: WPA. From 1935 to 1942 the Works Progress Administration (WPA) was charged with hiring all employable persons who were without work. In Michigan it met the challenge by hiring two hundred thousand workers at its peak and by spending over $500 million, three-fourths of which came from the federal government.[34]

Depression posed massive challenges to Michigan. The state's commitment to industrial leadership not only generated growth and prosperity but also made it most vulnerable to decreased industrial production. Workers attracted to industrial jobs depended on wages alone. Any stoppage of wages created an immediate crisis, for the industrial worker had no alternative means of support. Michiganians struggled to find ways to establish stability in a system subject to wild swings between optimism and despair and to create a community strong enough to endure vacillations in economic activity. The Great Depression demonstrated the need for and the effectiveness of federal intervention. Through direct assistance such as relief, public work programs such as the CCC, the CWA, and the WPA, and through sensitivity to the needs of ordinary people, the federal government, in partnership with the state, set in place institutions and principles to revitalize social, political, and economic life in Michigan. However, events beyond both the state and the national government brought full recovery, and placed Michigan at the center of another conflict in which it earned its title as the Arsenal of Democracy.

WORLD WAR II:
COMMUNITY CONTROL OF ECONOMIC LIFE

After 1935, when Italy attacked Ethiopia, the forces of fascism marched with chilling certainty across Europe. War was clearly their preferred tool. Awareness of this development in the United States emerged more quickly in some Americans than in others. From the ranks of labor organizers in Detroit and elsewhere came volunteers to fight on behalf of Republican Spain, at a time when national policy officially stood neutral. By 1939, when Nazi Germany invaded Poland, the movement for "preparedness" had mildly stimulated the state's economy, but support for allies did not mean willingness to enter the war on their behalf.

> By early 1940, Michigan's press, principal ethnic groups, and major labor federations had adopted a pro-Allied position, but all remained resolutely noninterventionist. Before the Japanese attack, no influential figure or groups in the state actively advocated American participation in the war.[35]

The war in Europe created a demand for American industrial output, but it was a demand with an uncertain future. How long would the war last, and who would be its victor? Was it really worthwhile to change one's productive capacity to new products tied to war, particularly when the war was being fought thousands of miles away? Did not the course of wisdom lie in continuing normal production, shifting only a portion of capacity to meet new, perhaps transitory, war demands?

During 1940 and 1941, Michigan industry, including auto assembly companies, vacillated in their response to these questions. To encourage the manufacture of war goods, the federal government agreed to build huge new factories which were turned over to the auto companies' private management. For example, the Warren tank arsenal, begun in September 1940 and operated by Chrysler Corporation, built medium tanks. Other assembly companies began to convert some productive capacity to war goods. Packard built Rolls Royce engines, and Continental Motors, Murray Corporation, and Briggs began to build aircraft subassemblies.[36]

By far the most spectacular development in this early stage of war production was the creation and operation by Ford Motor Company of the Willow Run plant designed to construct the B-24 "Liberator" bomber. Plant construction began in April 1941. In 1942 the first Liberators rolled off the mile-long assembly line. By June 1945 the last

Michigan State Archives

World War II draftees arriving at Michigan Central Station in Detroit, 29 November 1940.

B-24—the 8,685th Liberator—had been built by a work force that had at its peak exceeded forty thousand.[37] The story of Willow Run's massive achievement serves well as a symbol of modern industrial warfare, for the industrial might of Michigan supplied allied and American troops with equipment and armaments that achieved victory on the battlefield and in the sky.

The war expanded the role of the federal government in Michigan's economic life. The coordination of industrial might by federal agencies had been prepared by the depression's economic developments. Many have argued, persuasively, that the war ended the depression in Michigan. No one doubts that the increase in industrial activity stimulated by war production created a boom in which profits and wages suddenly rose. The influx of workers, largely from the South, drawn by steady work and high union wages, reflected the reinvigoration of life in Michigan's urban centers.

Statistics attest to Michigan's decisive role in the winning of the production war. With 4 percent of the nation's population, the state obtained better than 10 percent, or $21,754,000,000 of the nearly two hundred billion dollars in major prime war supply and facility contracts awarded by the United States government and foreign purchasers from June, 1940, to September, 1945. . . . No American city, in any event, carried out more war work than Detroit did. . . . In addition, Genesee and Ingham Counties each received more than one billion dollars in war orders, and nine other counties secured at least one hundred million dollars in armament contracts.[38]

In the Upper Peninsula, mining picked up, and war contracts—gliders were built in Iron Mountain—stimulated local economies. Sault Ste. Marie immediately felt the war with the ore to make weapons passing through the locks. Soldiers set up defensive emplacements around the locks and patrolled against sabotage as barrage balloons and antiaircraft guns guarded against attack from the skies.

To coordinate this massive effort, Michigan contributed William S. Knudsen, president of General Motors, whom Roosevelt appointed as one of two directors-general of the Office of Production Management (OPM) in 1940. His challenge could be simply stated: how could the economy be best managed to produce the goods and services necessary to support our allies' war efforts and to achieve military victory?

Auto plants converted to war production during World War II, earning Michigan the title Arsenal of Democracy. This Reo plant in Lansing produced army trucks.

Michigan State Archives

Stating the problem did not make the solution clear. It was clear, however, that to accomplish that task the federal government would interject itself in the economy of the nation, especially Michigan. Through myriad agencies, the most important of which were the Office of Production Management (OPM), the Office of Price Administration (OPA), the War Labor Board (WLB), the War Manpower Commission (WMC), and the War Production Board (WPB), the federal government coordinated Michigan's economic life. It set prices, allocated scarce resources, assigned manpower, let and administered contracts for goods and services, regulated working conditions and wages, and thereby managed the American economy as it had never been managed before.

The wartime emergency, like the depression emergency before, justified this broad intervention. It must be noted, however, that in both cases the community exercised its right to regulate economic life, even to achieve goals that were not themselves economic. For example, the WPA supported painters and writers who interpreted Michigan in murals and travel booklets, as well as architects who designed libraries and auditoriums. The CCC advanced conservation in stream and forest. By the end of World War II, the nation and the people of Michigan had so accepted this intervention that it lost some of its controversial aura.

During the depression, direct relief and work relief helped people meet immediate needs for food, shelter, and clothing. Economic security programs like Social Security and unemployment insurance tried to prevent the need for that relief. Regulation of commerce and banking helped stabilize an economic system prone to boom and bust. The war extended this principle of intervention and made economic health the business of the community.

◆

NOTES

1. Sidney Fine, *Frank Murphy: The Detroit Years* (Ann Arbor: The University of Michigan Press, 1975), 205.

2. Ibid., 400.

3. Karl Polanyi, *The Great Transformation: The Political and Economic Origins of Our Time* (Boston: Beacon Press), 30.

4. Ibid.

5. Bruce A. Hardy, "American Privatism and the Urban Fiscal Crisis of the Interwar Years: a Financial Study of the Cities of New York, Chicago, Philadelphia, Detroit, and Boston, 1915–1945" (Ph.D. diss., Wayne State University, 1977), 4.

6. At the end of World War I, United States Attorney General A. Mitchell Palmer initiated a national search for "subversives" who, he believed, threatened the nation. Members of the Communist party, labor organizers, politically left activists, and war critics—particularly recent immigrants—were rounded up en masse, detained, interrogated, and even deported without careful review by the judicial system. Historians generally characterize these raids as an hysterical reaction to dissent.

7. F. Clever Bald, *Michigan in Four Centuries* (New York: Harper and Brothers, Publishers, 1954), 390.

8. Ibid., 388.

9. Ibid.

10. Willis F. Dunbar, *Michigan: A History of the Wolverine State* (Grand Rapids: William B. Eerdmans Publishing Company, 1965), 566.

11. Ibid., 680.

12. Ibid., 388.

13. Bureau of Business and Economic Research, *Michigan Economic Charts* (East Lansing: Graduate School of Business Administration, Michigan State University, 1962), 7, 41.

14. *Michigan History* (January/February 1983): 38.

15. *Michigan's Economic Past Basis for Prosperity*, Technical Report Number 10A (Lansing: State Resource Planning Program, Michigan Department of Commerce, March 1967), 4.

16. *Detroit Free Press*, 2 April 1931, 1.

17. John Kern, *A Short History of Michigan* (Lansing: Michigan History Division, Department of State, 1977), 52.

18. Fine, 258.

19. *Detroit Free Press*, 8 April 1931, 2.

20. Bald, 405.

21. Ibid.

22. Fine, 257.

23. Bald, 415.

24. Ibid.

25. Hardy, 439.

26. Samuel Eliot Morrison, *Oxford History of the American People* (New York: Oxford University Press, 1965), 955.

27. Roger L. Rosentreter, "Roosevelt's Tree Army: The Civilian Conservation Corps in Michigan," *Michigan History* (May/June 1986): 22.

28. Bald, 414.

29. Ibid., 420.

30. Ibid., 407.

31. Bruce A. Rubenstein and Lawrence E. Ziewacz, *Michigan, A History of the Great Lakes State* (St. Louis, Mo.: Forum Press, 1981), 209.

32. Bald, 411.

33. Ibid.

34. Ibid., 417.

35. Alan Clive, *State of War: Michigan in World War II* (Ann Arbor: The University of Michigan Press, 1979), 15.

36. Ibid., 20.

37. Ibid., 219.

38. Ibid., 34.

◆

SUGGESTED READINGS

Bald, F. Clever. *Michigan in Four Centuries.* New York: Harper and Brothers, Publishers, 1954.

Clive, Alan. *State of War: Michigan in World War II.* Ann Arbor: The University of Michigan Press, 1979.

Dunbar, Willis Frederick. *Michigan: A History of the Wolverine State.* Grand Rapids: William B. Eerdmans Publishing Company, 1965.

Fine, Sidney. *Frank Murphy: the Detroit Years.* Ann Arbor: University of Michigan Press, 1975.

Hardy, Bruce A. "American Privatism and the Urban Fiscal Crisis of the Interwar Years: a Financial Study of the Cities of New York, Chicago, Philadelphia, Detroit, and Boston, 1915–1945." Ph.D. diss., Wayne State University, 1977.

Kern, John. *A Short History of Michigan.* Lansing: Michigan History Division, Department of State, 1977.

McLaughlin, Doris B. "Putting Michigan Back to Work: Bill Haber Remembers the 1930s." *Michigan History* (January/February 1982).

————. "Our Readers Remember. . . ." *Michigan History* (January/February 1982).

Rosentreter, Roger L. "Roosevelt's Tree Army: The Civilian Conservation Corps in Michigan." *Michigan History* (May/June 1986).

Rubenstein, Bruce A., and Lawrence E. Ziewacz. *Michigan, A History of the Great Lakes State.* St. Louis, Mo.: Forum Press, 1981.

1837-1945

JEREMY W. KILAR

A professor of history at Delta College, Jeremy Kilar teaches Michigan and business history. His major research interests are social and economic history with special emphasis on Michigan's lumbering and entrepreneurial experiences. He has contributed articles to several journals including the *Journal of Forest History* and *Michigan History*. Professor Kilar's book about Michigan's lumbertowns will soon be published. He received his bachelor's degree from the University of Detroit and a doctorate degree from The University of Michigan.

rom Forest & Field to Factory:

Michigan Workers and the Labor Movement

The lumber barons of Muskegon who gathered around the green felt tables in the card room of the exclusive Occidental Hotel in the spring of 1882 should have been looking forward to another profitable year. It had been four years since the Panic of 1873–78; and five years since the bloodshed and coast-to-coast rioting of the great railroad strike of 1877. In those intervening years the lumbermen had revolutionized the lumber business. Muskegon had changed from a stump-strewn, frontier logging town into a mechanized, industrial city in the wilderness. Logging railroads stretched into the hinterlands and brought timber to riverbanks and rollways. Modern steam engines powered new and speedier circular, band, and gang saws. Muskegon and many other logging towns in Michigan had entered the industrial age.

Despite four years of prosperity, however, the sawmill owners gathered at the Occidental could not disguise their apprehensions; the new year began ominously. Strikes, lower profits, and fears that the nation was soon to slide into another murky period of depression and labor unrest dampened their enthusiasm. Before the spring cutting season began, Muskegon would be shut down by sawmill workers demanding ten hours or no saw logs. Events in Muskegon and in other lumber towns throughout the state reflected the changing economic conditions that affected industrial societies nationwide in the last quarter of the nineteenth century. Capitalists everywhere made repeated attempts to bring order and stability to a work force adapting to the new industrialization. Industrial hardships, declining wages and bitter conflicts reinforced a belief among workers that now they were indeed a separate and exploited class. There arose a call for solidarity. Michigan no longer seemed to be the land of opportunity for new agricultural settlers and industrial workers.

The lumber barons themselves remembered a bygone era when opportunities to make money were found everywhere in the new state. Michigan was the West, the place where hard work and individual striving often reaped reward. During the decade after statehood, 1837–47, thousands of New Englanders and immigrants from Ireland and Germany managed to clear land and plant farms from the Saginaw Valley to the southern tier of counties. A good number of these settlers arrived with only the bare essentials, although some prosperous migrants came better equipped.

Life on the farm was difficult for the early laborer. Clearing the land was the most demanding task. Trees were "girdled," felled, and burned—a destructive process that appalled no one but later generations. Timber was perceived, as furs had been, as an inexhaustible resource. Once the crops were sown, women and children were recruited to keep a vigilant watch against blackbirds, squirrels, and deer who might devour new crops. Long days and hard work took a heavy toll. Dampness, cold, mosquitoes, and primitive sanitation facilities that spread contagious diseases debilitated many pioneers. Life on the farm seldom brought instant reward, and many farm families eventually moved to the city. Some farmed around Detroit or other cities where produce often brought better prices, but many other immigrants and migrants moved permanently and established workshops or stores in the rapidly burgeoning communities.

By midcentury Michigan's ample supply of lumber, copper, and iron ore began to feed fledgling industries in and around Detroit. Early factories were small affairs and seldom used more than thirty workers. The largest employer in midcentury Detroit, the Michigan Central Railroad, employed two hundred men.[1] Most hands were skilled and semiskilled laborers who often effected a leisurely work pace. Although they might work ten- or twelve-hour days, breaks were frequent and camaraderie within the work place often resembled that of an extended family. When employee organizations formed, such as the Detroit Typographical Society in 1839, they were largely social welfare societies pledged to further the intellectual, moral, and physical conditions of their members.

Periodically, though, minor disputes arose. The Detroit carpenters banded together to protest wage cuts brought on by the recession of 1837. As industrialization progressed and technology improved, master workmen were gradually replaced by an ever-increasing work force of common, unskilled laborers. Other labor disputes occurred among Detroit's printers, tailors, and carpenters. These quarrels grew more intense by the Civil War period, and workers began to organize into trade unions. Pledged to protect jobs as well as to seek self-improvement, these unions gradually began demanding improved working conditions, better wages, and shorter hours.

By the end of the Civil War, railroad connections east and west had created a national market for Michigan manufacturers. New technology and machinery accelerated the pace of industrialization, and small shops merged or gave way to the large-scale factory, sawmill, or metal foundry. In the late 1870s, forty-five factories in Detroit had one hundred or more employees. The Pullman Palace Car Company had seven hundred; Detroit Stove Works six hundred; and Pingree's Shoe Company had five hundred workers. In the state's northern interior, lumbering created industrial sawmill towns. John McGraw's sawmill operation in Bay City covered six hundred acres, employed over three hundred fifty men, and, in 1877, was considered to be the largest sawmill in the world.[2]

Throughout all of this, the number of skilled artisans dwindled, and the craftsman often became just another factory hand. The displaced or seasonal farmhand and the European immigrant likewise became mere parts of their machines, doing the same repetitive task eleven or twelve hours a day. Wages remained low: unskilled laborers in Detroit averaged only $1.33 a day in the 1880s; sawmill workers in the Saginaw Valley averaged $1.56 a day in 1882. In addition to meager incomes, a wide range of work was seasonal. Railroad construction, sawmills, and the building trades closed during the winter months. Layoffs were frequent, and workers were often fired for tardiness, absenteeism, or drunkenness. Even in the best of times, the workingman could seldom foresee much of a future. In Wayne County in 1884, only 6 percent of male workers responding to a survey found it possible to open a savings account.[3]

The leisurely work pace of earlier times also disappeared. Machinery not only replaced craftsmen but intensified and regimented the work

Jeremy W. Kilar

Michigan State Archives

Thayer Lumber Company's Anderson Camp at Grass Lake, Kalkaska County, 1906.

routine. Men were now driven by supervisors who often bragged about new production records. "Sawmill men are part of their machines," noted a Bay City attorney in 1885. "They could not even stop for a drink of water but must keep up the labor just as the inanimate machinery. The men are a cog in a vast machine."[4] Shipbuilders' ears rang incessantly from the noise of pounding rivets resounding within a ship's hull. Deafness was often their only escape. Carpenters in barrel, box, or furniture plants came out of the factory coughing and spitting quantities of oak or black walnut dust. Sawmill workers fed flesh and bone to the steel blades that often ran twenty-four hours a day. Around Saginaw, Muskegon, Manistee, or Menominee, a millman was easily recognized by his missing or grotesquely misshapen fingers and hands. There was seldom any accident insurance or compensation to provide for the injured or their families. A few employers sometimes made gifts of money or provisions; but, in most cases, the maimed and debilitated were considered responsible for causing their own injuries through carelessness or intemperate living.

Women and children did not escape the adversities of the work place. Foreign-born women and children entered the work force in large numbers in order to pool family resources to purchase a home. Native-born

240

children worked almost as frequently as the sons and daughters of recent arrivals. Paying a woman eighty-two cents a day or a child fifty cents a day cut labor costs in half.[5] In 1884 the State Bureau of Labor and Industry surveyed child labor in Michigan and found children often working from sunrise to sundown. Young girls labored in brickyards, and match, tobacco, knitting, and sewing factories. Beginning at twelve years of age, boys could be found in almost every heavy industry. Fewer than half the children over twelve attended school. Not surprisingly, despite the fervent belief in the "American Dream," wage earners who avoided education and worked long hours seldom moved up to become better than their fathers. Only one of every ten laborers who stayed in Detroit advanced into a professional or business occupation.

Still, times were good for many wage earners who could maintain their jobs and health. Working conditions in Michigan were better than in Europe and in many mining or steel towns back east. Moreover, the rapid population growth of several Michigan cities did not produce the densely-packed, four-story tenements that were built in large eastern cities. Cheap and available land enabled cities like Detroit, Saginaw, Cheboygan, Calumet, and Grand Rapids to build neighborhoods that expanded outward rather than upward. Wage earners in Michigan cities lived in small two-bedroom frame houses, often built by themselves or by neighborhood carpenters. Living rooms and porches faced the streets. Neighborhoods were created by the workers; they wanted to watch and communicate with each other. Workers and their children walked to work or school, and there were few geographic barriers to neighborliness. Even if the wage earner's home was built cheaply and covered with inexpensive paint, it was still kept neat and clean. Eventually, workers could envision paying off their mortgages or freeing themselves from rent. Owning a home was the one most achievable and conspicuous step up the ladder of success.

Prosperity meant a great deal more than home ownership to the self-made industrialist who profited by the labor of the wage earner. The "new rich" often developed strong social-Darwinist beliefs that their success not only signified Christian virtue but was a reward for hard work and persistence. As successful businessmen, they felt little compassion for those "lesser" mortals who could not climb to the top. Many of the wealthy frequently showed contempt for those immigrants and unskilled laborers they ruthlessly exploited in their factories. Labor unions and the collectivism they represented was seen as un-American. The poor, the workers, should "shift for themselves, like all Americans."

Reformers once again became active in trying to alter the wage system during the Panic of 1873. Economic stagnation and the end of western railroad building threw the nation into a severe depression. Indebted farmers became involved in the Patrons of Husbandry (the Grange), a national organization that sought regulation of railroad rates and the establishment of farm cooperatives. Farmers and industrial workers also supported the Greenbackers after 1876. Advocates of currency reform, the Greenback party argued that, until the laborer and the farmer had access to low-interest credit, they could never expect to be debt-free or to become independent producers or manufacturers.

By 1877, the fourth year of depression, unemployment worsened, sales plummeted, and workdays were lengthened; the national mood was explosive. In the summer of 1877, workers in dozens of states demonstrated and declared a general railroad strike. Business and government panicked, and local authorities called upon the police and state militia to shoot protesting workers. The bitter and violent conflicts of 1877 confirmed the belief among laborers in Michigan that workingmen had to organize and use force, if necessary, to receive their fair share.

The strikes of 1877 stirred people into action. Laborers realized that they needed a nationwide organization to represent and coordinate their demands. The Knights of Labor became the first representative national organization of workers—men and women—in America. Established in Philadelphia in 1869, the Knights grew rapidly after the depression years under the leadership of its Grand Master Workman, Terence V. Powderly.

In 1881, the Knights held their annual convention in Detroit. Two of the most tireless leaders representing the Knights in Michigan were Richard Trevellick and Joseph Labadie. Trevellick, a British-born carpenter, settled in Detroit in 1862 and immediately began organizing skilled hands. He had been instrumental in founding the National Labor Union in 1866 and the Greenback party in 1878, and had stumped the state for shorter workdays and currency reform. A dynamic speaker, Trevellick spurred the union movement away from welfarism toward the vigorous political involvement that the Knights espoused.

Like Trevellick, Joseph Labadie was an outspoken supporter of economic reform and political action. A native of Paw Paw and a rather large, jovial character, Labadie, a descendant of a Potawatomi leader, was often affectionately called the "Big Injun." He had organized the first assembly of the Knights in Detroit in 1878 and was the society's leading state organizer. Similar to the Knights, Labadie at first accepted the new industrial order. In time, however, he developed a distrust of capitalism and often spoke against free enterprise. He may well have been the pioneer socialist in Michigan and was an active organizer for the Socialist Labor party. The Knights, though, remained a good steppingstone toward Labadie's goal of worker reform, and throughout the era, he participated diligently in the union's organizational activities.

Through the efforts of Labadie and Trevellick, the Knights grew rapidly during the prosperous years of the early 1880s. In 1882, there were a number of local assemblies in Detroit, followed by Bay City, Grand Rapids, Saginaw, Muskegon, and several other communities. By 1886 there were thirteen thousand members in Detroit and twenty-five thousand statewide, representing perhaps as many as 10 percent of the state's nonagricultural work force.[6]

The Knights had important converts outside of Detroit as well. In 1881, two young Muskegon attorneys, Francis W. Cook and Nelson DeLong, breathed life into an embryonic labor movement among that city's sawmill workers. When Muskegon lumbermen refused a demand for ten-hour workdays, Cook and DeLong, with the aid of Trevellick, organized the millworkers into the state's first Workingman's party. DeLong became mayor of Muskegon in 1882, and Cook became the first Workingman's state representative. In the spring of 1882, DeLong and Cook rekindled the previous year's strike. Although they won few concessions from the powerful lumber barons, their political success confirmed labor's commitment to political action as a means to redress grievances.

By 1885 there were eighteen Knights-Workingmen in the state legislature. The Knights were responsible for the creation of a state bureau of labor in 1883 and some child labor legislation and safety laws. Cook and Thomas Barry of Saginaw spearheaded the state's first ten-hour law through the legislature in 1885. Still, much of the Knight's legislative success was short-lived. Labor legislation, like the ten-hour law, often had escape clauses where individual contracts between employer and employee could void the law's provisions.

The 1885 ten-hour law is often seen as one of the factors that prompted sawmill workers in the Saginaw Valley to undertake what has often been described as the most significant strike in nineteenth-century Michigan. The so-called Great Strike in the Valley began in the spring of 1886 when a number of the seven thousand sawmill hands demanded a reduction in working hours from eleven or twelve hours to ten. A drop in the price of lumber that spring had prompted lumbermen to cut the average wage from $1.98 to $1.77 per day. While the mill workers accepted the new pay rate, they demanded a ten-hour workday in June, prior to the September implementation date of the new hour law.[7]

When the lumbermen in Bay City, many of whom were absentee owners, refused to consider shorter hours, laborers left the work place on
6 July and roamed the city closing down all the sawmills. After shutting
down Bay City, the millmen went by barge upriver to nearby Saginaw.
They marched through the streets carrying placards demanding "Ten
Hours or No Sawdust." Thomas Barry became the spokesman for the
strikers and tried to restrain their sometimes violent attempts to close
Saginaw's sawmills. By the evening of 10 July, all mills in the Saginaw
Valley were shut down.

The Knights of Labor mustered in support of the strike. In Bay City
especially, reaction against the large number of intransigent, absentee
mill owners encouraged newspapers and businessmen to back the
Knight's local assemblies. However, in Saginaw, where there were more
resident lumbermen, labor could never secure widespread community
support or overcome the paternalistic political power of the wealthy mill
owners. Moreover, skilled sawmill workers in Saginaw resented the
invasion by Bay City's millhands and were lukewarm in their support of
the Knight's actions.

Minor skirmishes offered a rationale for the lumberman-mayor of
Saginaw to request the services of the Pinkerton Detective Agency.
Often seen as hired thugs and strikebreakers, the Pinkertons' presence
further alienated the workers. Soon, Gov. Russell Alger, a wealthy lumberman, appeared in Saginaw and Bay City. Alger, also an investor in a
Saginaw sawmill, perceived the strike as the responsibility of a few
labor agitators. He ordered Barry and other leaders arrested and
immediately brought in several companies of the state militia to protect
the sawmills.

Following the governor's actions, events in the Saginaw Valley settled
into a relative calm. Owners remained firm in their unwillingness to
negotiate a settlement. Powderly, who often opposed strikes, came to
the valley and encouraged the workers to return to work. Skilled hands
in Saginaw gradually returned to work in late August. Transient
employees were hired, and by early September many of the Saginaw
mills were running eleven hours a day. When Bay City lumbermen
began to ship their logs to Saginaw to be cut, resistance weakened.
Sawmill laborers needed some income prior to the shutting down of the
mills in the fall. Gradually, they too returned to work in Bay City at old
hours and wages.

Strikers could not overcome the power of the lumber barons. Any
really effective labor action in the milltowns would inevitably have
resulted in many mills simply being closed for good. The lumbermen
could easily pack their machinery and move westward. There were too

many logs, too many mills, too many machines, and too many available workers. At the end of the century, despite significant organizational and political success, workers still could not change established patterns of industrial capitalism.

By 1900 the white pine era had passed and the lumber barons moved on to greener forests. They left behind cut-over and scorched forest land that railroad companies, local boosters, and the state of Michigan tried vigorously to sell as rich agricultural homesteads. Thousands of displaced sawmill workers and immigrants bought cheap lands and tried to eke out a living on what was actually marginal sandy soil. When they did not prosper, local railroad and town boosters often blamed their failure on laziness or bad habits. Poor soil, unreasonable credit rates, and high retail prices in northern counties brought many a cut-over farmer to his knees by 1920. Thousands of abandoned homesteads symbolized the heartbreak of those settlers who believed the promoters.

Displaced loggers and farmers often migrated northward in the years before World War I. There was plenty of work to be found in the copper and iron ranges of Michigan's Upper Peninsula. Immigrants—Finns, Slavs, French-Canadians, Poles, and Italians—many barely able to speak English, also arrived in the Keweenaw Peninsula in the early years of the twentieth century. The Copper Country had developed an image of an industrious and rewarding environment, one in which the copper bosses provided comfortable and affordable housing, libraries, gymnasiums, and free medical care. Wages, while not as good as those earned in Montana's copper mines, were about $2.36 a day in 1909, reasonable by contemporary standards. Also, work in the copper mines was relatively safe; the Michigan mines were not the mankillers that eastern coalmines had become.[8]

However, fatal accidents occurred often enough—about forty a year between 1885 and 1920—that no one could become indifferent to the dangers. In 1912, after several years of declining wages, extra-long workdays, and the introduction of the dangerous one-man drill, the militant Western Federation of Miners (WFM) organized many of the unskilled laborers. In July 1913 union locals in the town of Calumet struck the large Calumet and Hecla Mining Company after the owners refused to respond to a WFM petition. The closing of the mines provoked some initial violence, and the entire state militia was sent northward by Gov. Woodbridge Ferris. In August, the companies sought to break the union and the strike by importing replacement (scab) labor and reopening some mines. Two striking miners were killed by private police in August; three strikebreakers were shot in December. The

245

Jeremy W. Kilar

Bentley Historical Library, Michigan Historical Collections, University of Michigan

Miners underground in the Champion Mine at Painsdale. Printed in O. F. Tyler, *Tyler's Souvenir of the Copper Country: Upper Peninsula of Michigan,* 2d ed. (Grand Rapids: James Bayne Co., 1904?).

shootings made any reasonable settlement with the union impossible. In another attempt to reopen the mines and ease tensions, the mine owners granted an eight-hour workday and raised wages.

Outside of the most militant, workers accepted the changes, and order was restored for the moment. However, late in the afternoon of 24 December, the union held a Christmas party for striking miners and their families on the second floor of the old Italian Hall in downtown Calumet. Just before the party of seven hundred broke up, someone at the front of the hall yelled, "Fire!" Children and adults stampeded down the narrow stairwell. In the panic several tripped and fell, and others piled on the fallen bodies. The mass of entangled legs and arms took over an hour to remove—seventy-two people, mostly children, suffocated; there had been no fire. Woody Guthrie's immortal labor ballad blamed the "copper boss thugs" for crying out "Fire!"—however, authorities were unable to determine responsibility.[9]

The tragedy cast gloom and depression over the Copper Country. While union resistance was briefly renewed, the WFM could not continue paying benefits to striking miners. On 12 April 1914 the remaining strikers voted to go back to work. Laborers abandoned the union and returned to the mines. Unionism would not come to the Copper Country for another twenty-five years. Other disillusioned workers left the region and drifted southward during World War I to find jobs in the rapidly expanding war industries and new automobile factories of Flint and Detroit.

Like the European immigrants and migrants arriving from the South, miners and displaced Michigan farmhands were drawn to Detroit by reports of jobs and high wages in the auto industry. Newcomers often filled the lowest-paid, least-skilled jobs in the industrial cities. The Michigan Federation of Labor had been founded by Labadie

Michigan Technological University Archives and Copper Country Historical Collections, Michigan Technological University

Striking miners demonstrate on the streets of Calumet in 1913. The worker in the center is reading a copy of *Tyomies,* the local Finnish language newspaper, while a miner in back holds a placard with a picture of James MacNaughton, general manager of the Calumet and Hecla Company.

in 1889 and later became a state affiliate of the American Federation of Labor (AFL). The federation replaced the old Knights of Labor and, for a time in the first decade of the twentieth century, effectively organized skilled hands in the auto and other industries. However, the federation shunned workers who offered muscle power but few skills. Despised because they were often immigrants, blacks, or women, these workers rarely managed to form labor unions. They had little job security and no control over the work place. Rapid industrial growth and new technology, coupled with aggressive anti-union practices by early Detroit industrialists, also weakened labor organizations. Consequently, in 1911, less than 9 percent of Detroit's work force was unionized.

It was also during these early years of the auto industry and World War I that the quest for efficiency by owners and managers transformed the state's industrial landscape. Industrial capitalists constantly sought ways to reduce the skilled work force while spurring production and cutting labor costs. Frederick Taylor, the nation's leading architect of so-called scientific management, believed worker productivity could be increased by simply eliminating skill and brainwork. If the job could be simplified into a series of repetitive tasks, skilled workers could be replaced by almost anyone and productivity vastly increased. The shop floor was redesigned, work rules rewritten, and craft unions weakened.

Henry Ford was an important convert to Taylorism. His massive new assembly plant in Highland Park employed 14,000 largely unskilled workers. Ford standardized parts and inaugurated the auto industry's first moving assembly line. His Highland Park plant vastly increased production and cut costs. Unfortunately, workers were so driven during their nine-hour workday that few wanted to work at the plant for long. In 1913, in order to keep a full 14,000-man work force, Ford had to hire 52,000 workers during the year.[10] Despite these turnover rates, efficiency compelled the entire industry to adopt Ford's methods. By 1920, 150,000 workers toiled among the repetitive monotony of the "Motor City's" machines. Workers experienced mental and physical collapse, and often there were debilitating injuries. In 1916, at the Highland Park plant alone, there were 192 amputated fingers and over 76,000 other major and minor injuries.[11]

There was also little in the way of steady employment. Plants shut down for six weeks in late summer for retooling, and there was no guarantee of getting one's job back. Disabled or out-of-work auto workers had little compensation; most relied on the beneficence of family and aid societies to tide them over frequent hard times.

Unions never played a major role in the auto industry until the New Deal years of the 1930s. Wages were somewhat higher in the auto industry, and in the 1920s manufacturers added such benefits as death insurance, medical facilities, and social and educational clubs to dissuade unionization. Labor spies increased, and strong-arm tactics and blacklists enabled the industry to become a nationwide example of open shop industrialization. The AFL made a half-hearted attempt to organize Detroit workers in 1926, but skilled craft unions within the AFL feared the addition of common laborers. Timid union leadership, wary of conflict, remained reluctant to challenge the industrial order.

The depression brought the dark winter that had been encroaching for years upon the auto workers. After 1929 people stopped buying cars, and by 1932 thousands of auto employees had lost their jobs. Unions formed to protect jobs and wages. A strike by tool and die makers in Flint, Pontiac, and Detroit resulted in union recognition in a few small shops. In 1936, when the newly-organized Congress of Industrial Organizations (CIO) began to enlist auto workers under its affiliate union the United Auto Workers (UAW), thousands of workers swarmed into union halls. Unemployed and employed alike supported the new militant union; overnight, Detroit, Flint, and other motor cities became union towns.

Emboldened by federal New Deal legislation that recognized the right of workers to bargain collectively, the UAW quickly set out to organize the nation's largest automobile firm—General Motors (GM). After a series of minor disputes and sit-down strikes in other states, GM officials, in December 1936, refused to meet with UAW representatives. Tensions were high, especially in Flint where speed-ups on the line and longer hours embittered workers. On 30 December, after GM cancelled a meeting with union officials and rumors spread that dies were being moved to plants outside of Flint, the local union spontaneously called for a sit-down strike. The sit-down was much more effective than a walkout, because it prevented GM from moving in scab replacements and held expensive machinery hostage. Although it was not the first sit-down strike, the Flint protest was important because it set a pattern for other successful sit-down strikes and led to eventual recognition of the UAW as the sole bargaining agent for GM workers.

The UAW not only wanted recognition but also demanded amnesty for strike leaders, shorter hours, better wages, and an end to speed-ups. GM refused to bargain until the workers abandoned the plant. On 2 January 1937, GM secured an injunction from a sympathetic judge ordering the strikers evicted.[12] The workers remained defiant, and GM shut off heat and water to one plant. On 11 January, the mayor of Flint ordered the police to remove the strikers. The workers fought back, throwing bolts, door hinges, and ice water. The police retreated, and victory for the strikers in the so-called Battle of the Running Bulls marked a turning point for the labor movement in Michigan. The UAW's struggle gathered nationwide support.

Gov. Frank Murphy, a recently-elected Democrat, sympathized with the strikers. He ordered the National Guard to Flint but instructed them to remain neutral and not attempt to evict the strikers. In the meantime Governor Murphy pushed the two sides toward negotiations. Just as it appeared a compromise was possible, GM vice president William Knudsen broke ranks and attempted to strike a bargain with a rival, company-sponsored workers' alliance. The UAW, through a shrewdly conceived ruse, now occupied the Chevrolet engine plant, a key unit in the entire GM complex. As negotiations stalled, Governor Murphy considered forcefully evacuating the plants. Finally, on 11 February, a truce was signed. GM agreed to a national contract with the UAW and recognized the union as sole bargaining agent for workers in its eighty-two plants.[13]

The UAW and workers everywhere won major victories in 1937. Following the Flint sit-down, strikes occurred throughout the state's industries. In the spring of 1937, six thousand lumberjacks in the Upper Peninsula engaged in a sixteen-week strike that enabled industrial unionism to make inroads into the north country's lumber business. Chrysler and Hudson motor workers sat down in their plants, and simultaneous sit-downs hit Detroit's ironworks, packing plants, drugstores, groceries, and clothing stores. Governor Murphy again stepped in and effected a negotiated settlement at Chrysler. Unionism accelerated throughout the state, and many workers looked successfully to the UAW and CIO for help and guidance in their efforts to secure recognition.

Henry Ford held out much longer against the union onslaught. Ford used hired spies and thugs to ferret out union men at his giant River Rouge complex. When, in May 1937, Walter Reuther led a UAW force to Rouge to distribute union literature, he and his associates were met by Ford thugs who beat the union men mercilessly at the famous Battle of the Overpass. Photographers captured the violence on film, and the entire nation witnessed Ford's "negotiating policies." Although the courts ordered Ford to refrain from prohibiting union activity, he continued to fire union supporters. Finally, in 1941, the UAW struck the Rouge plant. When Gov. Murray Van Wagoner refused to order the National Guard to break the strike, Ford capitulated. After an election was held and 70 percent of Ford's employees voted for the UAW, Henry Ford met with union leaders and signed a generous, far-reaching contract.

The UAW and the closed shop became entrenched in Michigan, but labor agitation continued into World War II. Wartime labor shortages

Archives of Labor History and Urban Affairs, Wayne State University

Flint Sit-Down Strike outside Fisher Body plant number one during 1937.

strengthened workers' positions and encouraged them to demand wage increases and better working conditions. However, new workers from the South and rural Michigan, including thousands of women, were unfamiliar with unions and initially did not appreciate what the unions had recently accomplished.

Women hired during the war especially found unions indifferent and insensitive. The employment of women in Detroit jumped from 41,000 to 260,000 in the first three years of the war.[14] Wages remained about two-thirds those of men, and industries often treated women as temporary employees with few rights. Wartime work, nevertheless, prompted recognition that women could indeed do "men's work" and accelerated the movement toward job and pay equality.

Government, because of military demands, also was less sympathetic to union activities during the war. In 1944, however, there were hundreds of short, sporadic shutdowns over wages, supervisors, and disciplinary firings. The war created a climate in which union leadership was at times hard pressed to maintain the balance between wartime patriotism and the membership's militant demands.

A century after the state's workers first organized, Michigan had become the nation's union flagship. In many ways, Michigan was a social laboratory in which the laborer worked to develop an environment where American workers could enjoy the rights and privileges that were often only bestowed on a wealthy few. Lumbermen, copper bosses, and giant corporations had unintentionally spurred unionization through intransigence and attitudes that repeatedly exploited the working classes. Auto workers and other laborers finally took a stand that truly effected change. Michigan became a union state. When critics impugn the labor movement and argue that unions are obsolete, they exhibit a historical amnesia that ignores the exploitative patterns of earlier generations and continuing labor/management conflict. The labor movement shaped the state's destiny, guaranteed for many a respectable standard of living, and put value into workers' lives.

◆

NOTES

1. Steve Babson, *Working Detroit: The Making of a Union Town* (New York: Adama Books, 1984), 3.

2. Olivier Zunz, *The Changing Face of Inequality: Urbanization, Industrial Development, and Immigrants in Detroit, 1880–1920* (Chicago: University of Chicago Press, 1982), 17–18; and Rolland H. Maybee, *Michigan's White Pine Era, 1840–1900* (Lansing: Michigan Historical Commission, 1960), 50.

3. Babson, 7.

4. *Detroit Labor Leaf,* 22 July 1885.

5. Zunz, 233–35; and Babson, 8.

6. Doris B. McLaughlin, *Michigan Labor: A Brief History from 1818 to the Present* (Ann Arbor: Institute of Labor and Industrial Relations, The University of Michigan-Wayne State University, 1970), 23; and Babson, 11.

7. *Michigan Bureau of Labor and Industrial Statistics, Third Annual Report* (Lansing: Thorp & Godfrey, 1886), 103, 125.

8. Larry D. Lankton, "Died in the Mines," *Michigan History* 65 (November/December 1983): 34.

9. For the most thorough and recent evaluation of the Christmas tragedy, see Arthur W. Thurner, *Rebels on the Range: The Michigan Copper Miners' Strike of 1913–1914* (Lake Linden, Mich.: John H. Forster Press, 1984), 138–207.

10. Babson, 31.

11. Ibid., 31–32.

12. Judge Edward S. Black of the Circuit Court, who issued the injunction, owned 3,665 shares of GM stock worth approximately $219,000. See Thomas A. Karman, "The Flint Sit-Down Strike, I," *Michigan History* 46 (June 1962): 103–4.

13. The UAW "leaked" a plan that workers would occupy and engage in a sit-down in Chevrolet Plant Number Nine. When the Flint and private police went to protect that plant from a small decoy force of workers, five hundred union men took Plant Number Four, the key engine plant. See Karman, "The Flint Sit-Down Strike, II" *Michigan History* 46 (September 1962): 231–33.

14. Babson, 120.

◆

SUGGESTED READINGS

Babson, Steve. *Working Detroit: The Making of a Union Town*. New York: Adama Books, 1984. A compilation of photographs and text, Babson's narrative is a keen analysis of disparate data that makes it an indispensable resource for Detroit's labor history.

Fine, Sidney. *Sit-Down: The General Motors Strike of 1936–1937*. Ann Arbor: The University of Michigan Press, 1970. Fine's book is the best account of the sit-down strike in Flint and its effects on the state's labor movement.

Kilar, Jeremy W. *The Lumbertowns: A Social-Economic History of Michigan's Lumber Communities, Saginaw, Bay City, and Muskegon, 1870–1905*. Detroit: Wayne State University Press, 1989. An examination of town growth, the role of the entrepreneur, and labor-capital conflict during Michigan's white pine era.

McLaughlin, Doris B. *Michigan Labor: A Brief History from 1818 to the Present*. Ann Arbor: Institute of Labor and Industrial Relations, The University of Michigan-Wayne State University, 1970. McLaughlin's short monograph is an excellent introduction to major labor-capital conflicts and union political involvement within the state.

Thurner, Arthur W. *Rebels on the Range: The Michigan Copper Miners' Strike of 1913–1914*. Lake Linden, Mich.: John H. Forster Press, 1984. Thurner's monograph is the first full-scale study of labor conflict and copper mining history on Michigan's Upper Peninsula copper ranges.

H

Since 1945

JEFFREY D. KLEIMAN

Currently professor of history at the University of Wisconsin-Marshfield Center, Jeffrey Kleiman previously taught at Michigan State University and Ferris State University. The writer of numerous articles and papers on economic and labor history, he is also the author of *Restoring Urban Democracy: Response to the Progressive Urban Legacy*. Professor Kleiman received his bachelor's degree from Lindenwood College, his master's degree from the University of Cincinnati, and a doctorate degree from Michigan State University.

ard Times —
Good Times:
The Michigan Economy

Michigan has a remarkably diverse economy. Too often we think of Michigan's fate as tied exclusively to the fortunes of the auto industry. Yet, it would be misleading and unnecessarily worrisome for us to focus on that aspect of our recent past. Michigan—and Detroit—is more than automobiles.

Noting the high trends in unemployment, especially among highly paid union workers, we assume things today are in a way they have not been before. We assume that somehow, somewhere, there was a Golden Age of continuously employed, well-paid, prosperous workers.

By taking a longer view of our immediate past, even though barely a generation ago, we can appreciate what has happened and where we now stand. Consider for a moment the fact that Michigan has never had a low unemployment rate compared to the national average. Even during the "Nifty Fifties," our state maintained a significantly higher rate of unemployment; only briefly from 1966 to 1968 did we experience a period of prosperity and unemployment levels below the national average. We need to look at the twenty years before and after that short span to gain a better sense of our state's economic history in the years since 1945 (Table 1). What we see is a transition no less uncertain and shaky as that when Michiganians moved off the farms and into the factories a century ago.

World War II saved Detroit. Beyond mere recovery, beyond a sustained revival, the war brought Detroit—and Michigan—back from the economic grave. Factories, machinery, and large pools of skilled workers remained idle, but still available, until "Hitler's War of Vengeance" stirred our state back to life. Billions of dollars were pumped into the economy for the war effort, transforming Michigan into the "Arsenal of Democracy."

From Michigan's contribution to the war effort flowed the shape of Michigan's future in the postwar world. The reemergence of heavy industry slowed diversity, keeping the state's economy yoked to its most dynamic region—the area around Detroit. Change and experimentation were left to the more marginal areas. It would not be until the first oil crisis of the mid-seventies, and then the sustained challenge of high-technology computer-oriented developments, that the basic pattern established in the wake of peace would change.

The demands of World War II worked with the materials and capabilities that were already in Michigan. Tanks, planes, and personnel

TABLE 1

Unemployment Rates for the United States and Michigan (Selected Years)

Year	Michigan	United States
1956	6.9	4.1
1958	13.7	6.8
1960	6.7	5.5
1965	3.9	4.5
1970	6.7	4.9
1975	12.5	8.5
1977	8.2	7.0
1980	12.3	7.6
1982	15.5	9.7
1985	9.9	7.2

Source: David I. Verway, ed. *Michigan Statistical Abstract 1986–1987*. Detroit: Wayne State University, 1987, 99.

carriers remained variations on old themes in the Motor City. With pistons harnessed to pull a load, did it matter all that much whether the load was flying over Berlin, carrying soldiers to the front, or driving an automobile down the road?

If the draft took millions of able-bodied men off the streets and unemployment lines, the attendant job opportunities brought hundreds of thousands of others to Michigan in search of work, including thousands of women. Chances for high-paying jobs moved entire communities from the South, as tens of thousands of people, black and white, came to Michigan. Wayne County alone increased its population by nearly 20 percent, while neighboring Oakland and Macomb counties nearly doubled.[1] This new pool of labor found itself ready to keep working in a postwar celebration. Americans were ready to celebrate, not merely with the victory over dangerous enemies, but also with continued prosperity.

Consider for a moment what the world must have looked like in 1945 to a person who had grown up around 1919. For almost ten years, until 1929, there had been good times. Leaving school to take any of the abundant factory work, a young man could have started a family, made the down payment on a small frame house, and purchased a car and some furniture on time payments—confident in the future.

Then disaster—the economic crash and depression of the 1930s reduced hours, wages, and the existence of jobs. For another ten years there was nothing but struggle and hardship; even with additional jobs from wartime production in 1942, there was little to buy. Wartime meant rationing: gasoline, tires, butter, meat, and clothes. In a little over twenty-five years there had been prosperity, hardship, and a return to work; but then there was no way to spend the money. What could they do with all that overtime pay except bank it? Suddenly, with the war's end, people found themselves with savings.

In Michigan, the return to peacetime did not disturb the flow of prosperity. Thousands of additional workers drawn from returning soldiers meant less overtime but no less work, because Americans had saved during the war years. Now, they could release years of pent-up demand. Nearly fifteen years had passed since most Americans could afford a new car, a home, or furnishings! Four years had gone by since the last new model had been introduced in the auto showrooms. When the United States had geared up for war, all nonessential items had disappeared from the stores and factory assembly lines.

The exuberance of war's end combined with new money and jobs enabled Michigan and the nation to begin again where they had left off in 1929. For the first time in nearly a decade, people had enough confidence in the future to have children, to pursue the "American Dream" with hope for advancement, and not merely get by and make do. Families, homes, and the promise of a better life beckoned to Americans.

Yet, this return to earlier patterns after 1945 did not spread around the state. In fact, separate paths were taken in the postwar world with important consequences—although no one could have imagined it then. Michigan split into two economies.

The first economy was in the eastern part of the state—the revival of life in the industrial corridor from Detroit northward to Pontiac, Flint, Saginaw, and Bay City. Old and new forges, assembly lines, and tool and die works appeared among farmers' fields. Here was the mainspring of wage-earning work most Americans had remembered before the depression. From Toledo to Saginaw Bay, heavy industry—best exemplified by the auto industry—dominated the landscape.

In the western and northern Lower Peninsula and Upper Peninsula less-industrial activities germinated. The significance of these developments would not be determined for another twenty years. In fact, during these years the outstate economy led the state's fledgling service sector—competing with, supplementing, but always overshadowed by the more robust industrial landscape. Tourism, retail and wholesale outlets, banking, and insurance emerged slowly as the principal staple of that service economy. The scale was much smaller, the rate of growth slower, and the wages and available work force unable to capture the popular interest.

THE GENEROUS YEARS, 1948–1968

America reigned as undisputed economic giant during the years 1948–68. Despite several periods of a faltering economy at home, it was a sputter but not a stall. Citizens were angry when unemployment climbed to 4 percent in 1955–56.[2] However, inflation was not a major concern. Several things occurred to make the American industrial economy robust, and with it, the Michigan economy one of the healthiest.

Both at home and abroad, there seemed an endless demand for American manufactured goods. These in turn created a highly skilled and highly paid work force that sent its good fortune on down the line as they bought on credit and dealt with other skilled, unionized workers (such as electricians, plumbers, and carpenters).

One reason for Michigan wage earners' good fortune, in comparison with other factory-oriented economies, stemmed from unionization of the work force and the nature of the available industries. These capital-intensive industries, such as auto manufacturing, which were located in the Midwest before the war, especially benefited during and after the war from the continued demand for manufactured goods. By 1950, the Great Lakes region had one of the highest percentages in the nation of work force engaged in the capital- to labor-intensive industries, and certainly the highest number of workers in these industries.[3] This meant that Michigan contained proportionately a great many well-paid industrial workers, a far greater percentage than the region or nation.

This wealth stemmed in part from the nature of factory work. It also meant that the growth of this area of the economy was tied to the continued growth of the same sort of factory work. The trickle of dollars to others who provided goods and services depended on a disproportionate number of wage earners in this sort of industry. From 1947 to 1954, this was reflected in a rate of wage increases above the national average.[4] Thus, when the system was upset after the period from 1973 to 1977, the distress in Michigan was proportionately greater than in the rest of the nation.

As population and homes spilled out of the city into the suburbs, roads ribboned out. States were encouraged by the passage of the Federal Highway Act of 1956 to link cities with each other, sending suburbs sprawling along the way.

Indeed, Michigan was a leader in the new programs to pave state-owned roadways, not only adding miles of good highway, but also thousands of jobs. Tying the state together with tar and cement took a number of years—even before the massive undertaking of completing the interstate system—with impressive results. We forget how rural most of Michigan was and how bad the roads; by 1950, there were still more than twelve hundred miles of unpaved state roads.[5] Yet, in slightly more than a dozen years, there were no unpaved state roads.

Along with the expansion of the state highway system, Michigan could look at the industrial corridor that sprang up along Interstate 75 as a symbol of the state's vitality. The rate of growth in Wayne, Oakland, Macomb, and Saginaw counties was astounding—in many cases, more than doubling every five years![6] Soon, the automobile took on a life of its own, shaping our habits. Fast food outlets, malls, and motels all created new fields of opportunity for franchising and jobs.

In all this, too, we need to remember that American prosperity was fueled by exports and the lack of world competition. We were helping to rebuild war-torn Europe with cash, credits, and loans from the Marshall Plan of 1948. Michigan shipped crates full of tractors and machinery across the ocean. The same thing can be said for the reconstruction of Japan. America sold at home and abroad in the fifties and early sixties because we were virtually unchallenged.

Yet, fueling this period, quite literally, was the availability of cheap imported oil. Until the postwar period, the United States had been an oil-exporting nation. (Negotiations with Japan on the eve of Pearl Harbor dealt with renewal of oil and scrap iron shipments.) In our ambitious postwar industrial march and rebuilding of the world, we consumed gallon after gallon of oil; wasteful and exuberant, we plowed along the highway, heated homes, lubricated machinery, and experimented with the new wonder material of the age—plastics.

Michigan agriculture, both as product and way of life, reflected these national trends. After 1945, the number and size of farms combined to give us fewer, but larger, farms as consolidation increased average acreage from 104 at the war's end to 144 acres in the mid-sixties.[7] At the same time, fewer children remained on the farm. The lure of city wages and living combined with higher productivity and uncertain markets to reduce the number of farmers in Michigan. Nearly one in twelve Michiganians farmed for a livelihood in 1945; twenty years later, the number had dropped to less than one in twenty. While the number of farms and farmers has continued to drop, until in the late 1980s less than 3 percent of Michiganians farm for a living, the first twenty years after the war witnessed the most dramatic plunge.[8]

Much of this farmland has been lost to increasing population and to the demands for development around the major cities. From 1945 onward, the residents in southeast Michigan increased fourfold.[9] Farm lands were eliminated to make way for roads, parking lots, homes, shopping malls, offices, factories, service stations, and the eventual ribbon of fast food franchises. The greatest losses occurred in areas with the most people. The process continues today as cities like Grand Rapids, Lansing, and Ann Arbor follow the supply and demand of the marketplace by filling out their existing municipal boundaries and annexing other parcels.

During this period, with the decline of mining, the economy in the Upper Peninsula was forced to rely more heavily on nonindustrial and service-centered jobs. Though operating with a robust thirty-six mines during World War II and for a few years afterward, the decline came quickly and relentlessly. By 1977, only six mines kept alive the rugged spirit of mine life. This stress on the state's economy was multiplied by the hardship experienced by thousands of downstate residents caught in the throes of the industrial shake-ups caused during the oil crisis of 1973 to 1977.[10]

THE LIMITS OF EXPANSION:
YEARS OF CRISIS, 1967–1982

The benefits of economic expansion and unchallenged growth were passing. It became obvious that not everyone had gained access to the expanding economy. This economic deprivation helped to spark the riots in Detroit and across Michigan in 1967.

Benefits of the vigorous—but fitful—industrial expansion were not shared equally among Michigan's citizens. Blacks had felt the brunt of hard times, and failed to gain a proportional share of the good times after 1945. Immediately following the war, black unemployment tended to be double that for whites, both in Michigan and across the nation.[11]

Angry at the growing gap between rich and poor and at the increasing connection between poverty and race, blacks struck out at policies that alienated them from the movement to the suburbs, and left them behind—concentrated in the cities, where fewer citizens meant a smaller tax base. In turn, this segregation meant worse city services and accelerated the flight to the suburbs, keeping the whole cycle alive.

This physical destruction of the city was accelerated by highway construction projects that brought new eight-lane roads into and around the cities. Businesses and homes were torn down to make way for the highways. Increased dependence on the automobile, combined with reduced population density in the cities, also meant less public transportation. This led to an increased demand for parking lots, which, in turn, meant more taxable land taken off the rolls. The cycle could not keep going indefinitely; and the riots in Detroit, Grand Rapids, Kalamazoo, Battle Creek, and Jackson during the years 1967 to 1969 were but one of the most visible signs that something had to change.

These violent eruptions, however, served as a prelude to the real economic crisis. In the years immediately following the long, hot summers, the supremacy of the American dollar was broken.

The first great shocks fell in the early 1970s. Americans had made the dollar the measure of all currency after World War II with the Bretton Woods Agreement. The dollar's great strength had made it possible for investment and expansion during the next two decades. Yet, American appetite for all sorts of items from Europe and Japan created a growing trade deficit.

This flood of goods coming into the country and the growing trade imbalance, however, was only a prelude to the greatest shock of all—the oil embargo of 1973. The cartel, or trust, of Oil Producing and Exporting Countries (OPEC) decided to cooperate in order to enforce production quotas, thereby raising the price of their commodity—oil—at the

Jeffrey D. Kleiman

Ford Expressway under construction in Detroit during August 1951 dramatically illustrates how highway construction displaced residential neighborhoods.

Michigan Department of Transportation

wellhead. Increasing shipping and refinement costs also added to the rising price of oil.

The effect of the oil embargo came as a bombshell. At first suspending all shipments of crude oil in a protest of America's Israeli alliance and sympathies, then curbing production as part of a hardheaded use of monopoly power, OPEC member countries drove up the cost of crude petroleum by more than five times in the next two years.

What did this mean in practical consequences? Imagine, on one day, paying twenty-five cents for a gallon of gasoline for a car, whose tank capacity of twenty-one gallons would take you about eleven miles to the gallon. The next morning the cost of gas was thirty-five cents a gallon, a month later fifty-five cents a gallon, until by the end of a year you now paid seventy-five cents a gallon for gasoline.

Americans felt this immediately. One result was a demand for smaller, lighter, and more fuel-efficient automobiles. Other nations had built such

262

cars for years in order to negotiate narrow streets and long lines at government-regulated gas stations. American automakers, however, had continued to produce large, gas-guzzling, but more profitable models. Suddenly, American luxury needed to be traded for efficiency.

A second shock came as Americans decided to hold onto their old clunkers another year or two as prices increased for the cars manufactured at home, and as demand for foreign autos cranked up their prices as well. As a result, during 1973–77, there was a significant increase in the number of older cars on the road, and nearly a 20 percent decline in cars less than a year old on the road. Such a figure could only bode ill for auto-industry-based Michigan.[12]

A third shock came to all consumers doing their everyday shopping, since so many goods were moved by truck. Prices increased along with the cost of diesel truck fuel. Production costs also jumped, even if the processes involved remained the same. The cost of canning peas went up with the escalating price of electricity, most likely generated from a petroleum-driven power plant. And what of the people working the line and driving the trucks? How were they supposed to keep pace with the cost of living?

Soon, the high rate of unionization among industrial, governmental, and other workers which led to successful demands for wage increases, plus the desire of business to maximize profits, created a game of pass-along. Added costs for doing business, increased salaries, and rising profits were passed along to the consumer. What emerged was a series of Cost of Living Adjustment (COLA) wars, where everyone who could do so bargained for an increased COLA. Private workers and public employees pushed for higher wages in order to keep pace with the cost of living brought about by the oil price increase. Even welfare recipients and unemployed workers received slight increases from the government, adding to the upward cost spiral. But this artificial prosperity could not continue. It collapsed under the strain of inflation in the years after 1976.

More dollars had been sent into the economy to purchase no more than the usual volume of goods. Michiganians were not necessarily buying any more gasoline, radios, tires, or peas, but they were spending more for these items. Dollars became worth less and less, promoting inflation. As profits shrank at home, businessmen looked elsewhere to increase profits. The competitive edge gained by foreign producers increased, and industries closed at home. Investors turned elsewhere to get a more solid return for their investment. The late seventies saw a rash of plant closings and overseas relocations. Weaknesses in the industrial sector became breakdowns.

Jeffrey D. Kleiman

THE MATURING ECONOMY:
A TALE OF TWO CITIES AND MORE

A look at two Michigan cities can help us appreciate what happened to the Michigan economy. We frequently compare Detroit and Grand Rapids, yet they are not really comparable. Detroit is a city of national scope, one of the industrial Goliaths, more fit to compare with major European or Asian cities. To contrast Detroit and Grand Rapids misleads us. Instead, we must look to Flint and Grand Rapids for a better sense of our immediate past and its implications.

At opposite ends of Route 21, these cities are also at opposite ends of the economic route traveled by Michigan. Drawn into Detroit's industrial orbit, Flint prospered through twenty years of American world economic domination. As General Motors and the auto industry went, so, too, went Flint. Its population and prosperity climbed rapidly, bringing the city to number two ranking in Michigan by 1960 (Table 2).

Grand Rapids, long considered to be Michigan's second city, found itself frustrated by the huge gulf in terms of prosperity and population that separated it from Detroit. Grand Rapids' industrial assets had not remained intact during the depression. The household furnishings industry moved south. Once the war began, large portions of the population had been uprooted in the search for jobs in the larger metropolitan centers like Detroit or Chicago. Nor had the war years been especially kind in reviving Grand Rapids' local industry. As a center for the manufacture of household furnishings, what could the war effort ask of Grand Rapids? Unlike Detroit and Flint's huge capacity for metal working and skilled tool and die employees, what could the western city offer? The fortune of Grand Rapids seemed at a low ebb.

TABLE 2

Population Figures for Flint and Grand Rapids

	1940	1950	1960	1970	1980
Flint	151,543	163,143	196,940	193,317	150,400
Grand Rapids	164,292	176,515	177,313	197,649	181,843

Source: Ann Golenpaul, ed. *Information Please Almanac* (New York: Information Please Almanac, 1977), 697–98; *Rand Atlas 1958*, 232; *Rand Atlas 1977*, 292; *Rand Atlas 1987*, 382.

While the impact of the 1970s oil embargo and inflation hit across the state, they did not fall with equal impact. The western portion of Michigan fared slightly better. This was, in part, due to planning but also to a pattern of diversity forced upon Grand Rapids when World War II's demands for heavy industry bypassed that city.

Through a curious twist, the manufacture of home furnishings fled south during the depression; but the manufacture of office equipment and furnishings took root in the Grand Rapids area. Banks, insurance companies, investment firms and government agencies (the growing portions of the American economy) all demanded desks, cabinets, and partitions. The growth of office space in the sunbelt cities of the South and in California's Silicon Valley area benefited Grand Rapids' regional industry.

Grand Rapids continued a slow but steady rate of growth during the seventies, as the oil embargo played havoc with the economy. The service arm of the economy, with its diverse wholesale and retail outlets, coped more readily in Grand Rapids than did Flint's industrial base. Flint lost more than thirty thousand residents in the five years after 1973,[13] while racking up the dubious distinction of having the nation's highest unemployment rate. Flint never recovered. Residents have not yet returned to Flint. Grand Rapids' downtown, however, continues a sustained recovery in both housing and commerce.

The central reaches of the Lower Peninsula also benefited during the seventies with the revival of the oil and gas fields, considered too costly to operate in the fifties and sixties. Suddenly, the race for natural mineral wealth was on. Old mineral leases were renewed, new ones opened, and a small boom carried more rural portions of the state into some degree of prosperity. Both the volume produced and the price received for Michigan oil increased dramatically. For thirty years, from 1947 through 1977, the price per barrel hovered around $3.00 or less. In 1974, the price more than doubled, and by 1975 another 20 percent increase brought the market price up to $10.74 per barrel.[14]

Western Michigan farmers also reaped economic benefits during the seventies and eighties. Americans have changed their eating habits over the past twenty years. Increasingly concerned about health, they now consume more fruits and vegetables. This increase in demand can be seen in the twofold jump in prices received for Michigan-grown fruits and vegetables in the decade after 1958, and a similar—although not quite so huge—leap in the two decades after that.[15] The western portion of the state, with its lake-fed climate, can boast of gains in the sale of apples, pears, and asparagus. Even grapes and wine now form a larger part of the state's economy, as nearly two dozen wineries compete for changing public tastes.

Jeffrey D. Kleiman

Michigan and Family History Room Department, Grand Rapids Public Library

The renewal of downtown Grand Rapids is graphically shown in these two photographs. Above is a 1960 view looking south on Canal Street from the corner of Michigan Street. Below is the same corner in 1988 (Canal is now Lower Monroe Avenue).

Some areas of Michigan have also witnessed an increase in their service sector economy with an increase in tourism during the last three decades. The natural beauty of the Lower Peninsula's western shore and the Upper Peninsula made this area a haven for tourists, more and more of whom were coming into the state for winter and summer sports. The American dollar's decline, as well as increased cost of travel, brought Americans home in search of quiet ruggedness. The attractions of western and northern Michigan are an important factor in the growth of the service economy outside Detroit and the Interstate 75 corridor.

The dramatic increase in tourism over the past two decades can be seen in a variety of ways. Since the mid-sixties, sales of outstate fishing and hunting licenses have more than doubled, as has the use of national forests in Michigan and the number of visitors to Isle Royale National Park. All these figures attest to the strength of the state's tourist industry and its continued potential for growth.[16]

GROWTH AND TRANSITION: 1980s

Unlike Massachusetts or California, Michigan has not spent the last two decades building a high-technology corridor. The state must play catch-up with state economies that have a twenty-year head start.

This is not to say Michigan cannot compete for new technology firms and jobs, nor must the state abandon all hope in the traditional fields of manufacturing. The needs of new industrial growth will have to come alongside the advent of service sector technologies. A look at some of the fastest-growing business research centers in Michigan suggests the trends for the future. Located around the state are the bioengineering laboratory in East Lansing, a polymer research facility at Midland, and the Industrial Technology Institute at Ann Arbor—all products of the shifting economy of the early 1980s.

Despite the shift and decrease in heavy industry reflected in the state's automotive and ancillary products decline, other areas of the Michigan economy are promising. Michigan remains a major producer of appliances, although layoffs approaching 40 percent have occurred. Five active plants turn out washers and driers, air conditioners, freezers, and vacuum cleaners.[17]

In an ironic turn-around, Japanese auto makers began to locate plants in the United States during the 1980s. Mazda Corporation in September 1987 started operations at its Flat Rock plant. By August 1988, 22,000 cars a month were in production and 3,300 workers employed.[18]

The future of economic development for the state has not been neglected. The role is a difficult one, trying to assist the movement from dependence on well-paying, unionized, capital-intensive factory jobs to the new postindustrial and service society. One of the strategies of the administration of Gov. James Blanchard has been to create the Michigan Strategic Fund in order to aid new enterprises to relocate or start up.

Retraining of the state's skilled labor force has also been a priority of the Blanchard administration, and some notable progress has been made in this area since 1983. Despite the near depression-level unemployment that has plagued the state, more than a half million new jobs have been created; nearly 80 percent in nonmanufacturing industries. These jobs were created in spite of 140,000 layoffs by the Big Three auto makers.[19] Early in 1988, the state appropriated $100 million for retraining unemployed workers in a program administered by the commerce and labor departments.

The strength and increasing diversity of Michigan's economy can be seen in the fact that *Financial World* magazine recently placed the ten leading companies of Michigan in their top third ranking of the world's most valuable businesses. Traditional heavy industrial giants like Ford, General Motors, Chrysler, and Whirlpool were listed; but other more versatile corporations including Dow and Upjohn, as well as K Mart and Kellogg, were included.[20]

Michigan's internal shifts toward a service-oriented economy have produced ten fast-growing businesses, which were assessed recently in the third annual *Michigan 100 Growth Report*. Among them are: Inacomp Industries, a microcomputer retailer; Highland Appliances, a retailing chain specializing in home appliances and electronics goods; MSE Cable Systems; and Zeeland-based Gentex Corporation, which produces a variety of electronics equipment for the home. Nearly a dozen new businesses are working to establish a research center some thirty miles north of Detroit near Oakland University. Oakland Technology Park promises to be the third largest such complex in the nation, and by 1990 to employ twelve thousand workers.[21] All these developments reflect the service and technology side of Michigan's shifting economy and the state's ability to cope with change.

Of equal concern to economic development is the human cost as the traditional manufacturing economy gives way to a new mix of service and high-technology jobs. Although auto production has surpassed 1979 levels, it has done so with only two-thirds of the workers. Is an entire generation of workers, lacking enough seniority to avoid layoff and too old to recall or retrain, lost? Are these people, who have built

Rick Smith, Oakland University

Comerica Building in Oakland Technology Park near Rochester.

their lives on the hopes of a middle-class income and who cannot support their families on something slightly better than minimum wage, destined for continual poverty? Even though the riots of those long, hot summers are decades behind us, have the inequities that spawned them lessened? Or have they become larger and more difficult to overcome, given the uncertainties of our economy in transition?

Michigan's future looks bright despite these troubles associated with change. The state possesses an abundance of skilled, educated, and hard-working people. Nationally known institutions for product research and development and work force training are also found in Michigan. The generation next to come will build on these strengths.

Jeffrey D. Kleiman

◆

NOTES

1. *Rand McNally Commercial Atlas and Marketing Guide* (Chicago: Rand McNally, 1958), 229. (Hereafter cited as *Rand Atlas* with corresponding date.)

2. David I. Verway, ed., *Michigan Statistical Abstract 1978* (East Lansing: Michigan State University Press, 1978), 304. (Hereafter cited as *Michigan Abstract*.)

3. Harvey S. Perloff, et al., *Regions, Resources and Economic Growth* (Lincoln: University of Nebraska Press, 1960), 574.

4. Ibid., 583.

5. Verway, *Michigan Abstract 1978*, 880.

6. *Rand Atlas 1960*, 267; *Rand Atlas 1977*, 292; *Rand Atlas 1987*, 382. The following table may prove interesting:

TABLE 3

Michigan Population Growth by Selected Counties

	1940	1950	1960	1970	1980
Macomb	107,638	184,961	405,804	625,309	694,600
Oakland	284,068	396,001	620,259	907,871	1,011,793
Saginaw	130,468	153,515	190,752	219,743	228,059
Wayne	2,015,623	2,435,235	2,666,297	2,670,368	2,337,843

Source: *Rand Atlas*, 1960, 1977, 1987.

7. Verway, *Michigan Abstract 1978*, 733.

8. Ibid.

9. See Table 3 above, note 6.

10. Verway, *Michigan Abstract 1978*, 783.

11. William K. Harris, *The Harder We Run: Black Workers Since the Civil War* (New York: Oxford University Press, 1982), 125–26.

12. Verway, *Michigan Abstract 1978*, 890.

13. *Rand Atlas 1987*.

14. Verway, *Michigan Abstract 1978*, 964.

15. Ibid., 183, 746; Verway, *Michigan Abstract 1986–1987*, 300.

16. Verway, *Michigan Abstract 1978*, 719–20.

17. "Appliance Industry Shrinks as Firms Modernize, Go South," *Grand Rapids Press,* 20 January 1988, sec. C, p. 5.

18. *Lansing State Journal,* 27 August 1988, sec. B, p. 3.

19. "State Plans New Worker Training Fund, Ross Says," *Grand Rapids Press,* 20 January 1988, sec. C, p. 26.

20. "Ford is Top Michigan Firm, Magazine Says," *Grand Rapids Press,* 16 March 1988, sec. B, p. 6.

21. "Corporate Kings are Flocking to Technology Park," *Grand Rapids Press,* 8 May 1988, sec. A, pp. 17–18.

SUGGESTED READINGS

Perhaps the best way to check the economic pulse of Michigan is to read the business section of any major regional daily paper, along with business and economic news in several national papers. Columnists usually feature stories about trends and developments in both the public and private spheres and their impact on our daily lives.

The annual *Michigan Statistical Abstract* provides a convenient way to create a thumbnail sketch of the economic environment over the long and short term. Do not be put off by the rows and columns of figures. Very often curiosity, persistence, and common-sense observations (accompanied, perhaps, by a hand calculator) will get you from one cover to the other.

We tend to overlook the very fine work done by *Rand McNally* available in their annual *Commercial and Marketing Atlas.* This is a wealth of information for professional businesses, economics students, or curious taxpayers. The Atlas has been published for more than a century and can give even the most casual user a sense of change within Michigan and the Great Lakes region as a whole.

The Rand McNally atlases use the most recent government census material for banking, industry, and population and interpret the data to present subtle, but important, shifts in both how we make and spend money. Most libraries subscribe to the *Commercial and Marketing Atlas,* and a quick look at the table of contents will open a new door to knowledge.

1945-1980s

L

GEORGE WEEKS

Journalist-author George Weeks is political columnist for *The Detroit News.* He is the author of *Stewards of the State: The Governors of Michigan* and *Sleeping Bear: Its Lore, Legends, and First People.* Mr. Weeks is also co-author of *The Milliken Years: A Pictorial Reflection,* and a contributing author to *A Handbook of African Affairs.* During fourteen years with United Press International, Weeks was Lansing bureau chief. He also was press secretary and chief of staff to Gov. William G. Milliken. A Traverse City native, Mr. Weeks has a journalism degree from Michigan State University.

eadership in a State of Change

The mid- and late-twentieth century produced profound change in the state of the state of Michigan and in its political parties. It also produced some remarkable political leaders, including governors whose careers rode the roller coaster cycles of boom/bust/rebound that affected Michigan government and politics throughout the first 150 years of statehood. Dominant political figures of the 1945–1988 period included:

- Republican United States Sen. Arthur G. Vandenberg, who served from 1928 until his death in 1951 and who abandoned his leadership of isolationism to become an internationalist and leader of postwar bipartisan United States foreign policy.
- Six-term (1949–1960) Democratic Gov. G. Mennen Williams, a politician-diplomat-jurist, whose public career spanned the last third of Michigan's first 150 years of statehood and ended with his retirement as chief justice of the Michigan Supreme Court a year before his death in 1988.
- Democratic United States Sen. Philip A. Hart (1959–1976), a former

Future Media Inc., Lansing

Five Michigan governors posed for this picture 17 November 1981 during a panel discussion on the changing role of the governor. From the left are governors: G. Mennen Williams, George W. Romney, Murray D. Van Wagoner, William G. Milliken, and John B. Swainson.

legal adviser and lieutenant governor under Williams, whose reputation as "conscience of the Senate" was reflected in the fact that it named one of its three Capitol Hill office buildings after him.

- Republican Gov. George Romney (1963–1969), former head of American Motors Corporation, who championed rewriting of the Michigan Constitution; was elected governor in his first bid for statewide office; and succeeded in adding Michigan to the majority of states imposing an income tax.

- Republican Gov. William G. Milliken (1969–1982), a former state senator and lieutenant governor, who became Michigan's longest-serving governor; built a progressive record in environmental, transportation, urban, and other programs; and was selected by his peers in 1976 as the nation's most effective governor.*

———————————

*Based on responses by governors to a survey conducted by the *U.S. News & World Report.*

• Democratic Gov. James J. Blanchard (1983–), a former congressman who ended twenty years of Republican rule when elected governor in 1982; presided over Michigan's 1980s economic comeback; and was reelected in 1986 by a margin of 878,091 votes—largest for any of Michigan's first forty-three governors.

These men were among leaders of a period that saw some of the biggest changes in Michigan politics since the Republican party (GOP) was founded "under the oaks" at the outskirts of Jackson in 1854. There was upheaval in both parties, as well as fading loyalties and roles for political parties in a television age in which politicians launched and advanced careers through paid media rather than parties. They "paid their dues" to paid media.

In the mid-1940s, the Democratic party was in eclipse. Republicans maintained the overwhelming majorities in both houses of the legislature that they acquired in 1938. Republican Gov. Harry F. Kelly had been reelected in 1944 and acquired a reputation as a solid administrator, by establishing a trust fund to aid veterans, revamping mental health programs, and expanding postwar building at colleges and universities.

Both of Michigan's United States senators were Republicans during this time, and on 10 January 1945, Senator Vandenberg gave a speech to the Senate on postwar foreign policy described by historian George S. May as

> the most important speech of his career and probably the most important speech delivered by any Michigan senator or representative.... The speech, widely praised and compared by some to the great orations of Daniel Webster and Henry Clay, established a new spirit of bipartisan cooperation in the development of an internationalist foreign policy.[1]

From that day onward, observed historian Clever Bald, "Senator Vandenberg became a statesman of world-wide influence and reputation."[2]

Vandenberg had been a symbol of isolationism—or "insulationism," as he liked to say. But the former Grand Rapids editor, who wrote a diary on a portable typewriter, said "my convictions regarding international cooperation and collective security for peace took firm form on the afternoon of the Pearl Harbor attack. That day ended isolationism for any realist."[3]

Vandenberg was touted for the presidency by isolationists in 1940 and internationalists in 1948. The 1948 GOP nomination, however, went to Owosso, Michigan, native Thomas E. Dewey, long-time governor of New York. Dewey lost to Democrat Harry S. Truman, but unlike 1944, when he lost Michigan to Franklin Roosevelt, Dewey managed to beat

Truman in Michigan by about thirty-five thousand votes out of more than two million cast.

In 1946 Vandenberg was reelected to the United States Senate by a margin of 567,647. Republicans won 95 of 110 state House seats, 28 of 32 in the Senate, and all state offices. "The Michigan Democratic party hit bottom in the election of 1946," wrote G. Mennen Williams' biographer, Frank McNaughton. "In that year, it lost everything in sight, including its self-respect."[4]

Also elected in 1946 was Republican Gov. Kim Sigler, a dapper, flamboyant corruption fighter known as Hollywood Kim. During the last years of the Kelly administration, Sigler was special prosecutor in a grand jury investigation of legislative corruption involving payoffs from lobbyists which produced 130 arrests and 62 convictions. It also resulted in the murder of state Sen. Warren Hooper of Albion on 11 January 1945, on M-99 south of Lansing three days before Hooper was to testify before the grand jury against former (1925–1930) state treasurer Frank D. McKay, a long-time Republican national committeeman and party kingpin. Multimillionaire "Boss" McKay was one of the most powerful and controversial figures in twentieth-century Michigan politics and an elusive target of Sigler's investigations.

The legislative corruption and unsolved Hooper slaying reflected one of the darkest chapters in Michigan government and politics. A 1987 book, *Three Bullets Sealed His Lips* by professors Bruce A. Rubenstein and Lawrence E. Ziewacz, accused Sigler of "laxity and impropriety in his handling of the case. To avoid embarrassment and political ruin, Sigler desperately hid the fact that he had deliberately permitted the assassins to remain anonymous and unpunished while he engaged in an abortive vendetta against Frank McKay."[5]*

Although Sigler was replaced as special prosecutor in 1946 when a new judge took over the cases, his reputation as a crime fighter vaulted him into the governorship when he defeated former Democratic Gov. Murry D. Van Wagoner by 359,338 votes. Sigler instituted improvements in management of state government, but, as did so many other governors, he left a deficit. He inherited a surplus of about $25 million

---

*The book cited previously-unreleased documents to support its contention that Sigler knew that the triggermen in the Hooper slaying were imprisoned Purple Gang mobsters who, with knowledge of prison authorities friendly to McKay, used the car of a deputy warden at Southern Michigan Prison at Jackson, drove to the ambush site, pumped three bullets into Hooper's skull, and returned to the prison where they had officially remained "on count" within its walls at the moment of the crime. Rubenstein and Ziewacz said Sigler was more intent on uncovering the identity of the person who financed the assassination than on disclosing names of the assassins. He did neither.

and left with a general fund deficit of about $20 million, largely because of the 1946 constitutional amendment decision by voters to divert a portion of all sales tax collections to schools, cities, and townships.

One of Sigler's biggest mistakes was appointing G. Mennen Williams to the Liquor Control Commission, "touching off the fuse on a political bomb that would blow the Michigan Republican party sky-high. . . ."[6] The job gave Williams a chance to win friends, travel the state, and develop a name and contacts to help him reach a goal he had already set—to become governor.

THE WILLIAMS YEARS

Williams was a self-described "liberal Democrat in a rock-ribbed Republican state."[7] He came from a Republican family (grandfather Gerhardt Mennen founded the Mennen line of shaving lotions; hence, Williams' nickname Soapy); and, at Princeton, he was president of the Young Republicans Club. But Williams said: "As a sophomore in prep school, I decided to make my career one of public service so as to help the underdogs. In college, I decided to be governor. In law school, I decided to be a Democrat rather than a Republican."[8]

Williams won the Democratic nomination and overthrew a weak and splintered party leadership with the help of such allies as Hicks Griffiths, who became party chairman; Hicks's wife, Martha, who went on to a twenty-year career in Congress and became lieutenant governor in 1983; Neil Staebler, who became Democratic state chairman from 1950 to 1961; Michigan CIO president August Scholle, a power throughout the Williams years; and campaign manager Larry Farrell, who became executive secretary to Governor Williams. These Democrats, along with Democratic vice-chairman Adelaide Hart, National Committeewoman Margaret Price, and Mildred Jeffrey, long-time party officer and United Auto Workers (UAW) organizer, were among those forming what George May said became by the 1950s "probably the most formidable political organization in Michigan history."[9]

A protégé of former Gov. Frank Murphy, Williams, who had begun his public career in 1936 as an attorney for the Social Security Board in Washington, won the nomination by beating two primary opponents, including one backed by Teamsters president James R. Hoffa.

In the general election, Williams had the help of veterans, conservationists, ethnics, and other groups. At one point, organized labor other than the Teamsters considered forming a third party out of anger at both Republicans and Democrats over workers' compensation. Instead it formed an alliance with Williams that helped sustain the longest Democratic control of the

Michigan State Archives

From left to right, former Gov. G. Mennen Williams, Gov. John B. Swainson, Pres. John F. Kennedy, and Neil Stabler in Detroit, 6 October 1962.

governor's office since the founding of the Republican party.

Williams said, "We wouldn't have won the campaign without the UAW and the AFL and the CIO, which were three separate groups then. But if that had been all we had, we wouldn't have won, either."[10]

Williams, at age thirty-seven, defeated Sigler by 163,854 votes; but two years later he barely won a recount election over ex-Governor Kelly by 1,154 votes—the closest gubernatorial election of the century and the state's second closest ever.*

Williams won four more terms before deciding not to run again in 1960. Soon thereafter, he became assistant secretary of state for African affairs, and later, an unsuccessful candidate for the United States Senate, United States ambassador to the Philippines, and chief justice of the Michigan Supreme Court.

---

*Out of 29,860 votes cast in 1837, Stevens T. Mason defeated Charles C. Trowbridge by 768 votes.

In 1953 Williams warned the legislature: "Already we have suffered some of the preliminary symptoms of financial collapse. Our treasury has been unable to meet in an orderly manner the obligations imposed by the Constitution for the support of our public schools."[11]

It became more desperate in 1959. A stalemate between the Democratic governor and the Republican senate on funding proposals led to a payless payday for state workers, a black eye for Michigan, and the demise of Williams' hopes for the White House.*

Long after leaving the governorship, Williams acknowledged that part of his problem with "Neanderthal" senators was his own stubbornness. Compromise, said the man who made green and white polka dot bow ties a political trademark, was a word that didn't fit into the vocabulary of "the young Williams."[12]

Asked to cite his proudest accomplishments, Williams said he brought Michigan "a real two-party system" and "into the 20th century" in social services, civil rights, mental health and highways. But he quipped, "I made myself a failure by not having two or three headline achievements, outside of maybe the Mackinac Bridge"—which was built in 1957.[13]

A failure? In truth, Williams' fifty-year career, which included an unprecedented six successful campaigns for governor and two for the Michigan Supreme Court, made him Michigan's politician of the twentieth century.

After leaving office, Williams ran unsuccessfully in 1966 for the United States Senate against ten-year House Republican Robert P. Griffin. Griffin had been appointed by George Romney to the Senate in May 1966 upon the death of Democrat Patrick V. McNamara; became minority whip in the Senate; was defeated in 1978 by Democrat Carl Levin; and, in 1986, in an ironic political twist, was elected to the Michigan Supreme Court seat vacated by Williams.

. When Williams, as governor, decided against running for the Senate in 1958, his lieutenant governor, Phil Hart, ran against and defeated Republican Charles E. Potter by 170,000 votes. Although overwhelmingly reelected by 90,640 votes in 1964 and by 886,246 votes in 1970, it was not necessarily strength at the polls but strength of conviction that distinguished Hart.

In 1972 Hart cast the lone "no" vote when the Democratic caucus selected segregationist Sen. James Eastland of Mississippi as president pro tem of the Senate, a position third in line in succession to the presidency behind the vice-president and speaker of the House. . "Jim

---

*A half-century earlier, a cash crisis in 1908 had also prompted Republican Gov. Fred M. Warner to delay pay for a few weeks to state employees.

Eastland would make an excellent president pro tem but an outrageous president," said Hart, who was floor manager of the 1964 Voting Rights Act and opponent of antibusing legislation.[14]

Hart, a consumer advocate and the Senate champion of national no-fault auto insurance, was described by the *Almanac of American Politics* in 1974 as "the kind of man who tries to see merit in the positions taken by his adversaries, even when he considers the consequences of their views horrifying. But his gentle nature is admixed with some steel."[15]

One of Hart's legacies is Sleeping Bear Dunes National Lakeshore along Lake Michigan in Leelanau and Benzie counties. Hart's leadership in establishing it was recognized by the National Park Service when it opened the lakeshore's Philip A. Hart Visitor Center in Empire.

When Hart left the Williams administration in 1958 he was replaced as lieutenant governor by Democratic state Sen. John B. Swainson, who was elected governor in 1960 at age thirty-five. Swainson, who lost both legs in World War II, was the second youngest man elected governor of Michigan (Stevens T. Mason was twenty-four when first elected in 1835) and the youngest to serve in all three branches of government. He later became Supreme Court justice at forty-five.

As governors before and after, Swainson inherited economic troubles, telling the legislature upon taking office, "Michigan is dotted with deep pockets of economic distress."[16]

Swainson picked up the fight by Williams and earlier governors for tax revision, particularly enactment of an income tax, arguing that Michigan's patchwork tax structure failed to meet reasonable tests of adequacy, permanency and equity. But the polarization with the Republican-controlled legislature that marked Williams' years continued during Swainson's term.

Swainson took the politically unpopular step of vetoing a bill that would have exempted suburbanites who worked in Detroit from that city's income tax. Ironically, the man who was to win legislative approval of a state income tax was a Republican, George W. Romney, who defeated Swainson in 1962.

THE ROMNEY YEARS

George Romney embodied most of the underlying forces in Michigan politics occurring during the last half of the twentieth century. He came to office from outside the political structure—from the auto industry, the fortunes of which have had so much to do with the careers of

Michigan politicians. He was a citizen activist who championed constitutional change. As governor he grappled with forces of social change,
including racial tensions that led to rioting in 1967.

In 1959 Romney founded Citizens for Michigan, which campaigned
for convening the convention that produced Michigan's Constitution of
1963. The new constitution greatly enhanced the power of Michigan
governors, extending their terms from two to four years without any of
the restrictions on serving consecutive terms as those imposed by
twenty-seven other states. Michigan also joined twenty-one other states
in providing that the governor and lieutenant governor would run as a
team.

Romney ended fourteen years of Democratic rule by defeating
Swainson by the relatively narrow plurality of 80,573, but he twice won
reelection by big margins.

After inheriting an $85 million deficit, Romney reported in 1965 that
"a sizable deficit has been replaced by a sizable surplus"[17] and, in 1966,
that "recession has been replaced by an unprecedented boom," and the
general fund surplus was $136 million.[18]

Romney, who as head of American Motors championed the compact
car as an alternative to "gas-guzzling dinosaurs," championed and won
legislative approval of an income tax in 1967. Romney saw downsizing
of cars and upsizing of the state budget. He presented Michigan's first
billion-dollar budget.

At one point, Romney was a leading candidate for the 1968 Republican presidential nomination that was won by Richard M. Nixon. But
Romney withdrew after being haunted ("cut to pieces," in his words) by
the media for his remarks about the "brainwashing" that he received
from United States military-diplomatic briefings in Vietnam.[19]

After this abortive bid for the nomination, Romney was named secretary of housing and urban development in 1969 by newly-elected President Nixon.

Romney and others tried, but Gerald R. Ford was the only Michiganian to become president—and without trying. The Grand Rapids lawyer entered Congress in 1949 and spent twenty-five years in the
House—eight of them as Republican leader—before being nominated by
President Nixon to replace Vice Pres. Spiro T. Agnew, when Agnew
resigned in 1973. Upon Nixon's own resignation in 1974 following the
Watergate scandal, Ford became president—the first to serve without
being chosen as president or vice-president in a national election. In his
own bid for the presidency, Ford lost to Jimmy Carter in 1976.

The White House

Pres. Gerald R. Ford and Gov. William G. Milliken (right) confer in the Oval Office while Sen. Robert P. Griffin (left) and a White House aide listen in the background.

THE MILLIKEN YEARS

During Michigan's first 150 years of statehood, six lieutenant governors became governors, but only two of them—Swainson and Milliken— were elected to the governorship. Milliken initially inherited the job when Romney went to Washington; but three times he was elected to four-year terms.

Milliken, a state senator from Traverse City like his father and grandfather, was another in a long line of progressive Republican governors often at odds with conservative Republican legislators (e.g., Civil War governor Austin Blair; turn-of-the-century governor Hazen Pingree, and governor from 1911 to 1912, Chase S. Osborn). In 1961, Milliken, who became Senate majority floor leader, was among moderate Republicans who drafted a liberal agenda for mental health, civil rights, education and other fields that later was written into the state party platform.

During the Milliken years, Michigan had some of the nation's most innovative environmental and other programs and, at one point, the nation's biggest property tax-cut program. He won acclaim for initiating programs to attract robotics and other high-technology industries, as well as criticism for state handling of contamination when PBB, a toxic chemical flame retardant, was accidentally mixed with cattle feed and entered the food chain in 1973.

Demonstrating broad appeal to ticket-splitting independents and Democrats, Milliken was reelected in 1974 by a plurality of 391,229—a margin that had been exceeded by only three other Michigan governors—and was the first Republican to carry Wayne County since 1946. He also became chairman of the National Governors' Association.

Except for brief GOP control of the Senate, Milliken faced a legislature run by Democrats. Although the legislature rejected some of his tax proposals designed to avoid a looming deficit, Milliken's was in large part an era of executive-legislative cooperation. "Despite his perennially boyish appearance and his low-key style, Milliken would prove even more adept [than Romney] in building and maintaining an effective coalition of moderates from both parties that could deal with the problems of the succeeding decade," said historian May.[20]

In his last term, as had been the pattern with Michigan governors, Milliken faced economic downturn. He said in 1982: "Since I have been governor, there have been four national recessions. But Michigan has not been hurt as much as it hurts now."[21]

Outstater Milliken, a Republican who grew up in wealth along the shores of Grand Traverse Bay, developed an odd-couple relationship with black Detroit Democratic Mayor Coleman A. Young, who said:

> Bill Milliken proved that you can appeal to people's best instincts and be a very successful politician in Michigan. His administration understood the importance of Detroit to the rest of Michigan and carried out policies which recognized the interdependence of the city and the state.[22]

Young himself has carved out a niche in Michigan political history as Detroit's longest-serving mayor, a builder of coalitions, rebuilder of downtown Detroit, a power within the Michigan Democratic party, and a target (and generator) of much of the outstate and suburban hostility toward predominantly black Detroit. Young blamed the hostility on "racism that still permeates our society."[23]*

---

* Asked by *Metropolitan Detroit* magazine in 1985 to comment on anti-Detroit hostility in "the political history of this city, especially its recent history," Young said: "I think it's a sad comment on the racism that still permeates our society. For one reason or another, the white population has been declining on a proportional basis in this city for the last 20 years or more. The exodus of whites—both of residents and businesses—accelerated after . . . the riots of 1967, notwithstanding the fact that there was no clash between whites and blacks. [The riot of] 1967 was a clash, basically, between a primarily white police department and a black community. . . . I think another characteristic of what has happened here . . . is that many whites find it impossible to live in a situation where they don't dominate, they don't control. . . ."

Gov. William G. Milliken (left) at a news conference with Detroit Mayor Coleman A. Young.

Also establishing records in the last half of the twentieth century were Attorney General Frank Kelley and Secretary of State Richard H. Austin. Kelley, who took office in 1961, after 1986 had won eight elections and was dean of the nation's attorneys general as well as Michigan's longest-serving attorney general. Austin, who took office in 1971, by 1986 had won five elections and was Michigan's longest-serving secretary of state. The tenure of these two Democrats, both of whom made unsuccessful attempts at the United States Senate, has served to deny Republicans use of offices that earlier had been steppingstones to the governorship.

When Milliken decided in 1982 to leave the governorship after twenty-two years in public office, the Michigan GOP resumed its more conservative tradition, began turning to candidates from outside the party for major statewide office, and suffered a series of losses. The 1980s began a period when Democrats held all major statewide offices, both United States Senate seats, a majority in Michigan's eighteen-member congressional delegation, and control of the state house. The lone Republican stronghold in the capitol was the senate.

284

THE BLANCHARD YEARS

In 1982 the Republican gubernatorial nominee was conservative insurance executive Richard H. Headlee, who, like Romney, was a businessman active in citizen crusades but not in the party. Congressman James J. Blanchard beat six primary opponents to win the Democratic nomination. Helped by infighting within the GOP and by the effects of a national recession under a Republican administration, Blanchard won by 191,709 votes.

In 1983 Blanchard won legislative approval of a 38 percent temporary increase in the income tax—and lost popularity. His approval rating fell to 30 percent, a record low for the era of public opinion surveys, and he faced a vigorous but unsuccessful recall effort. Yet by 1987 Blanchard was able to report: "Four years ago our state budget showed a $1.7 billion deficit. Our credit rating was the worst in the nation. Today, our budget is balanced. Our tax rate is below where it was four years ago. Our credit rating is the best in the nation."[24]

In 1986, Republicans tried to unseat Blanchard by recruiting Wayne County's county executive William Lucas, an ex-Democrat who had switched to the GOP a year earlier and who sought to be the nation's first elected black governor. Blanchard, campaigning as "the comeback governor of the comeback state" and staking out the political middle that was so successful for Romney and Milliken, won with a record landslide. Again, he was helped by divisions within the Michigan GOP.

Republicans accused Blanchard of designing a state promotion program to promote himself more than Michigan and said credit for Michigan's comeback belonged to President Reagan for leading the national economic recovery. But by 1988, Blanchard had established himself as one of the nation's most successful governors and was cited by national publications for his innovative programs to create jobs.

In addition to going outside its party farm system for the 1982 and 1986 battles against Blanchard, the Michigan GOP nominated ex-astronaut Jack Lousma, never before active in politics, for what became an unsuccessful challenge to incumbent Carl Levin for the United States Senate in 1984.

Michigan's senior senator during the 1980s, Donald W. Riegle, Jr., won Hart's seat in 1976 and, by 1988, had more than twenty years in Congress. He first went there at age twenty-eight as a Republican congressman from Flint but became a Democrat in 1973. The 1980s dean of Michigan's congressional delegation was Democratic representative John D. Dingell of Trenton, first elected in 1955 to fill the vacant seat of

Office of the Governor

Gov. James J. Blanchard was elected in 1982 and reelected in 1986.

his late father. The senior Republican, William S. Broomfield of Birmingham, was first elected in 1956.

In the 1970s and 1980s, presidential politicking also caused upsets and upheaval in Michigan's parties. In 1972 Alabama governor George Wallace upset eventual nominee George McGovern in the Democratic primary, benefiting from antibusing sentiment and crossover Republican votes. This prompted Democrats to lead a drive to switch Michigan from the primary to a caucus system that discouraged crossovers. In 1988, however, responding to destructive caucus infighting, the legislature returned Michigan to a closed primary system beginning in 1992.

In Michigan's last primary year before the switch to caucuses, George Bush, with a strong assist from Milliken, scored an upset in 1980 over eventual Republican nominee Ronald Reagan.

In 1988 the Reverend Jesse Jackson won an upset in Michigan's

Democratic caucus, fooling Mayor Young and others who said outstate whites would not vote for a black. That same year, another minister, ex-television evangelist Pat Robertson, displayed strong organizational abilities in the Republican caucus process. He eventually lost to Bush in the quest for 1988 Michigan delegates, but Robertson supporters for at least a period had the largest bloc in the Republican State Committee and served to move the Michigan GOP further to the right.

In truth, both parties became more conservative during the 1980s in Michigan. Blanchard himself was more centrist than Williams and other Democratic gubernatorial candidates of the mid-to-late twentieth century. After the resounding 1984 loss of Democratic presidential nominee Walter Mondale to Ronald Reagan, Blanchard was among Democratic figures who urged the party to be more centrist. As 1988 chairman of the Democratic Governors' Association and of the platform committee of the Democratic National Convention, Blanchard played a role in encouraging a move to the center.

Just as Michigan's economy rode rollercoaster cycles during the later twentieth century, so too did its political parties.

NOTES

1. George S. May, *Michigan: An Illustrated History of the Great Lakes State* (Northridge, Calif.: Windsor Publications, 1987), 179–80.

2. F. Clever Bald, *Michigan In Four Centuries* (New York: Harper & Brothers, 1954), 448.

3. Arthur G. Vandenberg, Jr., *The Private Papers of Senator Vandenberg* (Boston: Houghton Mifflin Company, 1951), 1.

4. Frank McNaughton, *Mennen Williams of Michigan: Fighter for Progress* (New York: Oceana Publications, Inc., 1960), 93.

5. Bruce A. Rubenstein and Lawrence E. Ziewacz, *Three Bullets Sealed His Lips* (East Lansing: Michigan State University Press, 1987), 203.

6. McNaughton, 96.

7. George Weeks, *The Detroit News*, commentary the day after Williams' death, 3 February 1988, 7A.

8. George Weeks, *Stewards of the State: The Governors of Michigan* (Ann Arbor: *The Detroit News* and the Historical Society of Michigan, 1987), 111.

9. May, 193.

10. Weeks, *Stewards of the State*, 112.

11. G. Mennen Williams, Message to the Legislature, 15 January 1953.

12. Weeks, *Stewards of the State*, 111.

13. Ibid., 114.

14. Richard A. Ryan, *The Detroit News,* 29 July 1972.

15. Michael Barone, Grant Ujifusa, and Douglas Matthews, eds., *Almanac of American Politics, 1974* (Boston: GAMBIT, Inc., 1973), 467.

16. John B. Swainson, Message to the Legislature, 1 February 1961, 1.

17. George Romney, Message to the Legislature, 14 January 1965, 1.

18. George Romney, Message to the Legislature, 13 January 1966, 1.

19. Weeks, *Stewards of the State*, 125.

20. Willis F. Dunbar and George S. May, *Michigan: A History of the Wolverine State* (Grand Rapids: Eerdmans Publishing Company, 1980), 667.

21. William G. Milliken, televised Report to the People, 10 March 1982.

22. Weeks, *Stewards of the State*, 131.

23. *Metropolitan Detroit*, December 1985, 98.

24. James J. Blanchard, State of the State Address, 5 February 1987.

◆

SUGGESTED READINGS

Bald, F. Clever. *Michigan in Four Centuries*. New York: Harper and Brothers, 1954. Valuable for material into the early 1950s.

Barone, Michael, and Grant Ujifusa. *The Almanac of American Politics 1988*. Washington, D.C.: National Journal, 1987. This annual publication includes political overviews for each state as well as election, campaign finance, voting records, and biographical information on United States senators and representatives. It also includes a profile of each congressional district and brief biographical and election material on governors.

Capitol Profiles 1987–88. Lansing: Capitol Publications, 1987. Includes profiles of elected officials.

Dunbar, Willis F., and George S. May. *Michigan: A History of the Wolverine State*. Grand Rapids: Eerdmans Publishing Company, 1980. May's revised edition includes material on Michigan's postwar years, through most of the 1970s.

May, George. *Michigan: An Illustrated History of the Great Lakes State*. Northridge, Calif.: Windsor Publications, 1987. Includes commentary on governmental and political developments through the first term of Gov. James J. Blanchard and an excellent chapter on Michigan at age 150.

Michigan Manual 1987–88. Lansing: Department of Management and Budget, 1988. Especially useful for biographical and election material.

1988 Michigan Government Directory. Lansing: Public Sector Consultants, 1988. Includes biographical and voting profiles on members of the legislature and congress, as well as useful research material on the judicial and executive branches, including directors and functions of state agencies.

Weeks, George. *Stewards of the State: The Governors of Michigan*. Ann Arbor: *The Detroit News* and the Historical Society of Michigan, 1987. Includes biographical material on the governors and highlights of political and governmental issues during their terms, with emphasis on common problems they faced.

Those desiring information to update political material in this chapter will find the annual editions of the *Michigan Manual* and the *Almanac of American Politics* especially helpful, as well as copies of Michigan newspapers that maintain bureaus in Lansing and Washington, D.C., including *The Detroit News,* the *Detroit Free Press,* Booth newspapers, and the *Lansing State Journal.*

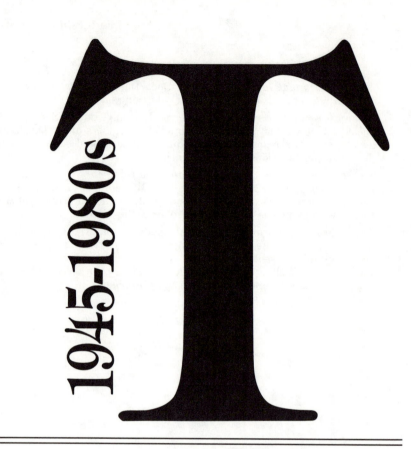

T
1945-1980s

DeWITT S. DYKES, JR.

DeWitt S. Dykes, Jr., is associate professor of history at Oakland University. His teaching and research specializations include Afro-American history, family history and biography, history of black American women, history of American cities, and oral history. He is currently president of the Michigan Black History Network. Professor Dykes received his bachelor's degree from Fisk University, and master's and doctoral degrees from The University of Michigan. He has contributed articles to many publications such as the *Dictionary of American Biography* and *Encyclopedia of Southern History*.

he Search for Community:
Michigan Society and Education

Many trends and movements affected the lives of Michigan's people and the nature of Michigan society in the years following World War II. Major trends included economic prosperity occasionally dampened by recession, increased labor union membership and greater benefits for workers, population growth due to a higher birthrate and migration, expansion of educational facilities and student enrollment, increased suburbanization, social unrest and social protest, two foreign wars, and changing federal policies toward states and cities. Any discussion of Michigan society during this time period should begin with population growth, urbanization, and the development of suburbs. These trends established the framework for other developments in the state's recent history.

In 1980, Michigan's population ranked eighth among the fifty states and third behind Illinois and Ohio in the Midwest. Michigan's growth from 5,256,106 people in 1940 to 9,262,078 in 1980 represented an increase of over 76 percent. Most people lived in the southern part of the state, close to the heavy industry and large commercial companies.

Southeast Michigan contained the greatest concentration of Michigan residents. Three counties—Wayne, Oakland, and Macomb—not only had 43.7 percent of the state's total population in 1980 but also contained more people—4,043,633—than the total population of thirty-six states. In addition, eight southern counties were home to 61 percent (5,688,151) of the population: Wayne, Oakland, Macomb, Washtenaw, and Genessee counties in southeastern Michigan; and Ingham, Kent, and Kalamazoo counties in central and western Michigan.[1]

CITIES AND SUBURBS

Michigan has been an urban state ever since the 1920 United States census revealed that 61 percent of its residents lived in cities of 2,500 or more people, the basic definition of "urban."[2] By 1978, Michigan's urban population had grown to be 81.3 percent of the state's total.[3] During the early 1940s the state's urban population had increased as large numbers of migrants, attracted by jobs in wartime industry, settled mostly in existing housing in cities such as Detroit, Flint, Pontiac, Saginaw, Willow Run, Ypsilanti, Grand Rapids, Lansing, and Kalamazoo. Multiple factors in the late 1940s and the 1950s combined to disperse urban populations onto wider and more scattered areas of land. This dispersion was accompanied by several social consequences. Thus, an analysis of the growth and direction of the urban population, its distribution within Michigan's metropolitan areas, and the resulting changes in Michigan's economic and social patterns is basic to understanding the major developments in Michigan society from the end of World War II in 1945 to the end of the 1980s.

Before 1945 suburban growth was limited and did not involve a large percentage of the population of any one region of the state. Suburbs were economically and socially dependent on the nearby central cities making it possible for the suburbs to develop. To recognize this symbiotic relationship between cities and suburbs and to standardize the collection of statistics on urban areas, the United States Census Bureau developed the concept now known as "Standard Metropolitan Statistical Area" or SMSA. An SMSA is an entire county or group of nearby counties that are economically and socially linked to a central city of at least fifty thousand population. The Detroit SMSA, the largest in Michigan, now has several cities of over fifty thousand population. Suburban cities, therefore, are directly tied to a larger nearby city and a significant portion of a suburb's residents take part in the daily economic and social activities of the central city and vice versa. By 1980, eleven areas wholly within Michigan had been designated as SMSAs: Ann Arbor-Ypsilanti, Battle Creek, Bay City, Detroit, Flint, Grand Rapids, Jackson, Kalamazoo-Portage, Lansing-East Lansing, Muskegon-Norton Shores-

Muskegon Heights, and Saginaw. In addition, Monroe County was listed as part of an SMSA with Toledo, Ohio, as its central city. Nine Michigan counties were listed as part of SMSAs in 1940. This number grew to twenty-five counties in 1980. It has been predicted that urbanization will spread so that eventually all counties south of a line from Muskegon to Bay City will be part of an SMSA. In contrast, there are no SMSAs in the northernmost part of the Lower Peninsula or in the Upper Peninsula.[4]

During the late 1940s, most of the population movement was into the newest sections of large cities and into the older, already established suburbs. Then, in the 1950s and 1960s, suburbs were established and grew at an astonishing rate, sometimes faster than the ability of the newly established cities to provide a full range of services to the new residents. This rapid, uncoordinated growth of suburbs was sometimes referred to as urban sprawl, resulting in a multiplicity of government agencies within a region and a duplication of municipal services. This growth of the suburbs on the fringes of Michigan's largest cities transformed life patterns, eventually affecting class structure, ethnic assimilation, and race relations. For example, by 1960 the suburbs in Michigan (and nationwide) contained as many people as the nearby central cities, and by 1970 suburbs were home to a majority of the residents of Michigan's SMSAs. This relocation of population from cities to suburbs came just as the civil rights movement of the 1950s and 1960s was seeking equality for black Americans. These population shifts made such equality harder to achieve and changed the basic assumptions and framework used to make many significant economic, social, and political decisions.

The collective motivations of thousands of individuals as well as national trends influenced the growth of Michigan's suburbs. Many middle-class families desired newer homes in smaller communities with less congestion than the larger cities. Some also wanted to escape from urban problems and to avoid paying the taxes associated with home ownership in cities. These individual desires were supplemented by larger forces.

Several national trends had a significant impact on the shaping of suburbs in Michigan. Increased availability of automobiles in the 1940s and 1950s, combined with prosperity for auto workers and the state's expanding economy, made it possible to live further from the job and to commute to work. The federal Interstate Highway Act of 1956 accelerated the rush to the suburbs by providing expressways from suburbs to central city job locations. Highway building financed solely by the state of Michigan further aided this development.

Federal programs made it easier for middle-class white families to finance the purchase of suburban homes. In the 1930s banks usually had required a 50 percent down payment on home mortgages and repayment within ten years, severely limiting access to home loans. During the 1940s and 1950s, however, the Federal Housing Administration (FHA) insured thirty-year bank mortgages ranging from 90 to 95 percent of home value, and the Veterans Administration (VA) insured them for 100 percent. Private banks not only welcomed the federally-insured mortgages but also liberalized terms for borrowers whose mortgages were not federally insured.

The new mortgage policies were of greater benefit in developing suburbs than in sustaining central cities. The FHA gave preference to buyers of single-family, detached houses—the type that could most easily be built in the suburbs—and offered less favorable terms to applicants desiring to improve older homes. Both the FHA and the VA preferred to grant home loans to middle-income buyers who could afford suburban homes. The FHA used a rating system to determine the degree of risk involved in insuring loans in different communities. This system resulted in high rankings for suburban areas, moderate rankings for the newest areas of large cities, and redlining—or an "undesirable" ranking—for older areas of central cities.[5]

Finally, business leaders decentralized their commercial and retail operations, transferring many downtown stores to regional shopping malls beyond city limits and taking jobs and commercial activities from central cities to suburban areas. Cities lost a major portion of their tax base, including middle-class workers, commercial and retail stores, and, eventually, factories. Ironically, for many years suburban residents in large numbers continued to work in central cities, but shifted their shopping and tax paying to the suburbs. This caused many cities to adopt income taxes on both residents and nonresident commuting workers in order to pay for the basic city services rendered to city employers and commuters who benefited from these services.

This trend of large- and medium-sized cities to merely maintain or lose residents while nearby suburbs increased in population occurred across Michigan. In the 1950s, Detroit had small but significant population losses while its suburbs grew by 131 percent.[6] For example, nearby communities in Oakland County showed considerable population increases in the same years. Oak Park increased 595.5 percent to 36,632 residents. Royal Oak grew 71.9 percent to 80,612, Warren increased over 12,000 percent to 89,246, while Detroit, by 1960, had lost 9.7 percent of its population.[7]

The process of suburban growth and central city decline continued in Michigan SMSAs throughout the 1960s and 1970s. Of eighteen Michigan cities with a population over 75,000 in 1970, only four of them experienced increases in population by 1980; the other fourteen registered population losses, ranging from 0.8 percent in Lansing to 20.5 percent in Detroit. The four with increases were Ann Arbor (7.3 percent), Southfield (9.1 percent), Taylor (10.8 percent), and Sterling Heights (77.6 percent).

ETHNIC AND RACE RELATIONS

The decline of central cities and the rise of suburbs profoundly affected relations among Michigan's ethnic and racial groups. The state's ethnic and racial mixture reflects considerable diversity. The English heritage has been dominant since the early nineteenth century, supplemented by French, German, and Dutch culture. During the latter nineteenth and early twentieth centuries, many nationality groups migrated in substantial numbers to Michigan. Some became identified with a particular place in Michigan: the Dutch in Grand Rapids and Holland, Germans in Frankenmuth and Westphalia, Poles in Hamtramck, and Finns in the Upper Peninsula. Southeast Michigan is home to large numbers of people whose origins are in Eastern Europe: Poles, Rumanians, Hungarians, Yugoslavs, and Ukrainians, many arriving after World War II.[8] In addition, Michigan is said to be home to the largest number of United States residents whose ancestry is Arabic, Bulgarian, Chaldean, and Croatian. Significant concentrations of Asian Indians, Armenians, Chinese, Filipinos, Koreans, Japanese, and Vietnamese, as well as other nationality groups, add to the ethnic and cultural diversity of Michigan.[9] Overall, more than seventy different ethnic, religious, racial, and nationality groups reside in significant numbers in Michigan. Of these, American Indians, Hispanics, and black Americans have had an especially significant impact on the state.

American Indians (native Americans) numbered 40,038, or 0.43 percent of the total state population, in 1980. Forty-seven percent of these lived in the southern counties of Wayne, Oakland, Macomb, Genessee, Ingham, Kent, and Muskegon. Another 9 percent resided in counties with modern Indian reservations: Chippewa, Menominee, Baraga, Isabella, and Ontonagon. The remaining 44 percent were dispersed throughout Michigan in rural areas and small towns, primarily in the northern two-thirds of the state. Native Americans comprised over 8 percent of the total population in each of three Upper Peninsula counties: Baraga, Mackinac, and Chippewa.

Hispanics numbered 162,398 in Michigan's 1980 census—1.75 percent of the total state population. Though they lived in both rural and urban areas, they were concentrated in the southeastern counties of Wayne (46,301), Oakland (14,478), Genessee (7,469), and Macomb

Robert Killips, Lansing

Anthony Guillen, his son Mark and daughter Michelle watch the festivities during the 1988 Hispanic Heritage Week on the steps of the Capitol in Lansing. About 23,000 Hispanics lived in the Lansing area in 1988. Most Hispanics in Michigan were born in Mexico or are descendants of Mexico-born ancestors.

(6,638), with significant numbers also in Ingham (10,523) and Kent (8,742) counties. Most of the other counties have some Hispanic residents, including Saginaw, Oceana, and Lenawee counties, where they make up more than 5 percent of each county's total population. Mexican Americans are the largest of the Hispanic cultural groups.[10]

The number of black Americans grew to 1,198,710, or 13 percent of the total Michigan population, in 1980. Of these, 69 percent (829,868) lived in Wayne County, which was 35.5 percent black. Other large concentrations of blacks were located in the southeastern counties of Oakland (47,962), Genessee (78,804), Saginaw (35,851), and Washtenaw (28,323) as well as in the outstate counties of Kent (31,460), Berrien (24,817), and Ingham (21,084). Lake County's 16.7 percent black population (1,285), which has centered around the mainly black resort community of Idlewild, was the only large concentration of blacks outside the mostly urbanized southern counties.[11] By the 1980s, blacks were the majority population in Detroit, Inkster, Highland Park, and Benton Harbor; comprised between 36 and 41 percent of the people living in the cities of Saginaw, Pontiac, Ecorse, and Flint; and made up 16 to 29 percent of the population of Kalamazoo, Grand Rapids, Albion, and Ypsilanti.[12]

The presence of a substantial black population in Michigan is new to the twentieth century. However, black settlement in Michigan dates back to the era of explorers and fur traders in the 1700s, to slavery in prestatehood Michigan, the operation of the Underground Railroad in pre-Civil War times, and to the settlement of former slaves. Blacks remained rural in residence and proportionately distributed throughout southern Michigan through most of the nineteenth century. However, by 1910, 71 percent of blacks lived in urban areas with more than 50 percent in cities of 25,000 or more population. Additionally, a larger percentage of the state's blacks began to live in Detroit: 26 percent in 1900, 33.5 percent in 1910, 68 percent in 1920, and no less than 63 percent through the 1980s.[13] The availability of jobs in the 1940s proved a special stimulus to black migration to Michigan, boosting blacks from 4 percent of the state population in 1940 to 6.9 percent by 1950. Each ten years' census for the last forty years has revealed an increase in the black population, a total increase exceeding 200,000 from 1940 to 1980, making blacks the state's largest minority group (see Table 1).

Blacks have experienced a wide range of discrimination in Michigan. During most of the post-World War II period, public and parochial schools were racially segregated, job discrimination was rampant, and housing was only available in limited quantity and quality in racially-restricted areas. Racial names and slurs were often hurled at blacks, and blacks could not expect police protection against the occasional physical violence practiced by whites against blacks. Nor did police usually treat blacks with the same courtesy shown to whites or enforce laws equally against both blacks and whites accused or suspected of breaking the law. Moreover, as middle-class whites moved to the suburbs, partly to escape the problems of city living, blacks were largely

TABLE 1

Black Population in Michigan in the Twentieth Century

Year	Total Population in Michigan	Total Increase in Michigan Population	Black Population in Michigan	Increase in Black Population	Black % of State Total
1900	2,420,982		15,816		.7%
1910	2,810,173	389,191	17,115	1,299	.6%
1920	3,668,412	858,239	60,082	42,967	1.6%
1930	4,842,325	1,173,913	169,453	109,371	3.5%
1940	5,256,106	413,781	208,345	38,892	4.0%
1950	6,371,766	1,115,660	442,296	233,951	6.9%
1960	7,823,194	1,451,528	717,581	275,285	9.2%
1970	8,881,826	1,058,632	991,066	273,485	11.2%
1980	9,262,078	380,252	1,198,710	207,644	13.0%

Source: Derived from the United States Bureau of the Census, *Twelfth Through the Twentieth Census of the United States, 1900 through 1980*; see also *Michigan Statistical Abstract, 1986–1987*, p. 12 ff.

confined to the central cities. Real estate agents, banks, and officials of the FHA and the VA cooperated to insure that blacks did not purchase or rent homes and apartments in the suburbs.[14]

Racial tensions in Detroit during World War II led whites to protest the admittance of blacks to the newly-opened Sojourner Truth Housing Project in a predominantly white neighborhood and to the promotion of black workers in factories. During the Detroit race riot of 1943, many whites hit and beat blacks, often within the sight of policemen. Police were aggressive in attacking blacks during the 1943 riot, even shooting and beating innocent black bystanders. However, police avoided using force to stop whites from attacking blacks or to cause white mobs to disperse. As a result, twenty-five of the thirty-four persons killed were blacks; seventeen of the blacks were killed by the police. At the time, and into the 1970s, police in Michigan limited their approach in stopping racial disorders to "surrounding, arresting, maltreating, and shooting" blacks while making "little attempt . . . to check the activities of whites."[15]

In the 1943 riot, the main activity involved white mobs physically attacking blacks, attempting to injure them. By contrast, the 1967

Detroit riot involved large numbers of blacks, and some whites, stealing from stores and setting fire to buildings in neighborhoods inhabited by a majority of blacks. Thus, many analysts term the 1943 event a race riot (attempting to injure or kill the members of a particular race) and the 1967 event a property riot, because the main purpose was to steal from white merchants who controlled the businesses in black neighborhoods. It was widely believed that these businesses profited at the expense of poor black residents. Still, the 1967 riot resulted in large numbers of blacks dead, mostly at the hands of the 95 percent white Detroit police, the National Guard, and the United States Army. Only two people were killed by rioters, and several were killed by store owners. Of the forty-three people killed, thirty-three were black and ten were white.[16] Smaller-scale civil disturbances occurred in Lansing and other cities in the later 1960s.

In spite of problems which remain in the 1980s, considerable improvement in the status of blacks has occurred in Michigan since the 1940s. These changes are a result of considerable crusading by black organizations in Michigan, greater racial integration initiated by the nationwide civil rights movement, the rising political strength of the rapidly growing black population, the greater involvement of black men and women in heavy industry and in labor unions, and the passage of far-sighted civil rights laws by the Michigan state legislature and some city councils.

In using state law to combat racial and sexual discrimination in employment and housing, Michigan has been a national leader. A 1955 law established the Fair Employment Practices Commission which became a part of the Michigan Civil Rights Commission in 1963, when Michigan became the only state in the nation to create a Civil Rights Commission by its state constitution. In 1966, Michigan laws were amended to prohibit sexual discrimination in employment, and a 1968 law prohibited racial discrimination in the sale or rental of housing. In the 1970s, the jurisdiction of the commission was broadened to protect additional categories of civil rights and to cover not only employment and housing, but also education, places of public accommodation and public service, and law enforcement.[17]

Blacks became politically influential in the 1960s and 1970s, electing mayors in seven of the state's fifteen largest cities, including Detroit, the state's largest city. A number of blacks serve on city councils and county commissions and the sixteen black members of the state legislature in 1988 constitute 11 percent of the total. Since 1970 Richard H. Austin has been secretary of state in Michigan, and two blacks, Otis M. Smith and Dennis W. Archer, have served on the Michigan Supreme

Court. Over forty blacks serve as judges in Michigan, including four federal judges: District Judges Anna Diggs Taylor, Julian A. Cook, Jr., Benjamin F. Gibson, and Sixth Circuit Court Judge Damon J. Keith. Thus, blacks have greater political representation and have used it to sharply reduce police brutality, to command fairer employment practices, to widen educational opportunities, and to achieve a greater stake in the business community. Though blacks as a group still have many problems and encounter social barriers, their overall economic, social, and political status has advanced and greater resources exist to address some of their needs.

EDUCATION

Race relations have also played an important role in the development of the state's educational system. Education in Michigan changed considerably after 1945 due to a sharp rise in the number of school-age children, the expansion of the total capacity of the educational system from kindergarten through the university level, the revision of curriculum to reflect changing values and societal concerns, new educational principles, rapid changes in science and technology, and the impact of social and racial issues upon all aspects of the educational system. In addition, state government increasingly played a larger role in financing local school districts, measuring the progress of students, encouraging the establishment of community colleges, and expanding the opportunities for higher education in state-supported colleges and universities.

Nationwide, birthrates increased sharply after World War II, resulting in a larger proportion of school-age children. In addition, Michigan's population was continuing to grow at a high rate as many people came from other states seeking jobs in industry. Indeed, the state's population growth during the 1950s—over 22 percent—ranked third in the nation, outpaced only by California and Florida[18] (see Table 2). As a result, enrollment in Michigan elementary schools increased by 48.4 percent from 696,289 in 1950 to 1,032,980 in 1960, and high school enrollments grew 58.9 percent from 372,582 to 592,184 during the same time period.[19] During the 1970s and early 1980s, however, school enrollment in Michigan declined. School districts across Michigan were forced to close schools and lay off teachers. By the later 1980s, however, school enrollment once again began to slowly increase.

The greatest impact of these changes was felt in urban areas as older cities and newer suburbs during the 1950s and 1960s built schools, hired additional teachers, and changed curriculum. Increasingly, local

TABLE 2

Michigan Population Growth, 1940–1980

Year	Population	Increase	Percent
1940	5,256,106	—	—
1950	6,371,766	1,115,660	21.2
1960	7,823,194	1,451,428	22.8
1970	8,881,826	1,058,632	13.5
1980	9,262,078	380,252	4.3

Total Increase	Total Percent Increase
4,005,972	76.2

Source: Derived from the United States Bureau of the Census, *Twelfth Through the Twentieth Census of the United States, 1900 through 1980*; see also *Michigan Statistical Abstract, 1986–1987*, p. 12 ff.

school districts sought financial aid from state government to help finance their expanded services. Local districts, limited in the amount of income they could raise from their traditional source of revenue—property taxes—sought part of the surplus funds state government had received in the early 1940s from the state sales tax. A 1946 Sales Tax Diversion Amendment to the state constitution required two-thirds of state sales tax income to be returned to local school districts and one-sixth of state sales tax revenue to go to city, village, and township governments.[20] With such a large portion of the state's taxes being returned to local government units, state government experienced financial difficulties throughout the 1950s, which were only resolved with the adoption of a new constitution in 1963 and a state income tax in 1967. The new constitution and income tax provided a sounder basis for both state revenue and state aid to education.[21] Yet, local school boards still relied on property taxes for the major part of their financing, causing considerable variations in educational opportunities based upon variations in funding. In the 1970s and 1980s, voters were reluctant to approve property tax increases to meet educational needs. The 1978 Headlee Amendment to the state constitution further limited property tax increases and made state financial aid to local school districts an even greater financial necessity in the 1980s.[22]

By 1980, 68 percent of Michigan residents were high school gradu-
ates and 14.3 percent had completed four or more years of college.[23]
The kindergarten to high school (K–12) public school enrollment of
2,123,497 in the 1972–73 school year had declined 27 percent by the
1984–85 school year to 1,542,257, reflecting the drop in the birthrate of
the post-baby boom generation. During 1984–85, approximately 90 percent of Michigan students received their K–12 education in public
schools. The dropout rate for public school students fluctuated between
5 and 6 percent in the 1970s and 1980s, with some school districts having a 0 percent rate and others having a rate as high as 15 percent.
Statewide, approximately 24 percent of students entering the ninth
grade did not complete their high school education. Variations in dropout rates by racial/ethnic group also existed: 3 percent for Asian-
Americans, 5 percent for whites, 7 percent for American Indians, 8
percent for blacks, and 10 percent for Hispanics.[24]

Concern about the high dropout rate and the quality of instruction in
the public schools prompted the state in 1969 to establish the Michigan
Educational Assessment Program. Fourth and seventh grade students
were tested in the areas of math and reading. Testing of tenth grade
students began in the 1979–1980 school year. A science test was added
to the assessment during the later 1980s.

Efforts to lower the dropout rate in public schools coincided with the
broader issues of the overall quality of education and of expanding educational opportunities from kindergarten through university to all students, including the working class and racial minority groups. One
method often proposed to upgrade education for blacks was the desegregation of schools in the larger cities. Though it was often asserted
that racial segregation in Michigan schools was simply a result of segregated housing, it was discovered that school boards had often made
decisions that reinforced the segregation of neighborhoods and avoided
adopting any policy that would cut across or break down the existing
racial patterns. In a variety of ways, cities such as Grand Rapids,
Lansing, Kalamazoo, and Benton Harbor were confronted with the
issue of racial segregation in the schools. However, the most notable
lawsuits were filed in Pontiac, Ferndale, and Detroit, with considerable
national attention coming to focus on the Pontiac and Detroit cases.

The Pontiac lawsuit, begun in 1969, initially resulted in a federal district court ruling that the Pontiac school board had kept the public
school system segregated by decisions affecting placement of new
schools and teacher assignments. Judge Damon J. Keith ordered about
nine thousand children, or 37 percent of the system's students, to be
bused to thirty-six mostly-white schools, thereby achieving a black

enrollment at each school varying from 20 to 36 percent. Appeals by the Pontiac school board postponed the implementation of the order until September 1971. By then, two groups that opposed busing to achieve racial integration had started to devote their attention to the planned desegregation of Pontiac schools.

The National Action Group (NAG), composed of white mothers in Pontiac, opposed school busing to achieve racial integration. NAG preferred to keep segregated neighborhood schools, though it insisted that its opposition was not based on racial considerations. One of NAG's first public rallies attracted five thousand people and featured George Wallace, the governor of Alabama, who in 1963 had "stood in the schoolhouse door" in an attempt to keep blacks out of the University of Alabama. NAG officially took a stand against violence, but it sponsored boycotts and picketing, which led to violence and to the shouting of "nigger" at black students entering previously all-white schools. The

Detroit News

School anti-busing demonstration in Pontiac, October 1971.

Pontiac Police Officers Association contributed three hundred dollars to NAG and police officers acted very leniently toward white demonstrators, with the police chief admitting "if we wanted to get technical . . . we could have arrested hundreds." Police, however, did not hesitate to restrain or to arrest blacks protesting at Pontiac school board meetings. The "gentle persuasion and logic" reserved for white demonstrations was seldom used on blacks.[25]

A second opposition group was the Ku Klux Klan. On 30 August 1971, a week before school began, some criminals used dynamite to destroy ten school buses. The FBI arrested six alleged members of the Ku Klux Klan, charging them with conspiracy. Convictions resulted in members of the Klan, including the alleged Grand Dragon, Robert Miles, spending time in prison.[26]

The Ferndale case began in 1968 and took over twelve years of litigation before a mutually agreeable solution was reached. The result, in January 1981, was the integration of one all-black elementary school with nearby white elementary schools. The process included the busing of approximately three hundred children.[27]

The Detroit school integration lawsuit attracted national attention because of the size of the school district and the nature of the judge's ruling. Federal District Court Judge Stephen J. Roth ruled on 27 September 1971 that the state of Michigan and the Detroit Board of Education were guilty of maintaining racial segregation in Detroit's schools. Judge Roth stated that the Detroit board had continued and reinforced segregation through decisions on "site selection" for new schools, feeder patterns, and zoning decisions, which kept children from mostly-white and mostly-black neighborhoods from attending the same schools. The state of Michigan, he went on, was guilty of failing, until recently, to provide Detroit with money for busing students regardless of the students' poverty or distance from their assigned school, "while providing in many neighboring, mostly white, suburban districts the full range of state supported transportation."[28] The remedy, the judge suggested, was to draw up a three-county, cross-district busing plan that would include Detroit and its suburbs, since Detroit schools were already majority black, and any segregation in Detroit schools is "the responsibility of all of society." Judge Roth delayed a final order pending further consideration.[29]

Predictably, considerable opposition to the cross-district busing intention of Judge Roth arose immediately. Suburban homeowners and municipal leaders organized and lobbied their elected representatives. Previously, sixteen of the seventeen white United States congressional representatives from Michigan had voted against proposed laws to limit busing as a method of desegregating schools in other parts of the country. They were now faced with a possible unusually large-scale cross-district busing plan close to home. All seventeen now voted in favor of legislation introduced by Rep. William Broomfield of Michigan that would postpone the starting date of any federal court order requiring school busing until all appeals had been exhausted or the time for them had expired. This law would drastically delay any actual court order's effect. The United States House of Representatives overwhelmingly approved Broomfield's proposed law. Previously, Gov. William Milliken had announced on both television and radio that the state of Michigan would appeal Roth's pending decision because the judge went too far and that "children—white or black—don't learn by riding buses."[30]

In May 1972, Judge Roth made public his decision. The eleven-page order required cross-district school busing to integrate Detroit schools. His plan required 310,000 children to be bused, with black and white children assuming equal responsibility for the transfers. Four out of ten school children in the affected districts would ride up to twenty miles each day so that classrooms would be 25 percent black. This plan would have allowed Detroit's 290,000 students to have been effectively integrated with the 490,000 children in fifty-three nearby suburban school districts. Roth also required all schools to have no "less than 10 percent black faculty and staff."[31]

The plan was to be started in the fall 1974 school term. Before this could occur, Judge Roth died on 1 July 1974 after suffering his third heart attack in twenty months. On 25 July 1974, in a 5 to 4 decision, the United States Supreme Court reversed Judge Roth's cross-district busing order. Detroit proceeded with a Detroit-only busing plan to desegregate its schools. This plan was implemented through the late 1980s.[32]

Michigan's colleges and universities also faced the pressures of population growth and social change during the years after World War II. Higher education had experienced a continual increase in student enrollment throughout the twentieth century, with a substantial portion occurring after 1945. In 1920, approximately 30,000 students attended the state's private and public colleges and universities, but by 1950 about 100,000 were enrolled. These students included thousands of armed forces veterans whose education was financed by the federal government under the Servicemen's Readjustment Act, popularly known as the G.I. Bill. By 1960, the numbers had increased to more than 150,000.[33]

Michigan is unusual in that 70 to 80 percent of its college students have been enrolled in tax-supported schools rather than in private institutions, 20 percent higher than the national average. Thus, during the period from the 1950s through the 1970s, the state was forced to dramatically expand its higher education capacity to accommodate the baby-boom generation by expanding several colleges and universities and establishing new ones.

State financial aid to community colleges increased considerably, and laws were amended to grant governmental units more options and greater flexibility in starting and operating junior or community colleges. New schools added to the sixteen existing in the 1950s brought the total of public junior and community colleges to twenty-nine, with a total of thirty-eight campuses by the late 1970s. These schools now offer low-cost tuition, feature both vocational education and liberal arts courses, and are sufficiently numerous and geographically placed so that at least one is within forty miles of about 95 percent of Michigan's population. The schools vary considerably in size, ranging (in 1987) from Macomb Community College, with 32,141 students, to Kirtland Community College near Roscommon, with 1,023 students. An important part of the state's educational system, public junior and community colleges enrolled 212,855 students in the 1987 fall term, about 41 percent of the total 517,000 students enrolled in Michigan's public and private colleges and universities.[34]

Four-year colleges and universities also underwent change and development. Of the tax-supported schools, two—Ferris and Wayne State—became state institutions for the first time in the 1950s. Michigan College of Mining and Technology became Michigan Technological University. Three teachers' colleges—Central Michigan, Eastern Michigan, and Western Michigan—became universities in the 1950s and 1960s. Two universities that began as branches of larger schools—Oakland and Lake Superior State—became independent of their parent institutions, while two branches of The University of Michigan, at Flint and Dearborn, remained under Ann Arbor's control. Additionally, two schools were newly created—Grand Valley State and Saginaw Valley State.

All fifteen of the state-supported schools in the 1980s are known for specialized programs, overall high quality of instruction, and distinctive curriculums. Three Michigan institutions—The University of Michigan, Michigan State University, and Wayne State University—rank high among the top one hundred research universities in the United States. Individual programs at Michigan's universities are often lauded as excellent models or have high ranking in their fields. In 1985, Michigan was tied for the ninth highest number of public universities among all states in the country. In the fall term 1987, Michigan's fifteen state-supported universities enrolled 244,288 students, approximately 47 percent of all college students in the state. Private colleges and

Kirtland Community College, near Roscommon, was established in 1966. Fall 1988 enrollment at the college was 1,044 students.

universities enrolled approximately 62,000 or 12 percent. Indeed, Michigan provides not only a quantity of educational opportunity but also an excellent quality of higher education.[35]

As Michigan's youth took advantage of increasing educational opportunity during the postwar years, labor unions continued to organize and represent the state's work force. Labor unions had expanded and enhanced their role in Michigan society as a result of the historic union-organizing activities of the 1930s and 1940s. The pattern-setting bargaining agreements reached by the United Automobile Workers (UAW) in the late 1940s and 1950s and union advocacy of a variety of social and political changes were designed to improve the quality of life in American society. Nationally, and in Michigan, union membership increased considerably, achieving record levels in the 1950s and then declining in the late 1960s and 1970s. The ups and downs of the Michigan automobile manufacturing industry played a major role in the number of union members in Michigan. For example, in the 1930s Michigan employed over 60 percent of all auto workers nationwide, but only about 47 percent by 1958. The processes of automation, decentralization of auto manufacturing to other states, and a decline in the number of defense contracts awarded to Michigan firms had combined to reduce the number of employed auto workers.[36] Increasingly, over the last thirty years, Michigan workers and unions have had no connection with the automobile industry, but the large number and concentration of workers in that industry continues to give their economic and social standing unusual influence on Michigan's society.

One labor union, the United Auto Workers (UAW), has a unique relation to the state of Michigan. Created in the state's historic labor-organizing activities of the 1930s, the great majority of its members lived in Michigan until after the decentralization of automobile manufacturing dispersed many jobs to other states. Still, even in the 1980s, Michigan contains the largest concentration of both auto plants and auto workers in the nation. Moreover, the UAW has kept its national headquarters in Detroit and its best-known president, Walter P. Reuther, had a Detroit connection throughout his adult years.

Walter P. Reuther, a West Virginia native who came to Detroit in 1927 at the age of nineteen, finished high school and attended Detroit City College (later Wayne State University) for three years while working a full-time shift in the auto plants. A co-founder of the UAW in the 1930s, he rose through the ranks to become UAW president in 1946, remaining so until his death in a plane crash in May 1970. Under Reuther's presidency, UAW unionism took on aspects of a social reform movement which sought to improve not only workers' pay and work conditions, but also the economic and social standing of all workers. Reuther acquired a reputation as a national leader, and his union's activities had considerable influence throughout the United States. UAW contract agreements with the auto manufacturers resulted in precedent-setting innovations such as cost of living allowances (COLA), company-financed pension plans, supplemental unemployment benefits (SUB), and profit sharing.[37] These advances in pay and worker benefits established a standard that unions nationwide demanded other employers meet. In the words of John Barnard, the UAW, under Reuther's presidency, "set the pace for a generation of workers in winning compensation that raised living standards, enhanced economic security, provided opportunities for workers' families, and added to self-respect."[38]

Archives of Labor History and Urban Affairs, Wayne State University

Walter Reuther addressing workers during the 1950 Chrysler Corporation strike.

WOMEN

Women also experienced significant changes in their economic, social and political status from the 1940s through the 1980s. Women's participation in the labor force sharply increased and the types of jobs available to women expanded considerably to include many nontraditional, previously all-male job categories. The level of education completed by women rose as life expectancy increased and family size (number of children per family) declined. Thus women lived longer, had fewer children, devoted a smaller percentage of their lives to pregnancy and child rearing, and a larger percentage to obtaining an education and gainful employment outside the home.

Women's choices expanded and they enjoyed greater opportunities for self-fulfillment and self-development. There were fewer restrictions from socially-prescribed sex role stereotypes. Yet these changes came slowly, involved considerable agitation and demand for the principles of equality and fairness, and necessitated adjustment of social attitudes and practices.[39]

World War II helped break some of the barriers which excluded women from traditionally male jobs in heavy industry, government, and streetcar conducting. The number of women workers in Michigan increased 49 percent from 391,600 in March 1940 to a peak of 799,100 in November 1943. Previously, most working women had been single and under the age of thirty, but by 1943 the number of married women equaled the number of single women workers, and those over the age of thirty were almost equal in number to those under thirty.[40] Large numbers of women were laid off after the end of World War II in 1945, but the number of women workers in Michigan began to slowly increase again in the late 1940s and 1950s, and at a faster pace in the 1960s to 1980s. Thus, women's participation in the Michigan labor force rose from 32.7 percent in 1960 to 40.2 percent in 1970, and to 48.5 percent in 1976.[41]

Nationally, among women, the labor force participation rate rose from 34 percent in 1950 to 52 percent in 1980, and to 54.5 percent in 1985.[42] Because of their greater need to earn money for basic family necessities, a larger percentage of minority women have worked. Thus, 48 percent of black women were in the United States labor force in 1960 and 57 percent in 1985; 43 percent of Hispanic women worked in 1975 and 49 percent in 1985.[43] As a result, by the early 1980s women made up 43 percent of the entire United States labor force and constituted almost 60 percent of its growth since 1970.[44]

In the 1980s, women are frequently employed as construction workers, heavy truck drivers, in police and detective work, as firefighters, auto mechanics, plumbers, miners, professional athletes, pilots, and navigators. In addition, the number of women engineers, editors, reporters, lawyers, judges, and computer equipment operators steadily increases. Women are achieving higher levels of management within businesses of all sizes and many women have become business owners. The barriers to women entering male-only occupations have been knocked down and previous employment ceilings are being pushed higher, even though income differentials based on race and sex still exist nationwide. For example, in 1980 white women as a group earned only 59 percent of the income of white males doing the same work, and blacks as a group received even less than either white men or white women.[45]

Michigan women also sought higher levels of education during the 1970s and 1980s. Their rate of high school graduation in the 1970s was higher than the national average for all ages, while the completion rate for Michigan men was higher than the national average only in the eighteen to twenty-four-year-old category. The rate of college

310

attendance for Michigan women was increasing but was still lower than the men's rate, with women showing a slightly greater tendency to enroll as part-time students in two-year colleges while men had a higher rate of full-time enrollment in four-year colleges.[46] Nationally, in 1979–80, almost half of all bachelors' and masters' degrees were awarded to women, primarily in the areas of the humanities, nursing, and education, rather than in the physical sciences, mathematics, or engineering. Yet national trends in the 1980s show women earning 30 percent of doctoral degrees, 30 percent of law degrees, 20 percent of medical degrees, and 14 percent of dentistry degrees.[47]

In the movement to attain equality between the sexes, Michigan women and Michigan women's organizations have played valuable and historically significant roles. Within the state, Michigan women have pressed for equalization of salaries in business and in colleges, more equitable treatment for female athletes and students, and an end to sexual discrimination in hiring, promotion, worker relations, and worker benefits.[48] One result has been several notable achievements for Michigan women. The Rev. Marjorie Swank Matthews became the first woman elected a bishop of the United Methodist Church. Three women have served on the Michigan Supreme Court, two as chief justice. Mary Stallings Coleman, the first woman elected to the Michigan Supreme Court in 1972, was chief justice from 1979 to 1982, and was probably the third woman in the nation to be a chief justice of a state supreme court. Patricia J. Boyle has been a supreme court member since 1983, and Dorothy Comstock Riley has been a member since 1985 and chief justice since January 1987.[49]

Women have also significantly increased their membership in the Michigan State Legislature since 1945. Since the first woman legislator served in 1921, fifty women have been members of the legislature: five between 1921 and 1945 and forty-five from 1946 to 1988. In 1987–88, twenty-two women made up 15 percent of the legislature's total membership.[50]

The position of lieutenant governor is the highest elective office held by a woman in Michigan. Martha Wright Griffiths was elected to this position in 1982, and in 1986, when Griffiths was opposed by Colleen Engler, both major parties nominated a woman for lieutenant governor.

On the national scene, Michigan women have played influential roles in the struggle for women's equality. As a congresswoman, Martha Griffiths played a decisive role in adding a clause banning sexual discrimination in employment to the 1964 Civil Rights Law, and she was a primary sponsor of the proposed Equal Rights Amendment (ERA) to

Office of the Lieutenant Governor

Martha W. Griffiths, a former congresswoman from Michigan, was elected in 1982 as Michigan's lieutenant governor. Since the 1940s she has been a power in the Democratic party and a strong supporter of women's rights.

the United States Constitution approved by Congress in 1972.[51] Betty Ford was not only an active supporter of the ERA, but was also known for her candor in speaking out on a variety of issues and for enlarging the customary role of First Lady while Gerald R. Ford was president.[52] Other Michigan women who were active supporters of the ERA included Elly M. Peterson, a former assistant chairperson of the Republican National Committee who, along with Helen Milliken, served as a national co-chair of ERAmerica (a group lobbying for the ratification of the proposed amendment by the required thirty-eight states), and Mildred Jeffrey, chair of the National Women's Political Caucus. The

Michigan legislature ratified the ERA in May 1972, two months after its approval by congress. Though the ERA did not become part of the United States Constitution, the efforts to have it adopted raised the consciousness of all Americans and focused attention on the need to end all forms of inequality between the sexes.

QUALITY OF LIFE

Women contributed directly to the improved standard of living Michigan residents experienced in the postwar years. The quality of life in Michigan can be illustrated briefly by reference to income and life expectancy. Most residents have benefited from the state's overall prosperity. During the 1950s to 1970s, however, between 13 and 20 percent of all Michigan families had incomes below the poverty level. Additionally, poverty was disproportionately distributed, with rural residents, racial minority groups, and families headed by females having higher rates of poverty, and urban whites having an overall higher income. The gap between income in rural areas and industrial areas also increased, and the unemployment rate in northern Michigan and in the poorer sections of Detroit rose to three or more times the statewide rate.[53] In the later 1980s, the great majority of Michigan's families were economically well off, but significant amounts of poverty remain in the state.

Life expectancy in the state in 1985 for all persons was 73.6 years, just below the national average of 73.8 years, ranking Michigan thirty-first among all states. There are also different average life expectancies for males, females, racial minorities, and the poor. Upper-income people can afford better medical care and a healthier diet. The poor, however, often cannot afford medical care and seldom see physicians until their health problems become serious, sometimes beyond the stage of effective medical intervention. For example, Michigan has a high infant mortality rate among blacks. This is attributed primarily to poor pregnant women not being able to afford adequate prenatal medical care. On the other hand, women tend to outlive men. The resulting average life expectancies in Michigan as of 1985 were 78.2 years for white females, 70.8 years for white males, 72.8 years for black females, and 64.1 years for black males.[54]

During the 1960s quality-of-life issues rallied protesters and revolutionaries. The civil rights movement and the Vietnam War, in particular, acted to fracture society; the state and nation nearly came apart. More than twenty-five hundred Michigan residents were killed in Vietnam. Opposition to the war, to racism in the South and at home, to poverty and economic inequality, and to what was termed an oppressive conformist society, brought thousands of New Left radicals into class-rooms, government halls, and the streets. Michiganians as diverse as Tom Hayden, Malcolm X, and John Sinclair played prominent roles during this political, social, and cultural rebellion. Legacies of the sixties movement—the good (peace, justice, tolerance), and the bad (cynicism, apathy, drugs)—continue to bind and divide Michigan residents more than twenty years later.

Though Michigan in the later 1980s still has problems of poverty, infant mortality, uneven economic opportunities, regional disparities, racial polarization, and sexual inequality, significant changes have occurred since 1945. To many, signs of hope appear bright that these problems will be addressed in the near future and ameliorated. Indeed, as this history of the state shows, the material, economic and human resources exist to solve these problems. A greater public interest and awareness appears imminent. Perhaps, to paraphrase William Faulkner, Michigan will be a leader in helping humans to not merely survive, but prevail over our common problems.

◆

NOTES

1. Lawrence M. Sommers, *Michigan: A Geography* (Boulder, Colo.: Westview Press, 1984), 9, 11.

2. Willis F. Dunbar and George S. May, *Michigan: A History of the Wolverine State* (Grand Rapids: William B. Eerdmans Publishing Company, 1980), 557.

3. Sommers, *Michigan: A Geography,* 21.

4. L. M. Sommers, J. T. Darden, J. R. Harmon, and L. K. Sommers, *Atlas of Michigan* (East Lansing: Michigan State University Press, 1977), 67, 71; *Michigan Statistical Abstract, 20th edition 1986–1987* (Detroit: Bureau of Business Research, School of Business Administration, Wayne State University, 1987), 618–19.

5. Richard Polenberg, *One Nation Divisible: Class, Race and Ethnicity in the United States Since 1938* (New York: Viking Press, 1980), 131–32.

6. Ibid., 128.

7. Figures taken from *City Profile* (Oak Park: Department of Community Development, City of Oak Park, Michigan, 1976).

8. Sommers, *Michigan: A Geography,* 30–31.

9. See James M. Anderson and Iva A. Smith, eds., *Ethnic Groups in Michigan* (Detroit: Michigan Ethnic Heritage Studies Center and Ethnos Press, The University of Michigan, 1983); Dunbar and May, *Michigan: A History of the Wolverine State,* 592.

10. Sommers, *Michigan: A Geography,* 37.

11. Ibid., 33–37.

12. DeWitt S. Dykes, Jr., "Black Population: Growth, Distribution and Public Office," in Anderson and Smith, *Ethnic Groups in Michigan,* 39–52.

13. Ibid., 40–41.

14. Joe T. Darden, *Detroit: Race and Uneven Development* (Philadelphia: Temple University Press, 1987), 72–73.

15. Thurgood Marshall, "The Gestapo in Detroit," *Crisis* 50 (1943): 232–33.

16. Darden, *Detroit,* 72–73.

17. See Michigan Department of Civil Rights, *Civil Rights Protections in Michigan* (Lansing, n.d.).

18. George S. May, *Michigan: An Illustrated History of the Great Lakes State* (Northridge, Conn.: Windsor Publications, 1987), 194.

19. F. Clever Bald, *Michigan in Four Centuries* (New York: Harper and Row, 1961), 470.

20. Dunbar and May, *Michigan: A History of the Wolverine State,* 637.

21. Ibid., 652, 661.

22. Ibid., 718.

23. *Almanac of the 50 States* (Wellesley, Mass.: Information Publications, 1987), 181.

24. *Condition of Michigan Education in 1986* (Lansing: Michigan State Board of Education, 1988), 19–20.

25. George R. Metcalf, *From Little Rock to Boston: The History of School Desegregation* (Westport, Conn.: Greenwood Press, 1983), 132–33.

26. Ibid., 132.

27. Ibid., 148–55.

28. Ibid., 160–61.

29. Ibid., 160–62.

30. Ibid., 162–63.

31. Ibid., 164–65.

32. Ibid., 165, 169, 188–93.

33. Bald, *Michigan in Four Centuries,* 458, 470–71; Alan Clive, *State of War: Michigan in World War II* (Ann Arbor: The University of Michigan Press, 1979), 216.

34. Dunbar and May, *Michigan: A History of the Wolverine State,* 671, 672; *1988 Michigan Government Directory* (Lansing: Public Sector Consultants, 1988), 436–47.

35. Dunbar and May, *Michigan: A History of the Wolverine State,* 669–72; *1988 Michigan Government Directory,* 534–47.

36. Dunbar and May, *Michigan: A History of the Wolverine State,* 634.

37. John Barnard, *Walter Reuther and the Rise of the Auto Workers* (Boston: Little, Brown and Company, 1983), 137, 138, 140, 141, 144–48.

38. Ibid., 212–13.

39. Lois W. Banner, *Women in Modern America: A Brief History* (New York: Harcourt Brace Jovanovich, 1984), 231–72.

40. Clive, *State of War,* 186.

41. Mary P. Andrews and Robert P. Boger, eds., *Michigan Family Sourcebook* (East Lansing: Institute for Family and Child Study, College of Human Ecology, Michigan State University, 1980), 50–51.

42. U.S. Bureau of the Census, *American Women: Three Decades of Change* (Washington, D.C., 1984), 15; Cynthia M. Taeuber and Victor Vald, *Women in the American Economy* (Washington, D.C.: U.S. Bureau of the Census, 1985), 2.

43. Taeuber and Vald, *Women in the American Economy,* 4.

44. Mavis Jackson Dion, *We the American Women* (Washington, D.C.: U.S. Bureau of the Census, 1984), 7.

45. Ibid., 7–8; U.S. Bureau of the Census, *American Women,* 21.

46. Andrews and Boger, *Michigan Family Sourcebook,* 119, 120, 129.

47. U.S. Bureau of the Census, *American Women,* 12–13; Taeuber and Vald, *Women in the American Economy,* 13.

48. "Battle of Ann Arbor," *Time,* 12 March 1973, 114–15; Albert Krichmar, *The Women's Movement in the Seventies: An International English Language Bibliography* (Metuchen, N.J.: Scarecrow Press, 1977), 675–78.

49. Telephone interview with the clerk of the Michigan Supreme Court, 23 August 1988; *1988 Michigan Government Directory,* 421, 423.

50. See *Women in the Michigan Legislature, 1921–1987* (Lansing: Michigan State Legislature, 1987); *1988 Michigan Government Directory,* 421–23.

51. Mary Frances Berry, *Why ERA Failed: Women's Rights, and the Amending Process of the Constitution* (Bloomington: Indiana University Press, 1986), 61–64; Emily George, *Martha W. Griffiths* (Washington, D.C.: University Press of America, 1982), 167–85.

52. "Women of the Year," *Time,* 5 January 1976, 19.

53. Dunbar and May, *Michigan: A History of the Wolverine State,* 640; Andrews and Boger, *Michigan Family Sourcebook,* 60–66.

54. "State is 31st in Life Spans," *Detroit News,* 7 November 1985.

----------◆----------

SUGGESTED READINGS

Almanac of the 50 States. Wellesley, Mass.: Information Publications, 1987.

Anderson, James M., and Iva A. Smith, eds. *Ethnic Groups in Michigan.* Detroit: Michigan Ethnic Heritage Studies Center and Ethnos Press, The University of Michigan, 1983.

Andrews, Mary P., and Robert P. Boger, eds. *Michigan Family Sourcebook*. East Lansing: Institute for Family and Child Study, College of Human Ecology, Michigan State University, 1980.

Bald, F. Clever. *Michigan in Four Centuries*. Rev. ed. New York: Harper and Row, 1961.

Banner, Lois W. *Women in Modern America: A Brief History*. New York: Harcourt Brace Jovanovich, 1984.

Barnard, John. *Walter Reuther and the Rise of the Auto Workers*. Boston: Little, Brown and Company, 1983.

Berry, Mary Frances. *Why ERA Failed: Politics, Women's Rights, and the Amending Process of the Constitution*. Bloomington: Indiana University Press, 1986.

City Profile. Oak Park: Department of Community Development, City of Oak Park, Michigan, 1976.

Civil Rights Protections in Michigan. Lansing: Michigan Department of Civil Rights, n.d.

Clive, Alan. *State of War: Michigan in World War II*. Ann Arbor: The University of Michigan Press, 1979.

Condition of Michigan Education in 1986. Lansing: Michigan State Board of Education, 1986.

Darden, Joe T. *Detroit: Race and Uneven Development*. Philadelphia: Temple University Press, 1987.

Dion, Mavis Jackson. *We, The American Women*. Washington, D.C.: U.S. Bureau of the Census, 1984.

Disbrow, Donald W. *Schools for an Urban Society*. Lansing: Michigan Historical Commission, 1968.

Dunbar, Willis F. *The Michigan Record in Higher Education*. Detroit: Wayne State University Press, 1963.

Dunbar, Willis F., and George S. May. *Michigan: A History of the Wolverine State*. Grand Rapids: William B. Eerdmans Publishing Company, 1980.

Dykes, DeWitt S., Jr. "Black Population: Growth, Distribution and Public Office." In *Ethnic Groups in Michigan,* edited by James Anderson and Iva A. Smith, 39–52. Detroit: Michigan Ethnic Heritage Studies Center and Ethnos Press, The University of Michigan, 1983.

George, Emily. *Martha W. Griffiths*. Washington, D.C.: University Press of America, 1982.

Krichmar, Albert. *The Women's Movement in the Seventies: An International English Language Bibliography*. Metuchen, N.J.: Scarecrow Press, 1977.

Marshall, Thurgood. "The Gestapo in Detroit." *Crisis* 50 (1943): 232–33.

May, George S. *Michigan: An Illustrated History of the Great Lakes State*. Northridge, Conn.: Windsor Publications, 1987.

Metcalf, George R. *From Little Rock to Boston: The History of School Desegregation*. Westport, Conn.: Greenwood Press, 1983.

1988 Michigan Government Directory. Lansing: Public Sector Consultants, 1988.

DeWitt S. Dykes, Jr.

Polenberg, Richard. *One Nation Divisible: Class, Race, and Ethnicity in the United States Since 1938*. New York: Viking Press, 1980.

Sommers, Lawrence M. *Michigan: A Geography*. Boulder, Colo.: Westview Press, 1984.

Sommers, L. M., J. T. Darden, J. R. Harmon, and L. K. Sommers. *Atlas of Michigan*. East Lansing: Michigan State University Press, 1977.

Taeuber, Cynthia M., and Victor Vald. *Women in the American Economy*. Washington, D.C.: U.S. Bureau of the Census, 1986.

U.S. Bureau of the Census. *American Women: Three Decades of Change*. Washington, D.C.: U.S. Bureau of the Census, 1984.

————. U.S. Bureau of the Census. *Twelfth Through the Twentieth Censuses, 1900–1980*.

Verway, David I., ed. *Michigan Statistical Abstract, 20th edition 1986–1987*. Detroit: Bureau of Business Research, School of Business Administration, Wayne State University, 1987.

Wolf, Eleanor P. *Trial and Error: The Detroit School Segregation Case*. Detroit: Wayne State University Press, 1981.

Women in the Michigan Legislature, 1921–1987. Lansing: Michigan State Legislature, 1987.

RICHARD J. HATHAWAY

Richard Hathaway is a consultant in the fields of Michigan history and
literature, libraries, and archives. Prior to his consulting practice, he was
for over twenty years with the Library of Michigan. During this time Mr.
Hathaway directed the development of the library's noted historical
research collections. He has also authored many articles and book reviews
for *Michigan History* and other magazines. Mr. Hathaway received a
bachelor's degree from Albion College and masters' degrees in history
and library science from The University of Michigan.

ichigan Vision:
A Usable Past

Historians do not always think of history as a discipline to be "used" in the sense that a knowledge of the past can assist in making decisions today and planning for the future. The academic attitude is often that the challenge of research and interpretation is sufficient reward. Likewise, the amateur history buff, or genealogist, is not searching for guideposts to the future; nostalgia and curiosity are sufficient. For public officials, legislators, teachers, and corporate executives, however, not paying attention to the lessons of the past may mean decisions made without an understanding of their impact on society or the corporate institution.

One method of interpreting Michigan's past as presented in the previous seventeen essays is as a series of continuing stress-lines or conflicting interests. Although many such areas of tension can be traced throughout this book, three seem especially significant: population diversity, economic dislocation, and business/labor conflict.

Richard J. Hathaway

POPULATION DIVERSITY

When the French arrived in the Great Lakes area during the mid-1600s, they encountered native Americans who had lived with the land for several thousand years. Thus began a conflict of cultural traditions and values which continues to the present. The French did not come to colonize the area with homes and farms. Instead, their purpose was to defend their new world empire with forts, control the lucrative fur trade, and convert the natives to Catholicism.

The British, who by 1765 had driven the French from the area, were likewise not interested in settlement. Like the French, their concerns were maintenance of a colonial empire and the fur trade. By 1796, when the British finally withdrew their troops, the newly formed United States took control of the area. Even though the aggressive Americans to the east were primarily settlers rather than soldiers, fur traders or missionaries, Michigan was not heavily settled for another forty years. The Territory of Michigan was established in 1805 with the capital at Detroit, but the population of the territory numbered only 4,800 five years later. Bad publicity which branded Michigan as a land of swamps and fever, and the events of the War of 1812, worked to prevent immigration.

Soon after the opening of the Erie Canal in 1825, which provided a direct water route to Michigan from the east, Michigan's population exploded. The great majority of these settlers came from western New York and New England. Their roots were English, with a mixture of Scots and Irish. The cultural values these farmers and mechanics brought with them remains until today as the dominant ethos of the state.

From the beginning of settlement, however, other peoples came to Michigan. The Irish and Germans moved to towns, farms and villages. The Dutch established colonies in southwest Michigan, where their influence is still predominant. During the latter part of the nineteenth century immigrants from eastern Europe came to farm, to work in the emerging factories of Detroit, to cut timber, or to labor in the mines of the Upper Peninsula. Poles, Italians, Jews, Slavs, Finns and other nationalities added to the ethnic mix of Michigan. More recently, Hispanics (Mexican, Cuban, South American), Asians (Chinese, Korean, Hmong, Vietnamese, Cambodian), and Arabs have made the state their home. But with this diversity of culture and language has also come conflict with the dominant "yankee" culture, and strife between the various ethnic groups. None of these divisions, however, has had the continuing impact of the struggle between black and white.

A few blacks had made their way to the frontier outpost of Detroit while the area was still under British rule. However, the first real settlement of blacks in Michigan did not occur until the two decades preceding the Civil War. Between 1830 and 1850 hundreds of blacks fleeing slavery came to the Detroit area. Occasionally, as in Cass County, a group of families established an agricultural settlement.

Although Michigan's already-established residents were opposed to slavery (especially the expansion of slave labor), they were not willing to accept blacks as equals or as entitled to the rights of citizenship. The denial of voting rights was only the political expression of overt racial hostility. In 1863, a Detroit black man, William Faulkner, was accused of raping two white girls. A white mob, intending to lynch Faulkner, attacked the jail where he was held. Guards fired shots and one rioter was killed. The mob then turned its fury on Detroit's small black community, burning homes and assaulting men, women, and children.

Robert Killips, Lansing

By the 1980s most Asians in Michigan were immigrants, or children of immigrants, from Hong Kong, Taiwan, and Korea. During the 1970s and early 1980s refugees from Southeast Asia came to Michigan, such as this Hmong family from Laos in Lansing. The Japanese presence in Michigan also increased during the 1980s as Japanese businesses located new facilities in the state.

Faulkner was soon convicted and sent to jail. A few years later the girls admitted that they had fabricated the rape story. Faulkner was pardoned.[1]

Lured by the prospect of jobs and less oppressive conditions, thousands of blacks moved from the South to Detroit and other Michigan cities during the first three decades of the twentieth century. Competition for jobs and housing increased tensions between black and white. In 1924, a black doctor, Ossian Sweet, seeking to escape conditions in Detroit's tightly segregated black ghetto, attempted to move into a white eastside neighborhood. A threatening white crowd gathered outside the house. From inside a shot was fired, and one of the crowd was killed. Sweet was put on trial for murder. An impassioned defense by his lawyer, Clarence Darrow, citing racial discrimination and the right to self-defense, led to Sweet's acquittal.[2]

The deadly Detroit riots of 1943 and 1967, and recent racial incidents in communities and on campuses, sadly prove that racial divisions continue. Blacks, whites, and other interest groups have, however, built alliances to further human relations, civil rights, and joint economic development. But no matter how one views the present racial/ethnic climate in the state, history as a guide shows that without awareness of these population divisions, and continuing efforts to minimize their impact, Michigan's future will be painful and bleak.

ECONOMIC DISLOCATIONS

The pattern of economic boom and bust endemic to a capitalist free-market economy has been especially evident in Michigan.

The Great Lakes area's first industry, the fur trade, had declined by the first decade of the nineteenth century. The necessary raw material, beaver, had been trapped almost to extinction. The trade moved farther west, although Mackinac Island remained an active command post of the business for the next thirty years.

The influx of settlers during the 1820s and 1830s, and the accompanying rapid economic growth, prompted a wave of land and money speculation. When settlers, promoters, and business interests demanded easy credit and internal improvements, the state responded with loose banking laws and grand schemes of state-financed railroads and canals. The boom collapsed in 1837, leaving a decade-long legacy of impoverished farmers, failed banks, and abandoned construction projects.

During the decade preceding the Civil War the economic basis of nineteenth century Michigan was established, and an economic boom period began. The rich farmlands of the southern counties continued to provide a stable agricultural base, while the new industries of lumbering and mining began to provide for capital accumulation and employment for new immigrants. Increased demand for lumber, copper, and iron during the Civil War further accelerated the state's economic development, including small manufacturing establishments in the Detroit area.

By 1873, however, the economy was once more in trouble. As purchasing power declined and economic growth slowed, the lumber, mining, and railroad interests, which controlled the state's economy and politics, came under attack from farmers and laborers. After a slight rebound during the 1880s, the state and nation plunged into a severe depression in the 1890s.

The effects of this depression were worse in Michigan than elsewhere. The twin peaks of Michigan's economy were already in trouble. The timber was nearly exhausted and the output of the mines would soon begin a rapid decline. Manufacturers in Michigan's cities—farm implements, carriages, stoves, tobacco products, shoes, furniture, food products, railroad cars, steel, shipbuilding, chemicals, and pharmaceuticals—saw their markets and credit disappear. Thousands of workers lost their jobs with no back-up system of relief to sustain their families.

The political and business leaders of the 1890s were, for the most part, content to let the market mechanisms take their course, believing that in time prosperity would return. One renegade Republican, mayor of Detroit Hazen S. Pingree, saw the needs of working people and, in his view, the callous attitude of the political and business community. Although he was unable to transfer most of his reforms to the state level when later elected governor, Pingree was an effective advocate of reform and a precursor of the "progressive" movement.

By the turn of the century Michigan and the nation were on the road to recovery. Reformist Republican governors like Fred Warner and Chase Osborn pushed for socially progressive legislation, including railroad regulation, taxes on utility companies, safety regulation in factories, limitations on child labor, and the adoption of a workers' compensation law.

Prosperity, with a boost from World War I, returned to Michigan during the first three decades of the new century. A slight economic downturn after the war was followed by a roaring economy led by the phenomenal development of the automobile industry. By the end of the 1920s, Michigan, led by the big three of Ford, General Motors, and Chrysler, had put the United States on wheels. As a result, Michigan's economy was dominated by the automobile industry.

Richard J. Hathaway

Michigan's reliance on the automobile industry was a major factor in the state's economic collapse during the "great depression" of the following decade. In 1929, prior to the October stock market crash, more than five million motor vehicles were manufactured; two years later the figure was slightly over one million. Consequently, Michigan was harder hit by the financial collapse than other areas of the country. The state's unemployment rate at the beginning of 1931 was 46 percent, nearly twice the national average. Michigan's nonmanufacturing sector was also destroyed as farm prices declined drastically, leading to reversion of tax-delinquent farm land to state ownership.

At first, the desperate plight of the unemployed was ignored as the self-correcting features of the market economy were thought to be the solution. The election of governors William Comstock in 1932 and Frank Murphy in 1936, however, signaled the application of President Franklin Roosevelt's "New Deal" to Michigan economic woes. The combined effect of New Deal programs and the industrial needs of World War II pulled Michigan back from economic collapse. Michigan became the "arsenal of democracy" as automobile plants retooled to produce jeeps, tanks, and airplanes. For the next thirty years the state enjoyed nearly continuous economic prosperity. Despite the grim lesson of the depression, however, Michigan's economy remained hostage to the fortunes of the automobile industry.

The Arab oil embargo of 1973 produced the first signal that Michigan's economy was once more in danger as gasoline shortages led to a reduction in new car sales. By February 1975, more than 16 percent of Detroit's work force was unemployed.[3] An upturn in car sales during the late 1970s provided a false sense of well-being. Only a loan guaranteed by the United States government saved Chrysler Corporation from bankruptcy in 1979. The continuing invasion of the world car market by Japanese and other nondomestic auto makers, and the relocation of automobile manufacturing outside of Michigan, still leaves the future of the state's major industry in doubt.

A review of Michigan's economic past shows that economic upswings and downturns will continue. Equally important is the lesson that concentration of the economy in one manufacturing area will worsen the effects of economic recession. Recent government, business and labor actions seem to indicate that these lessons are being learned. But will the response be quick enough, and effective?

BUSINESS/LABOR CONFLICTS

Michigan as the home of big business is also the home of big labor. A third consistent stress-line running through the state's history is conflict between the two.

As early as 1837, carpenters left work to parade the streets of Detroit with signs proclaiming "Ten Hours a Day, Two Dollars for Pay."[4] Thirteen years later, in 1850, the state's first permanent trade union, Local 18 of the National Typographical Union, was established in Detroit.[5]

Michigan's first large-scale industries, lumbering and mining, were the setting for many of the earliest business/labor confrontations. The most significant strike in Michigan, however, began in 1937 when auto workers in Flint sat down and took over General Motors' Chevrolet and Fisher Body plants.

For the next forty years automobile industry management, as well as business leaders in other industries, were forced to deal with a strong unionized work force. Of equal importance, no longer could management depend on government to forcibly intervene on its behalf during a labor dispute. At least in the automobile industry, big business and big labor also found themselves in a confrontational, but mutually

Michigan Technological University Archives and Copper Country
Historical Collections, Michigan Technological University

The Lake Angeline Iron Mine near Ishpeming, ca. 1885. The Pittsburgh and Lake Angeline Iron Company was formed in 1863, and by 1881 was shipping more than 18,000 tons of iron ore from this mine.

beneficial, relationship where corporate profits as well as workers' salaries increased.

The severe recession of the late 1970s and early 1980s brought this partnership to an end while, at the same time, laying the basis for a hoped-for era of cooperative production between management and labor. The critical juncture occurred late in 1979 with the near collapse of Chrysler Corporation. The United Auto Workers, in return for wage concessions and work rule changes, gained a greater voice in management decisions. Since then, during contract negotiations workers in the

Michigan Tourist Council/Michigan State Archives

State Capitol, Lansing, with the memorial to the First Michigan Sharpshooters Civil War regiment in the foreground.

automobile and other Michigan industries have declared job security as the primary bargaining issue. Management, on the other hand, has insisted on cost-cutting measures and joint quality-control programs.

The experience of the past few years does not necessarily lead to an optimistic projection for business in Michigan. From 1978 through 1987 more than 200,000 manufacturing jobs were lost. The total work force, however, has risen by more than 250,000 jobs. Most of these new jobs have been in the rapidly growing, and mostly unorganized, service sector of the economy.

Labor unions during the 1980s have also found themselves confronted by the tough stance of management and bitter accusations of "sellout" from their members. Wage concessions, benefit reductions, layoffs, plant closings, and plant relocations have all reduced the bargaining power of unions. A knowledge of our state's history, however, indicates that tensions and conflicts between management and labor will not disappear. Unions will, most likely, continue to aggressively recruit among government employees and the service sector, and industrial unions may be prepared for a new round of militancy in order to recapture the "givebacks" of recent years.

There are many such stress-lines woven through Michigan's past. Others include the struggle of women for political and economic equality; religious faith and the requirements of public education; southeast Michigan's contentions with the rest of the state; and economic development imperatives versus critical environmental concerns. A knowledge of the state's history illuminates all of these issues; allows us to step back and weigh alternatives based, in good measure, on past experience. Michigan has a usable past.

◆

NOTES

1. Willis F. Dunbar and George S. May, *Michigan: A History of the Wolverine State* (Grand Rapids: William B. Eerdmans Publishing Company, 1980), 391, 392.

2. Bruce A. Rubenstein and Lawrence E. Ziewacz, *Michigan, A History of the Great Lakes State* (Arlington Heights, Ill.: The Forum Press, 1981), 227.

3. Michigan Unemployment Security Commission, *Detroit Labor Market Review* 30, no. 5 (May 1976): 3.

Richard J. Hathaway

4. F. Clever Bald, *Michigan in Four Centuries* (New York: Harper and Brothers, 1954), 268.

5. Steve Babson, *Working Detroit: The Making of a Union Town* (New York: Adama Books, 1984), 5.

---◆---

SUGGESTED READINGS

Useful general histories include F. Clever Bald, *Michigan in Four Centuries* (New York: Harper and Brothers, 1954); Willis F. Dunbar and George S. May, *Michigan: A History of the Wolverine State* (Grand Rapids, Eerdmans Publishing Company, 1980); George S. May, *Michigan: An Illustrated History of the Great Lakes State* (Grand Rapids: Eerdmans Publishing Company, 1987); Bruce A. Rubenstein and Lawrence E. Ziewacz, *Michigan: A History of the Great Lakes State* (St. Louis: Forum, 1981); and Mileo M. Qualife and Sidney Glazer, *Michigan: From Primitive Wilderness to Industrial Commonwealth* (New York: Prentice-Hall, 1948, 1988).

Among the more specialized studies of the state's history are: Steve Babson, *Working Detroit: The Making of a Union Town* (Detroit: Wayne State University Press, 1986); Willis F. Dunbar, *All Aboard: A History of Railroading in Michigan* (Grand Rapids: Eerdmans Publishing Company, 1969); Calvin Goodrich, *The First Michigan Frontier* (Ann Arbor: The University of Michigan Press, 1940); Reginald Larrie, *Black Experiences in Michigan History* (Lansing: Michigan Department of State, Bureau of History, 1976); George S. May, *A Most Unique Machine: The Michigan Origins of the American Automobile Industry* (Grand Rapids: William B. Eerdmans Publishing Company, 1975); Angus Murdock, *Boom Copper* (Calumet: R. W. Drier, 1943, 1964); Richard A. Santer, *Michigan: Heart of the Great Lakes* (Dubuque: Kindall/Hunt Publishing Company, 1977); Lawrence M. Sommers, ed., *Atlas of Michigan* (East Lansing: Michigan State University Press, 1977); and Arthur R. Woodford, *All Our Yesterdays: A Brief History of Detroit* (Detroit: Wayne State University Press, 1969).

Interesting studies of Michigan's people include: James M. Anderson and Iva A. Smith, eds., *Ethnic Groups in Michigan* (Detroit: Ethnos Press, 1983); James A. Clifton, et al., *People of the Three Fires* (Grand Rapids: Inter-Tribal Council, 1986); Michael Delp, et al., *Contemporary Michigan Poetry: Poems from the Third Coast* (Detroit: Wayne State University Press, 1988); C. Kurt Dewhurst and Yvonne Lockwood, *Michigan Folklife Reader* (East Lansing: Michigan State University Press, 1987); Richard M. Dorson, *Negro Folktales in Michigan* (Cambridge: Harvard University Press, 1956, 1974); W. Vernon Kinietz, *The Indians of the Western Great Lakes, 1615–1760* (Ann Arbor: The University of Michigan Press, 1940, 1965); C. Warren Vanderhill, *Settling the Great Lakes Frontier: Immigration to Michigan* (Lansing: Michigan Historical Commission, 1970); and George Weeks, *Stewards of the State: The Governors of Michigan* (Detroit: *The Detroit News* and the Historical Society of Michigan, 1987).

Current statistics and information on the state are found in: Michigan Department of Management and Budget, *Michigan Manual* (Lansing: biennial); and two publications of Public Sector Consultants, Inc., *Michigan Government Directory* (Lansing: annual); and *Michigan in Brief* (Lansing: annual).

INDEX

Michigan: Visions of our Past

Production Editor: Julie L. Loehr
Design: Lynne A. Brown
Cover: Lynne A. Brown
Copy Editor: Dawn Kawa
Proofreader: Anne Forgrave

Text Composed by: the Copyfitters
on a Compugraphic Quadex 5000 in Tiffany for running headers
and footers, main heads and subheads; Helvetica light for captions
and footnotes; and Century II light for text

Cover composed by: Adventures with Nature
on a Linotronic L-300 in Tiffany and Helvetica

Printed by: BookCrafters
Text printed on: 60# Lakewood
Dust jacket printed on: 80# antique enamel
Cover ink: PMS 419
Text ink: black